Housing: the great British failure

Housing: the great British failure

Fred Berry

Charles Knight
London 1974

Charles Knight & Co. Ltd.
25 New Street Square, London EC4A 3JA &
Sovereign Way, Tonbridge, Kent

A member of the Benn Group

Copyright © 1974 Fred Berry

Set by Cold Composition Ltd.
Southborough, Tunbridge Wells, Kent

ISBN 0 85314 230 0

Printed in Great Britain by
Redwood Burn Limited
Trowbridge & Esher

Contents

Contents

Acknowledgements

No man is an island, especially when he is writing a book, and I would like to take this opportunity of expressing my sincere thanks to all those, friends, colleagues, acquaintances as well as those who had never even heard of me, who helped me. Particularly I would like to thank Ann Baker (formerly of SHELTER) who bore my incessant demands for information with great cheerfulness; Miss Power, the Librarian at Hunstanton for getting hold of all kinds of books and for letting me keep them far longer than I had any right to; Reg Freeson M.P. (former Joint Parliamentary Secretary at the M.H.L.G.) for his helpful letters; A. E. Holmans, Senior Economic Advisor at the D. of E., for useful comments and information; Miss Partington of the D. of E. Library for kind assistance; members of the staff of King's Lynn public library for ferreting out various snippets of information — nothing was too much trouble for them; Mrs Baker, formerly of the Housing Centre Trust, for access to the Trust's Library; Maureen FitzGerald, David Peschek and Chris Birch, editors respectively of *Local Government Chronicle, Municipal Review* and *Municipal Engineering,* who gave me great help, quite possibly without being aware of it; and my very special thanks to Henry Aughton, formerly Borough Treasurer of Hemel Hempstead and now Chief Executive of Dacorum, for reading the proofs and saving me from my worst faults. I am deeply indebted to them all. And though one way and another they supplied me with much information and a great deal of help, I must emphasise that the responsibility for all that appears in this book is mine and mine alone.

Lastly, may I extend my thanks to my dear wife Betty for

Acknowledgements

putting up with a good deal of bad temper as well as long periods of lonely boredom, and to my little daughter Nicola for the many happy playhours she had to forgo (and now, alas, lost for ever) because of my preoccupation with other things. These, fortunately, are debts one does not have to repay; to do so would in any case be quite impossible.

Fred Berry
Hunstanton

23rd November 1973

Introductory note

The Housing Finance Act, 1972 is likely to be repealed, and at the time of going to press I have added Appendix 7, in which I look, with caution, at possible future developments in housing. But changes will not, I hope, invalidate my discussion of the Housing Finance Act, which has in any case the historical value of indicating the attitude towards housing at that time.

This book is intended to be a discussion of the long-term issues involved in housing, rather than a contribution to a topical debate. Inevitably, the political aspect of housing means that as governments change, the immediate situation changes, but this does not, I believe, destroy the fundamental arguments I present.

1 An Englishman's home...

"Hunger, drink, sex", wrote Professor Laski, "and the need of shelter and clothing seem the irreducible minimum of human wants."* Few would quarrel with that. A human being can manage a few days, maybe weeks at the most, without food, a few days perhaps without drink, and, quite apart from its aspect as an immediate physiological need, without sex the whole human race comes to an end anyway. In the tropics perhaps clothing and shelter can be dispensed with for a while, but for most of mankind clothing and shelter alike are a prerequisite of continued existence. And in the colder climates, certainly in this country, we may take it for granted that, for the most part, those denied the protection and comfort of shelter and clothing cannot long survive.

The fundamental purpose of shelter is what the name implies, that is to keep wind and weather out and generally to protect from the elements. But only shelter at its most primitive is confined to this meagre role. We may, in the next few paragraphs, usefully consider what it is we now expect of housing and then go on to assess, if we can, the extent to which housing in Britain fulfils or, if you prefer, fails to fulfil this function. And if those experienced in housing matters find all this too elementary let them skip to page 3. It is in fact the elementary truths about housing that are too often overlooked.

Even at the primary level, much of our housing proves inadequate; damp, draughty, cold and even verminous, it fails to provide the most elementary protection. Yet we are

*H. J. Laski, *A Grammar of Politics,* London, Allen and Unwin 1948.

entitled to expect much more from a dwelling than that. A home should provide privacy, seclusion for the family from its neighbours and, when the need arises, from each other. It should provide opportunities for rest and relaxation in warmth and comfort. In a sense this is the essence of the place we call home; we must all have somewhere to sleep. If the worst comes to the worst we can put up with a chair or a table for washing at or eating from; what we cannot decrease (unless we are astronauts in flight) is the space we need for our beds and lying down on them. But this is to put things at their lowest; it is many years since living space was as basic as that. In the twentieth century it calls for privacy and security from surprise intrusion (for parents particularly), room to sit and read or watch television or play records without disturbing others, attend to one's bodily requirements, dress and undress, have easy access to washing and toilet facilities and provide comfort and warmth in time of sickness. It goes without saying that bedrooms should be capable of being heated and that the heating should be built in, not just an afterthought. Relaxation should not be confined to the bedroom but, with recreation and the pursuit of culture, should be a function of the main living area. Home is a place where a harmonious family life develops together with the relations between its members. This is not possible where space is so cramped that its occupants are constantly falling over each other and literally treading on each other's toes. Care of the body and the maintenance of hygiene demand, as a minimum, an internal W.C., a fixed bath or at very least a shower conveniently placed for use by all the family, a wash-basin (or more than one when the family is large), space for washing and drying clothes, a constant supply of hot water; all this appears to be the minimum acceptable provision for a twentieth-century home.

Home is where one prepares and eats one's meals, and the dwelling must be provided not only with the space but also the equipment to do this adequately. Here too one receives and entertains one's friends and this means, if nothing else, enough space, space for hanging up the hats and coats, room for the extra chairs or occasionally the extra bed (this is one of the instances where the case of those who insist on the house "matching" the family falls down). Home is a place for storing both personal and household possessions. Even the least affluent will in the course of a lifetime acquire cherished possessions to be preserved with sentiment and care; these must be safely stored away, not in an attic or a cellar, but somewhere reasonably accessible where from time to time they can be brought out and displayed with pride or contemplated with satisfaction and perhaps nostalgia. Finally, though this by no means exhausts the possibilities, a home is a "base for one's operations against the world", a kind of fortress, perhaps, from which one may sally forth to carry on the business of everyday life and to which one may retire to revive and gather strength against the morning. An adequate home in short is a basic requirement of civilised living, and it will be the burden not only of this chapter but of this book to say that we have denied this basic requirement to millions of our fellow-countrymen, often unwittingly, but frequently as the result of deliberate policy.

Let us now go on to examine, as far as we may, the extent to which housing in Britain matches up to its requirements. We may conveniently begin by assessing what proportion of our dwellings can be actually deemed as unfit, even by the very low standards which the law permits. Exceptional cases apart, the replacement of unfit housing is not, and for many years has not been (if it was ever), an activity which commends itself to private enterprise. Slum clearance has therefore willy-nilly been an activity undertaken principally by the State, which in this country has meant the local authorities. The local authorities have by and large accepted this task reluctantly. They have frequently been unwilling to admit that they have much in the way of slums within their borders and when from time to time they have been required to make some assessment of the size of the problem, they have been prone to report the numbers of unfit dwellings they felt they could deal with, or would wish to deal with, rather than make a detached, objective and accurate assessment. This has made it difficult for those responsible for policy to quantify the slum problem at any particular point of time, leaving aside the rather obvious point that it is ongoing, not capable of solution on a once-for-all basis. The

Housing: the great British failure

House Condition Survey of 1967* showed about 1.8 million dwellings as unfit, about 12 per cent of the total stock. (A survey carried out in 1971 puts the numbers a good deal lower, but there are grounds, which will be developed later, for treating this revision as suspect.) This is a very much larger figure, more than twice as large, than had previously been supposed. In addition just over 3¾ million supposedly "fit" dwellings were found to require repairs costing £125 or more (at 1967 prices). Moreover, of the dwellings classed as "not unfit" no less than 2½ million lacked one or more of the basic "amenities" (internal W.C., bath, wash-basin, and hot and cold water at three points). And of all the dwellings classified as "fit"† at that time no less than 4½ millions lacked one or more of the basic amenities or needed major repairs or both. These are staggering figures and they pointed in all to a total of no less than $6\frac{1}{3}$ million dwellings which were unsatisfactory even by the low standards applied. Numbers on this scale are largely meaningless, but it might help to consider that $6\frac{1}{3}$ million houses, built to a 20 ft. frontage, would occupy both sides of a street 12,000 miles long, or from London to the furthest point of Australia and beyond. Walking down such a street, day and night without stopping, would take five months.

But these figures, alarming as they are, show up the shortcomings of our housing only in respect of wind- and weather-tightness, stability, freedom from damp and lack of basic amenities. They say nothing about space for privacy, relaxation and entertainment, nothing about standards of finish and equipment, nothing in short about dwellings judged by twentieth-century standards. Moreover, the space available in a dwelling depends on how many people occupy it; overcrowding statistics might help if those which exist were reliable, but they are not, because so few authorities take much notice, much less keep accurate and up-to-date records. In any case the legal definition is much too low. The

---

*Old Houses into New Homes, Cmnd 3602, April 1968, Ministry of Housing and Local Government, published by H.M.S.O.

† Strictly speaking the classification was "not unfit", a nice distinction leading one to suspect that those responsible for drafting the Report could not bring themselves to say that these dwellings were actually "fit".

1966 Census showed that 2½ per cent of the population (over one million persons) were living at a density of over 1½ persons per room in England and Wales (Scotland was in fact much worse). Many of these people were living in slums but many were not. The 1964 Housing Survey* found that 1.4 million households (9 per cent) were living in accommodation which did not afford them the number of bedrooms they needed. In fact most of our houses are probably too small, as nearly two-thirds of them consist only of four or five habitable rooms.

And when we go on to examine facilities for sanitation and hygiene we find that 25 per cent of all dwellings (nearly 4 million) lacked one or more of the basic amenities. There will of course be some overlap between dwellings which are unfit and dwellings which lack these amenities; a slum by definition is a dwelling that is likely to be badly equipped. But this does not apply in every case. Of the 2.1 million dwellings lacking a fixed bath, 782,000 (36.6 per cent) were classified as "fit". Nearly 3 million dwellings were without an internal W.C., but over 1½ million (51.6 per cent) of them were classified as "fit". Over 3 million dwellings are not (or were not at the time of the Survey) equipped with a wash-basin. Nearly 1.6 million (52.3 per cent) of these were "fit". Hot and cold water at three points could not be found in 3.4 million homes; 1.88 million of these (55.3 per cent) were supposed to be "fit".

Finally (for the purpose of this chapter) there is the question of age. In many parts of the world sixty years is considered long enough for the lifetime of a house and in some countries it is even less. This for us is a convenient span as it takes us back to the years just before the First World War, which was itself a notable watershed in housing standards. Up to the time of the First World War it was still considered reasonable to build dwellings without bath or washing facilities, without internal W.C.s, with little or no control over density or layout except that afforded by the Public Health Acts, and arranged internally so that it was still

*Myra Woolf, *The Housing Survey in England and Wales*. An enquiry undertaken by the Government Social Survey for the Ministry of Housing and Local Government, 1964.

possible, say, to have to pass through one bedroom to reach another one. At the time of the 1967 House Condition Survey no less than 6 million pre-1914 dwellings were still in existence and these accounted for nearly 40 per cent of the housing stock. This is about the same proportion obtained by adding together the known slums with those dwellings needing major repairs. It seems not unreasonable tó conclude that something like four dwellings out of every ten are inadequate even by the low standards still permitted. (We are not talking about houses built to Parker Morris standards obligatory on local authorities — but not private builders — since 1969. These standards are comparatively high and they are on the whole acceptable, but even so they fall short of what is considered reasonable in other parts of Europe, as we shall see in Chapter 14.) In fact the proportion may be higher. Inadequate space, insufficient storage, poor heating arrangements, these are features of hundreds of thousands of pre-1919 dwellings which are fit in the Public Health sense and which possess the basic amenities. Nevertheless 40 per cent seems to be a reasonable figure for the purposes of argument.

Further, it will get worse. Current rates of clearance would in fact be sufficient to deal with no more than 1.8 million dwellings by the year 2000, assuming that current rates *can* be maintained. (It will become more difficult to do so as the main clearance effort moves from the clearance areas to the more difficult areas outside.) But by the end of the century another *4 million* dwellings will have reached the same age that a 1914 dwelling is now. Not all will be slums by standards then current, but they will hardly be in line with expectations appropriate to the opening years of the twenty-first century. The reason for this worsening situation is that for many years we have been building more houses than we have been demolishing. For the past sixty years the average rate of increase of the housing stock has been 1.3 per cent, whereas the demolition rate has been only 0.25 per cent*. The normal life of a dwelling in Needleman's sense† is

*Simon Pepper, *Housing Improvement: goals and strategy*, London, Lund Humphries 1971, p.15.
†L. Needleman, *The Economics of Housing*, London, The Staples Press 1965, p.41. Needleman defines the normal life of a dwelling as the number of years that elapse before half the dwellings built in a given year have been demolished.

at present 140 years. If current rates of demolition and growth (about 0.5 per cent and 2.0 per cent respectively) were maintained, this figure would still be about 120 by the end of the century. And this would mean that half the dwellings built in the year 2000 would still be standing in 2120. To replace all pre-1919 stock by the end of the century would require a clearance rate of 250,000 a year (Pepper, op. cit.). And to achieve the "ideal" normal life of sixty years by the end of the century it would be necessary to demolish 300,000 and build 500,000 a year from now on (Pepper, op. cit.). These are rates not yet achieved in this country and without radical change it is unlikely that they will be achieved.

This state of affairs did not come about overnight. From the time of Edwin Chadwick in the 1840s, through the period of the Earl of Shaftesbury's early housing legislation in the 1850s, the Public Health reforms of the 1870s, the Royal Commission in the 1880s, the Housing Reform campaigns at the turn of the century, the coming of subsidised state housing in 1919, the slum clearance campaigns of the 'thirties and 'fifties, right up to the time of Rachman, Cathy and Shelter, public disquiet about housing conditions has been massive and deep. But not deep enough, it seems, and not sufficiently sustained. This is not to say that very considerable sums of money have not been put into housing. It is difficult to estimate exactly how much; the Department of the Environment are unable to say and in fact the complete figures may not now exist. The author estimates that the capital cost of council houses in England and Wales between the two world wars amounted to something like £500 million and that since the Second World War the figure must be something in the order of £10,000 million. And subsidies granted by the Exchequer since 1919 cannot have amounted to less than £2,000 million to which the local authorities themselves must have added at least £650 million. These are all estimated at current costs; present-day costs would be very much higher, at least four times as much. In view of the sparse data available, it is quite likely that these figures could be a long way out, but in the author's opinion they are not very likely to have been over-estimated. These are admittedly very large figures. And if one adds the very substantial Exchequer aid to private house purchase by the way of tax relief on mortage interest, the under-estimation of Schedule A Tax prior to 1964 and its abolition since that date, then the contribution made by tax- and ratepayers must have been very great indeed.

Notwithstanding this considerable expenditure, the housing situation has not improved to the extent that one would have been expected and in many ways is getting worse. It is getting worse because we as individuals, as taxpayers and as ratepayers have not been willing to make sufficient resources available. It is getting worse because the best use has not been made of the resources that have been made available. Above all it is getting worse because the political will has been lacking, the will to determine the proper policies and then stick to them, no matter what adverse circumstances may arise.

It is difficult to avoid the conclusion that in this apparently elementary matter of providing ourselves with adequate shelter, as in so many other fields, what has for years been regarded with complacency and even with pride as a British success story is proving to be, with greater certainty every passing year, a great British failure.

2 The beginning of the story

It is frequently said, and commonly supposed, that our housing problems were brought about by the Industrial Revolution. This is only partly true and it could be argued that in a sense it is not true at all. So that we can be sure what we are talking about, let us define the Industrial Revolution as the great series of changes in technology, communications and financial and industrial organisation which began somewhere during the second half of the eighteenth century and continued well into the fifth and sixth decades of the nineteenth century. Or, to put it another way, from about the accession of George III in 1760 — this marked the beginning of the canal era and the revolution in communications — to the 1850s when the great period of railway building was coming to its end and the "coal and iron revolution" was almost complete.

England at the beginning of the eighteenth century was a predominantly agricultural nation. Such manufactures as existed were on a handicraft basis with the guilds still very much in evidence. The woollen industry was mainly a rural affair providing employment for women and children while the men worked on the land, and remained a cottage industry for the greater part of the century. Only a minor part of the process was undertaken in factories. Iron was still almost wholly dependent on charcoal for smelting and water power for the machinery. Agriculture was still at a primitive level and would have to wait on the improvements in communications, crop rotation and animal breeding and the extension of the enclosure movement which were not to come about until the latter half of the century. There was nonetheless sufficient to eat in the sense that, except for

9

years of bad harvest, there was a surplus of wheat for export, amounting at the beginning of the century to something like a million quarters and increasing to three or four times this figure by mid-century. In short the whole way and tenor of life was going on much as it had for centuries. But the great central factor which was to bring about dramatic changes, not only of the face of Britain but of the whole civilised world, was just beginning to make itself manifest: an unprecedented and unheralded increase in population.

The population of England and Wales had perhaps stood at about two million at the time of the Conquest and had increased steadily, apart from a setback at the time of the Black Death, until by the end of the seventeenth century it had reached about five million. During the next century it was to more than double and from then on the rate of increase was 10 per cent per decade right up to the First World War. The high point occurred during the intercensal period 1811-1821 when the increase was no less than 17 per cent. By twentieth-century developing-nation standards these figures are not particularly high and do not by any means approach what is biologically possible, but they were without precedent and brought with them greater changes to the lives and work of men than had all the previous centuries put together.

Just why this should have happened is not clear. Some attribute it to improvements in medical care, but this seems doubtful since such advances in medicine as took place in the eighteenth century were unlikely to have percolated to the great mass of the predominantly rural population, most of whom would never have seen a hospital and could not have afforded the new medical care even if they had known about it. The hospitals themselves are considered by many to have been of doubtful value, patients being more likely to survive if they kept out of them than if they went in. Work recently undertaken by Professor Sigsworth may well lead to a reconsideration of this view, but all in all it seems unlikely that at that time the hospitals had much effect on the population increase. Others feel that the reason lay in the change in popular drinking habits, from gin to beer, and certainly Hogarth expressed a similar view through his famous pictures. But the population increase was getting firmly under way in the 1750s, just when gin-drinking was at its height, so that theory too seems a non-starter. Improvements in sanitation did not really get going for another century and it is unlikely that improvements in personal habits of cleanliness and hygiene affected a significant proportion of the population until well into the nineteenth century. Another explanation is sometimes sought in the Speenhamland System of poor relief where in effect the poor rates were used to subsidise low wages, the subsidy varying with the cost of bread and the size of the family. But the Speenhamland Justices did not institute their famous arrangements until 1795 when the population explosion was already well established.

The answers (it is unlikely that any single explanation will suffice) must clearly be sought elsewhere. The collapse of the feudal system must have had something to do with it. A peasant population tends to remain stable because if families are too large it involves too great a division of land holdings: young men postpone marriage until they have a farm of their own. The enclosures removed this restraint, and the labourer could look forward to no possible improvement in his fortune for which it would be reasonable to wait. Moreover he needed a wife to look after him, whereas the practice of "living-in" — prevalent on farms and elsewhere — meant staying unmarried. The new trades now developing did not require the long apprenticeship customary under the guild system, and apprenticeship delayed marriage. In short, men and women were marrying earlier and having children at a younger and therefore more healthy and more fertile period of their lives. Children were less of a burden than had previously been the case, particularly in the textile areas where they could be put to work at an early age. The average age of marriage fell during the eighteenth century from around twenty-seven to nearer twenty, which in those days of low life-expectation meant that the child-bearing period was virtually doubled. The improvements in agriculture coupled with better communications probably led to an improved diet, leading in turn to a lower rate of infant mortality. With more babies surviving and growing up to marriageable age, such a process will become self-sustaining, as indeed it has been, except for a period between the great wars of the twentieth century, right up to the present day. Even this does not supply a completely satisfactory answer. Ireland, for example, was experiencing a similar rate of increase without the stimuli of industry, better communications or improved agriculture; at any rate up to the 1840s when the Malthusian restraint of famine followed by mass emigration intervened. The question therefore of whether the Industrial Revolution created its own work force or whether it was the other way round will continue to exercise the minds of social and economic historians; it does not appear likely to be resolved in any satisfactory way for our purposes.

Whatever the reason, the effect on housing conditions was disastrous, and would have been so even if the changes in industrial technology had not led to the concentration of the population in towns, which was the inevitable result. It is wrong to suppose that up to that time or indeed for a long time afterwards the working man had been adequately housed, but at least he lived in the open countryside where space and fresh air could to a great extent make up for lack of sanitation and other household inadequacies. But even the mean hovels in which he lived had to be built by someone, and one can see, if one stops to consider it for a moment, the effect of population pressure on the building industry. To take a hypothetical example let us suppose that, with population stable, dwellings become uninhabitable and are replaced after one hundred years. (In the circumstances of the time it is unlikely that working-class dwellings were replaced as often as that, but it will serve for the purpose of the argument.) This will mean that for every 1,000 existing houses, 100 new ones will be required every ten years. But if the population now starts to increase at 10 per cent per decade, then sooner rather than later a further 100 dwellings per decade will be required to house the additional people. Thus a population increase of 10 per cent has generated a demand for housing that has increased 100 per cent. Of course this is an over-simplification and the increased demand would not amount to 100 per cent every decade. But the fact remains that an increasing population demands additional housing at a higher rate than the increase of population itself. And the population of Britain has been increasing without pause (except for a short period between the two world wars) from the beginning of the eighteenth century to the present day, and it is this central fact of population expansion that created the worst of our housing problems in the first place and has made their solution so difficult ever since. Alfred Woods, the enlightened and extremely able Planning Officer for Worcestershire, put it to a National Conference in 1972 that the population ought to be drastically reduced. He was taken to task over it but he had the heart of the matter in him.

All this was made much worse by the rapid growth, by migration, of the new industrial towns. The new machinery called for the concentration of the work force in factories and these were built for convenience near to the source of raw materials or power, or close to convenient forms of communication. This process was already under way in the latter half of the eighteen century and became a flood in the nineteenth. Birmingham, Bradford, Cardiff, Glasgow, Northampton, Sheffield and Southampton, all these towns at least doubled their populations during the period 1821-1841 and many others grew only slightly less dramatically. The older towns such as Bath, Bristol, Norwich, Oxford and York were also growing, though not so fast. Large numbers of cheap jerry-built dwellings were run up as fast as possible, frequently by the factory owners themselves, as near to the factories as possible and without thought being given to any consideration of layout, light and air and, least of all, sanitation. Taken individually these dwellings, poor as they were, were probably no worse and may have been better than their occupants had been used to; it was not until later in the century when defects in their construction, equipment and layout became only too apparent that they came to be regarded as slums. But they could not be taken individually: a hovel in a rural setting is one thing, a thousand hovels crammed together without proper sanitary provision, water supply and rubbish disposal is something else again. And the occupants brought to an urban situation habits of life developed in a rural context. The result, not unnaturally, was widespread squalor and disease.

Housing: the great British failure

But in the early nineteenth century, squalor and disease, especially the latter, were considered as manifestations of divine displeasure, beyond the power of man to remedy even if he had the temerity to try. In any case most of this concentration was taking place in the new industrial towns, many of which had no municipal organisation, however feeble, in being. This was not put right until the Municipal Corporations Act of 1835, and even then the powers available to the new authorities were minimal even if they were prepared to use them, which most were not.

It was however about this time that, almost fortuitously, events were taking shape that were to bring to the notice of the nation in a dramatic way the dreadful housing conditions of the working classes. We have already mentioned Speenhamland and how in 1795 the Justices of that Berkshire parish laid it down that every poor and industrious person was to be assured a certain income "either procured by his own or his family's labours, or an allowance from the poor rate", and that this income should be on a sliding scale according to the price of bread. This practice, which incidentally has something in common with the family income supplement provisions of the present day, was soon to be widely adopted, and indeed the decision of the Justices came to be known as the "Speenhamland Act of Parliament" and was even believed by many to have the force of law. The consequences were obvious and were soon felt. No employer was going to pay proper wages when they could be supplemented by the poor rate, which naturally enough increased by leaps and bounds. In the middle of the eighteenth century the poor rate had averaged about £700,000 and had increased to about £2 million by 1790. It rose to nearly £4 million by 1800 and later to nearly £7 million. In only six of the years between 1810 and 1834 did it fall to below £6 million. The end result, though highly profitable to employers, was a crushing rate burden and the widespread pauperisation of the working people. It also, no doubt, gave a fillip to the already expanding population since children, far from being a liability, could now attract additional poor relief. The whole business came to an end in 1834 with the coming of the New Poor Law.

The new laws were completely in accordance with the spirit of the age in that it was commonly held that unemployment and poverty were the result of some moral shortcoming; the condition of the pauper therefore was to be "less eligible" than that of the least prosperous worker. Outdoor relief was abolished and every person in need of relief had to receive it in a workhouse. In the sinister language of the Poor Law Commission of 1834, every able-bodied person receiving workhouse relief must be "subjected to such courses of labour and discipline as will repel the indolent and vicious". What this meant in terms of human suffering and degradation is best left to the imagination.

In terms of the history of housing the results were two-fold, one immediate and one long-term. Immediately it meant that large numbers of rural workers who were able to get along under Speenhamland (at least they could starve in the open air) were driven to the towns to swell the ranks of cheap labour still required for the factories. As far as the towns were concerned this made a bad situation worse, with greater overcrowding and the hasty erection of jerry-built "dwellings" which were already slums before their hapless occupants moved in. The longer-term, and less vicious, effect lay in the central organisation of the Poor Law itself. Efficiency rather than democracy was the aim and it was entirely in accordance with Benthamite thinking that administration of the Act had deliberately been removed from popular control by the appointment of three independent commissioners. But the commissioners' secretary, Edwin Chadwick, was no ordinary man, and when the registration of births, marriages and deaths was added to the duties of the Guardians of the Poor, he had under his control a unique machinery for gathering information about the condition of working-class life and this he proceeded to use. The result was the monumental *Report on the Sanitary Condition of the Labouring Population and the Means for its Improvement* which came out in 1842 and which was, although ostensibly the work of the three commissioners, actually the work of Chadwick himself. The Report was a resounding condemnation of the appalling conditions under

15

which millions of working people had to live, and it is not too much to say that the movement towards improved housing conditions, painfully slow to emerge though it may have been, actually started at this point. Unfortunately Chadwick himself was far from popular and his Report might very well have finished up on the shelf had it not been for an outbreak of cholera shortly afterwards. As it was, Parliament relented and passed the first Public Health Act in 1848. The Act, being permissive rather than mandatory, soon became a dead letter and its details need not concern us here. All the same it was perhaps unfortunate, though probably inevitable, that the housing problem was first seen as a sanitary problem. This was a burden from which the housing reformers of later days were never able completely to free themselves; indeed it is significant that right up to the present day it is the Public Health Inspector and the Medical Officer of Health from whom representations must first come if housing conditions in an area are to be improved. Meanwhile back in the 1840s slum landlords were busy, in the best traditions of *laissez-faire,* promoting the good of all by pursuing their own self-interest, which in this case took the form of throwing up (the term is apt) atrocious slum dwellings from one end of the country to the other without any let or hindrance. It may have been the first decade of Victoria's reign but it was a dismal age.

Nor was contemporary philosophy on the side of the reformers. The following extract from *The Economist* in May 1848 has turned up in practically every treatise, learned and unlearned, ever written on housing in the nineteenth century, but it can stand quoting again: "Suffering and evil are nature's admonitions; they cannot be got rid of; and the impatient attempts of benevolence to banish them from the world by legislation, before benevolence has learnt their object and their end, have always been more productive of evil than good." Sadly, it has a strangely familiar ring.

Not everybody, however, agreed with the economists. Lord Ashley, later the Earl of Shaftesbury, a Victorian do-gooder in the very best sense of the term, had interested himself (and others) in the working-class condition since the 1830s, and in 1851 he managed to get the very first Housing

Acts through Parliament (see next chapter). They did not in fact amount to much and had little effect, but they were a beginning and from small beginnings great things may eventually come. They were followed in the 1860s by the Cross and Torrens Acts which aimed at dealing with bad housing conditions from a sanitary approach. Again these Acts were of little effect but they were the precursors of something better, in this case the great Public Health Act of 1875. It was this Act which at last gave local authorities the power to control house-building through the imposition of local byelaws. The term "Byelaw Street", now a term of disparagement and a synonym for monotony and drabness, also sprang from this Act, but in the 1870s a Byelaw Street was the model of what such things should be and a very great improvement on what had gone before. It says much for this Act and for the Parliament that passed it that it remained the principal Act in the field of public health for over sixty years with very little fundamental amendment. Its effect on housing built after 1875 was profound, and generations of those who came after had good reason to be grateful to the far-seeing Victorian reformers who had left such a distinctive mark on the face of the country's townscapes. But it also, in a sense, contained the seeds of its own failure.

Throughout the nineteenth century the main supplier of housing by a very long way was the speculative private landlord who obviously operated only under profitable conditions. The 1875 Act reduced the number of dwellings that could be built on any given area and because of improved standards it also increased the cost of building and therefore reduced the profitability of the investment. It can be said that the first hint of the decline of the private landlord dated from this Act, though it was to be another thirty years before that decline reached obvious and dramatic proportions.

Meanwhile Victorian charity and philanthropy were displaying themselves in other ways. Throughout the second half of the nineteenth century many commercial, philanthropic and charitable trusts came into being with the avowed intention of providing good housing for working people. Some of these — Peabody, Waterlow, Guinness — are familiar names today, others have long since disappeared. Some, although philanthropic in origin, insisted on an economic return on the capital invested, giving rise to the phrase "five-per-cent philanthropists". Almost all of these trusts and charities however confined their activities to London. In other parts of the country a few large employers built reasonable dwellings for their employees, in some cases laying out quite large estates and providing schools, churches, community centres and so on. Their names, too, have a familiar ring — Cadbury (Bournville), Leverhulme (Port Sunlight), Salt (Saltaire), Rowntree (Earswick). But the great mass of the working people of this country could only look to the private landlord for their accommodation.

That this accommodation was still grossly inadequate is evident by the decision taken in 1884 to appoint a Royal Commission to inquire into the whole matter. The Prince of Wales was appointed to the Commission and it is clear from the terms of its report that the other commissioners felt in no way dismayed or inhibited by this royal participation. Their report, published in 1885, dwelt particularly on the question of overcrowding which, they said, was more serious than ever. This was caused chiefly by high rents due to competition for houses and to scarcity of accommodation in proportion to the population. They felt that there had been a failure of administration rather than in legislation, in other words the law was not being used or enforced. It is sad to reflect that today many of the dwellings in existence at that time are still being lived in and he would be a bold man who would dare to say today, ninety years later, that the law in relation to overcrowding is being zealously observed.

The outcome of the Commission's report was an Act in 1885 and another, more important, Act in 1890. Parts I and II of the 1890 Act consolidated the Cross and Torrens Acts respectively, but it was Part III which laid the ground for the housing reform movement of the early twentieth century for it gave local authorities unequivocal powers to build working-class housing. Alderman William Thompson of Richmond (Surrey) was one of the first to see the possibilities opened up to local authorities by these powers and it was the success of the estate built there in the 1890s which led to the great housing reform movement in which for many years Thompson and Henry Aldridge, another notable campaigner, played a leading part. They gathered round them reformers, philanthropists, architects and others, some of whose names — Cadbury, Leverhulme, Unwin, Rowntree — are remembered to this day. History has been less than kind to Thompson and Aldridge, particularly when written by those with other axes to grind; it is not too much to say that between them they altered the face of Britain, and for the better.

While the housing reform movement was gathering strength, the position of the private landlord was becoming less tenable. Increasing prosperity at the end of the nineteenth century led to an increased demand for housing, not for the very poor indeed, but for the more prosperous artisan class. By 1900 house building in the United Kingdom was approaching 150,000 a year. But the rot had already set in, the private mortgagee was disappearing in the face of other, less onerous forms of investment which did not involve the time and effort that housing management demands. Money for house-building (and in the context of the time this meant building to rent) was no longer plentiful, and from 1904 onwards fewer and fewer houses were built each year until by 1914 the total was no more than 48,000. This is shown graphically in Figure 1 (p.116) and proves dramatically that the private landlord, far from being killed off by rent control — one of the more persistent myths — had already decided to go out of business long before rent control was ever thought of. Rent control was in fact not introduced until 1915, and although the immediate reason was the protection of munition workers in Glasgow, in reality it was introduced because of the feeling, held quite strongly during the First World War, that it was immoral to make a profit from a war situation. During the war very few new houses were built and, despite the slaughter, the shortage of houses at the end of the war had increased substantially over the 1914 figure, and amounted to something more than a million. It was this fact, coupled with the feeling that those whose lives had been at risk in war should not be less significant in peace, that led to the demand for "Homes for

Heroes" in 1918 and state intervention on a large scale. We will deal with that in a later chapter, but it is worth noting that in 1918 public health legislation had been on the statute-book for seventy years and some sort of housing legislation for almost as long. A Royal Commission had come and gone and for all the good it had achieved it might as well have saved its breath. Meanwhile Great Britain had become the workshop of the world, providing not only itself but countries throughout the world with the equipment that made modern technology and communications possible. Railways and steamships made it possible to move goods, food and raw materials on a scale unprecedented in all history, and American wheat, Australian sheep, South American beef, and New Zealand dairy products made it possible to sustain the population of this country at a level which would have been quite impossible a century earlier. But, although housing conditions in 1918 were undoubtedly better than those of 1818, they were very far from perfect, and it still seemed beyond the grasp of people and politicians alike to secure this basic need of shelter on an adequate scale. The reason then, as now, is not far to seek, the population was not prepared either collectively or individually to devote sufficient resources to this end. It is a hard lesson to learn.

3 State action: the sanitary principle

The purpose of this and succeeding chapters is to see how it came about that the State decided to intervene to improve housing conditions and the supply of new houses. Today, with more than five million dwellings in public ownership and at public disposal, it is clear that state intervention in housing affairs has been on a very large scale and it might be supposed that this was the outcome of the gradual evolution of a sense of social responsibility which in other fields brought about, say, the National Health Service or that group of benefits and protections loosely known as the "Welfare State". This would in fact be some way from the truth. For the period we are thinking of, the third and fourth decades of the nineteenth century, was not one of socially conscious radical reform. True, the long reign of the Tories had come temporarily to an end and the Whigs were in power. True, the Act of 1832 was now on the statute-book and the rotten, pocket boroughs abolished. But it was also true that the old Poor Law had been abolished and with it the Speenhamland system of family allowances; however catastrophic the effects of that may have been in other directions, at least paupers did not starve. The New Poor Law, born out of Benthamite Utilitarianism, was based firmly on the belief that poverty was the direct result of some lack of moral fibre which it was the duty of the better-off classes to put down as firmly as possible. No one was to be allowed actually to starve, starving people were an inconvenience, but as relief was to be granted only in a workhouse, to many starvation might have been an acceptable alternative, if only to escape the harsh application of the doctrine of less eligibility.

This was an age too where children eight years old were

Housing: the great British failure

put to work in the mills, standing at machines, many of them unfenced and dangerous, for as long as sixteen hours a day, six days a week. This was an age which still sent small boys climbing up chimneys, small boys being cheaper and more convenient than brushes. This delightful manifestation of *laissez-faire* economics was to continue virtually unchecked for another forty years. This was an age that still put women and children to work in coal mines under appalling conditions which only those who knew the mines could even begin to understand. This was the age of Malthus, Mill, Bentham and Ricardo; of the Iron Law of Wages, of classical economic orthodoxy. The spirit of the age was wholly against government intervention of any kind, that is unless the rights and privileges of the dominant classes in society were threatened.

It was also an age of epidemics. Cholera, the scourge of the East, had crossed Europe in 1831 landing in Sunderland in October and spreading to London by the next February. For once Government felt constrained to act, and the result was the Cholera Act of 1832. This made provision for compulsory entry into any home for the purpose of cleansing, fumigation and whitewashing. The cost of doing this was to be met from the poor rate, which seemed reasonable enough at the time, seeing that cholera was a disease of the poor, possibly brought about by their own moral and physical shortcomings. This was, however, one of the first, probably the very first, instance of state action to interfere with living conditions; as Brian Inglis puts it: "The cholera had forced recognition of what came to be known as the sanitary idea; that the State had not merely a right but a duty to its citizens to try to protect them from health hazards arising out of bad living conditions, even at the cost of interfering with the property rights of individuals."* This was revolutionary enough and could only have been brought about by the fear that cholera might not be such a respecter of persons as had first been thought. (This was right — the Prince Consort himself was to die of the disease in Windsor Castle thirty years later.) And although the epidemic brought

*Brian Inglis, *Poverty and the Industrial Revolution*, London, Hodder & Stoughton 1971.

to light, perhaps also for the first time, how wretched those conditions were under which the poor lived, public interest waned with the epidemic and, as the Cholera Act was to lapse as soon as the epidemic was over, it soon ceased altogether. But the "sanitary idea", i.e. the conviction that bad housing conditions arose from bad sanitary conditions rather than the other way round, was to bedevil the movement towards housing reform for another sixty years; indeed it is not too much to say that its influence lingers with us still.

Certainly the sanitary idea was very much in Edwin Chadwick's mind when he undertook his mammoth inquiry into insanitary housing conditions (see page 15). Today such a disclosure would precipitate a first-class scandal; in 1842 it evoked very little interest, though its revelations seem damning enough:*

... a report from *Mr. Bland,* the medical officer of the Macclesfield union, gives the following description of the state of the residences occupied by many of the labourers of that town:

"In a part of the town called the Orchard, Watercoats, there are 34 houses without back doors, or other complete means of ventilation; the houses are chiefly small, damp, and dark; they are rendered worse with respect to dampness perhaps than they would be from the habit of the people closing their windows to keep them warm. To these houses are three privies uncovered; here little pools of water, with all kinds of offal, dead animal and vegetable matter are heaped together, a most foul and putrid mass, disgusting to the sight, and offensive to the smell; the fumes of contagion spreads periodically itself in the neighbourhood, and produces different types of fever and disorder of the stomach and bowels. The people inhabiting these abodes are pale and unhealthy, and in one house in particular are pale, bloated, and rickety."

Mr. William Rayner, the medical officer of the Heaton Norris district of the Stockport union describes the condition of a part of the population of that place:

"The localities in which fever mostly prevails in my district, are Shepherd's Buildings and Back Water Street, both in the township of Heaton Norris. Shepherd's Buildings consist of two rows of houses

*Taken from *Report on the Sanitary Condition of the Labouring Population of Gt. Britain* by Edwin Chadwick, 1842. This edition edited by M. W. Flinn, Edinburgh University Press 1965.

with a street seven yards wide between them; each row consists of
what are styled back and front houses — that is two houses placed
back to back. There are no yards or out-conveniences; the privies are
in the centre of each row, about a yard wide; over them there is part
of a sleeping-room; there is no ventilation in the bedrooms; each
house contains two rooms, viz., a house place and sleeping room
above; each room is about three yards wide and four long. In one of
these houses there are nine persons belonging to one family, and the
mother on the eve of her confinement. There are 44 houses in the
two rows, and 22 cellars, all of the same size. The cellars are let off
as separate dwellings; these are dark, damp, and very low, not more
than six feet between the ceiling and floor. The street between the
two rows is seven yards wide,. . .''

Or again:

The Report of one of the medical officers of the West
Derby union, with relation to the condition of the
labouring population connected with Liverpool, will serve
to show that the evils in question are not confined to the
labouring population of the town properly so called.

"The locality of the residences of the labouring classes are in
respect to the surrounding atmosphere favourably situated, but their
internal structure and economy the very reverse of favourable. The
cottages are in general built more with a view to the per centage of
the landlord than to the accommodation of the poor. The joiner's
work is ill performed; admitting by the doors, windows, and even
floors, air in abundance, which, however, in many cases, is not
disadvantageous to the inmates. The houses generally consist of
three apartments, viz., the day-room, into which the street-door
opens, and two bedrooms, one above the other. There is likewise
beneath the day-room a cellar, let off either by the landlord or
tenant of the house, to a more improvident class of labourers; which
cellar, in almost all cases, is small and damp, and often crowded with
inhabitants to excess. These cellars are, in my opinion, the source of
many diseases, particularly catarrh, rheumatic affections, and
tedious cases of typhus mitior, which, owing to the over-crowded
state of the apartment, occasionally pass into typhus gravior. I need
scarcely add that the furniture and bedding are in keeping with the
miserable inmates. The rooms above the day-room are often let
separately by the tenant to lodgers, varying in number from one or
two, to six or eight individuals in each, their slovenly habits,
indolence, and consequent accumulation of filth go far to promote
the prevalence of contagious and infectious diseases.

"The houses already alluded to front the street, but there are
houses in back courts still more unfavourably placed, which also

have their cellars, and their tenants of a description worse, if possible. There is commonly only one receptacle for refuse in a court of eight, ten, or twelve densely crowded houses. In the year 1836-7, I attended a family of 13, twelve of whom had typhus fever, without a bed in the *cellar*, without straw or timber shavings — frequent substitutes. They lay on the floor, and so crowded, that I could scarcely pass between them. In another house I attended 14 patients; there were only two beds in the house. All the patients, as lodgers, lay on the boards, and during their illness, never had their clothes off. I met with many cases in similar conditions, yet amidst the greatest destitution and want of domestic comfort, I have never heard during the course of twelve years' practice, a complaint of inconvenient accommodation."

Or again:

Mr. Harding, medical officer of the Epping union, states:
"The state of some of the dwellings of the poor is most deplorable as it regards their health, and also in a moral point of view. As it relates to the former, many of their cottages are neither wind nor water tight. It has often fallen to my lot to be called on to attend a labour where the wet has been running down the walls, and light to be distinguished through the roof, and this in the winter season, with no fire-place in the room. As it relates to the latter, in my opinion a great want of accommodation for bed-rooms often occurs, so that you may frequently find the father, mother, and children all sleeping in the same apartment, and in some instances the children having attained the age of 16 or 17 years, and of both sexes; and if a death occurs in the house, let the person die of the most contagious disease, they must either sleep in the same room, or take their repose in the room they live in, which most frequently is a stone or brick floor, which must be detrimental to health."

Or yet again:

"These parts of the town (Stafford) are without drainage, the houses, which are private property, are built without any regard to situation or ventilation, and constructed in a manner to ensure the greatest return at the least possible outlay. The accommodation in them does not extend beyond two rooms; these are small, and, for the most part, the families work in the day-time in the same room in which they sleep, to save fuel."

Had it not been for another outbreak of cholera in 1848, Chadwick's Report might very well have been pigeon-holed for ever. As it was it led to the passing of the first Public

Housing: the great British failure

Health Act in that year with its provisions for local Boards of
Health acting under a General Board. As it was a permissive,
not a mandatory, Act it soon became a dead letter and it was
in fact repealed a few years later; it is of interest to us chiefly
because the local Boards were to be the vehicles chosen for
putting into effect the first housing acts proper, the
Shaftesbury Acts of 1851.

Shaftesbury was very definitely one of those of whom it is
true to say that the world is the better for their having lived
in it. As a social reformer he concerned himself with hours
and conditions of work in factories, with the plight of
women and children in the mines, with Parliamentary reform,
with the climbing boys, with bad housing conditions and
much else besides. Not only was he a reformer, he was a
Tory, a Tory of great influence and the Tories were once
again in power. In 1851 (he was then Lord Ashley) from his
place in the Commons he draw public attention to the
disgraceful conditions under which the poor lived and, in
moving for leave to introduce a Bill, he declared:

A return made in 1842 gave the following result of a house
to house visitation in St. George, Hanover Square, reported
to the Statistical Society; 1,465 families of the labouring
class were found to have for their residence only 2,174
rooms; of these families 929 had but one room for the
whole family to reside in, 408 had two rooms; 94 had
three; 17 four; 8 five; 4 six; 1 seven; 1 eight; the remaining
three families were returned "not ascertained". If this was
so in *one of the best parishes of London*, (My italics —
Author) what must be the condition of the over-populous
and more needy parishes in the East of London?*

It was also Shaftesbury who had discovered, in London, a
room with a family in each of its four corners, and a room
with a cesspool underneath its boarded floor. His
representations to the Commons led to the passing of not one
but two Acts, which incidentally he piloted through both
Houses of Parliament, he having succeeded to the title of
Lord Shaftesbury that year. They were: the Common
Lodging Houses Act, 1851 and the Labouring Classes
Lodging Houses Act, 1851. The first Act concerned itself

*The Times, 9 April 1851.

26

with regulating and improving conditions in common lodging houses (buildings with a kitchen used in common by all the occupants of the building). The second, despite the similarity of the title, aimed at increasing the supply of ordinary working-class housing. It was a cumbersome Act and an adoptive one, and in any case the bodies responsible for its administration outside London, the local boards of health, were soon to be dissolved. But it was a start and it went a great deal further than public opinion, the legislature or the philosophy of the times would have permitted even a few years earlier. It was also an outward and visible manifestation of the flowering of the evangelical conscience which was at once the mark and the saving grace of the Victorian age.

(If it appears that what follows is a recitation of a list of Acts of Parliament, this is to some extent inevitable since it is through Acts of Parliament that the legislature makes its commands known. If the State intends to intervene, whether in housing or in any other sphere, it is through legislation that that intervention will come.)

The Nuisances Removal and Sanitary Acts of 1855 and 1866 authorised proceedings to be taken for the abatement of overcrowding in a house occupied by more than one family. It seems to be true of housing, as it is of so many facets of human life, that there is nothing new under the sun. The regulations which could be made under these Acts included, *inter alia,* the registration and decrowding of dwellings in multiple occupation, a matter with which Parliament has concerned itself many times since and which is not satisfactorily resolved even today.

So far the State had not concerned itself with the removal of insanitary dwellings and indeed this was still regarded as an outrageous encroachment on the rights of private property. But it was only a matter of time. In 1868 came the first of a series of Acts known as Torrens's and Cross's Acts. The first, the Artizans' and Labourers' Dwellings Act, 1868 (Torrens's Act, 1868), applied only to individual houses and was based on the principle that "the responsibility of maintaining his house in proper condition falls upon the owner, and that if he fails in his duty, the law is justified in stepping in and compelling him to perform it." But it contained no provision for compensation and this coupled with its limitation to single houses meant that it was not much used. The second, the Artizans' and Labourers' Dwellings Improvement Act, 1875 (Cross's Act, 1875), applied to whole areas which "are so structurally defective as to be incapable of repair, and so ill-placed with reference to each other as to require, to bring them up to a proper sanitary standard, nothing short of demolition and reconstruction." But Cross, Disraeli's Home Secretary, had vastly underestimated the Act's financial implications; not only was the procedure to be followed clumsy in the extreme but it could take ten years or more to assemble the land required for redevelopment. True, compulsory powers were available for those authorities (there were not many of them) who were prepared to use them, but even then the compensation provisions were so generous that the owners of unfit dwellings would get as much as they would have got for sound, fit houses. Both these Acts were amended in 1879; compensation under Cross's Act was to be market value less the cost of removing the nuisance which had caused it to be included in a scheme in the first place, and Torrens's Act was amended to include provision for compensation which had been omitted from the original Act.

When these four Acts had been in force for some years it was realised that very little was being done under them. A Select Committee sat in 1881-82. The result was the Artizans' Dwellings Act, 1882, which did little more than reduce by half the rehousing obligations laid down in the principal Acts. This was all very well and might make things easier for the rehousing authority, but what was to become of the other half of those displaced? In any case none of these five Acts did anything to promote the provision of homes for those without them.

Meanwhile, there had come on to the statute-book one of the greatest pieces of Victorian legislation, the Public Health Act, 1875. This mapped out the country into sanitary districts, urban and rural, the former having wider powers. It gave considerable powers to local authorities to control the erection and maintenance of dwelling houses and to secure the closing of unfit dwellings. It introduced model bye-laws to regulate building standards and dealt with such aspects as ventilation, natural lighting, drainage, water supply, the width of streets and the areas of open space around dwellings. True, the Act did nothing positive to encourage the building of new houses but it did at least secure that those that were built were of a higher standard. At the same time it probably limited the number of houses built and by putting up the cost almost certainly put them beyond the reach of the poorer families. Moreover the closing of unfit dwellings meant worse overcrowding elsewhere. But this is with the benefit of hindsight and it should not blind us to the fact that for its day it was a remarkable, progressive piece of legislation.

There were now on the statute-book upwards of a dozen Acts directly or indirectly concerned with housing, but it was soon felt that very little was being done either to alleviate overcrowding, insanitary conditions or to provide decent new homes for working people. Early in March 1884 therefore, the Marquis of Salisbury moved in the House of Lords for the appointment of a Royal Commission to enquire into the whole matter. It was appointed almost immediately under the chairmanship of Sir Charles Dilke. The Commission reported the next year and commenced by saying that though there had been a great improvement in the condition of the houses of the poor, yet the evils of overcrowding were becoming more serious than ever. They pointed out that, although there was legislation to meet the evils, the existing laws were not enforced. The report ranged widely, drawing attention to the defective structures of working-class dwellings, inadequate water supply and defective drainage. It referred to the serious degree of overcrowding which it put down, rather naively, to the scarcity of housing. It expressed the view that medical officers should devote their whole time to their official duties. It was convinced that the situation had been brought about by *failure in administration rather than in legislation.* In short it found that although powers existed, they were not being used. Consequent upon the Commission's report another act (Housing of the Working Classes Act, 1885) found its way on to the statute-book, but it did little more than tinker with the existing legislation. It was not until the great reform of local government in 1888 which set up county and county borough councils, not forgetting the L.C.C., that the way was clear for the first comprehensive housing act, the Housing of the Working Classes Act of 1890. This Act was divided into no less than seven parts, of which only the first three need concern us here. Part One brought up to date the Cross Acts provisions for dealing with insanitary areas. Part Two did the same for the Torrens Acts provisions for dealing with individual unfit dwellings. Part Three, and this is the important one, gave unequivocal powers to local authorities to provide new homes for working people. This part was adoptive and placed no duty on the shoulders of the local authorities, but it gave the forward-looking authorities the opportunity to do something positive in housing provision and to meet the cost from the rates. (See page 18.)

An interesting point to note is that the 1885 and 1890 Acts mentioned housing of the "working classes", a limitation which was to accompany housing legislation until the term was dropped in 1949, mainly because of the difficulty of identifying who were the "working classes". Even the Victorians were not too certain of its definition; a contemporary work thought that the only clue appeared to be the definition of persons of the "labouring class" contained in the Standing Orders of Parliament. This definition ran as follows:

The expression "labouring class" means mechanics, artisans, labourers, and others working for wages, hawkers, costermongers, persons not working for wages but working at some trade or handicraft without employing others (except members of their own family), and persons other than domestic servants whose income does not exceed an average of thirty shillings a week, and the families of any such persons who may be residing with them.

This seems rather hard on domestic servants, but it is interesting to note that no other definition of "working class" was ever made manifest either in statute or case law over the whole period.

As far as this period is concerned we are almost at an end. There was a further Act in 1909 but this was a planning rather than a housing act. Further legislation was contemplated in 1912 and again in 1914, but the coming of war caused it to be deferred. The only other state intervention as such was the imposition of rent control in 1915, reasonable enough in the context of the time; its continuation, in one form or another right up to the present time, was however to cause problems enough for future generations. That is a story for a future chapter.

In this chapter we have spanned, however sketchily and inadequately, the seventy years from the first Public Health Act to the end of the First World War. We have seen how it was that the State was forced to take the first timid steps towards intervention in the housing field and how sheer pressure of events coupled with an awakening social conscience forced the Government, frequently in the face of bitter opposition, to move from point to point until by the turn of the century it was possible for local authorities, had they the will, to seize the nettle and make a massive contribution towards the health and well-being of the working people. That they did not do so must be counted among the first of many failures in housing and it was largely a failure of will, first and foremost a failure of will on the part of the Government which throughout the whole housing story consistently moved too little and too late. Time and time again the sweeping radical changes the reformers were looking for were watered down in Parliament until they emerged emasculated and totally ineffectual. Time and time again the Government of the day put off taking action until events forced their hand. The governments of the nineteenth century, Liberal and Tory alike, were imbued with a very strong sense of the rights of property, rights with which they were reluctant to interfere. They were convinced that an "Englishman's home is his castle", which was all very well for those who had decent homes, but the hovels described by Chadwick or Shaftesbury could hardly be described as homes, never mind castles. And throughout the period continued the interminable argument on the issue of self-help versus state help, a conflict which has not been satisfactorily resolved even today.

Finally there was the failure on the part of Government, local authorities and reformers alike to accept two vitally important facts. The first was that if the State decrees that certain standards must be achieved, whether in housing or anything else, somebody has to pay. This issue was shirked by all concerned, at any rate until 1919. The second was the fact that improving sanitary conditions by closure and demolition will, unless new dwellings are provided at the same time, result in worse conditions than before because of overcrowding. This seems to be so obvious as to be hardly worth mentioning, yet it did not seem to dawn on those involved until well into the twentieth century.

At the close of this period a great world war was raging; the adult manhood of the country was compelled to engage in foreign war on a scale unprecedented in the history of the nation. If the State could enjoin such risk and sacrifice on the part of its sons, perhaps the State could also be obliged to secure their health and comfort in time of peace. And so the way was prepared for the second great stage of state intervention in housing — state-subsidised local authority housing. To this we will now turn.

4 Subsidised housing 1919-1939*

We have seen how, under the twin spurs of epidemic disease and burgeoning social conscience, the State had been forced to intervene to improve the housing condition of the working population and later to increase the supply of working-class houses. These first steps were timid enough, for example if a local authority wished to take action under Parts I, II or III of the 1890 Act it had first to wait upon representations made to it by a medical officer of health, two justices or twelve ratepayers. It then had to prepare a scheme and advertise it for three consecutive weeks in September or October or November. Provisional Orders made by the Secretary of State confirming the scheme (or the Compulsory Purchase Order in the case of action under Part III) had to be confirmed by Act of Parliament. In the case of Part I the local authority could not, without the consent of the Secretary of State, erect new houses themselves, and if this consent were forthcoming they had to sell the houses within ten years; under Part II the Authority could erect dwellings but still had to sell after ten years; under Part III, however, if after seven years the houses became unnecessary or too expensive, they could be sold provided the Secretary of State consented, but this was not obligatory. The financial loss from such schemes fell entirely on the shoulders of the ratepayers and this was a burden that ratepayers were most

---

*This chapter deals with the development of state, i.e. municipal, housing in the period between the two world wars. I would like here to acknowledge the very great debt that I, and all students of housing, owe to Dr. Marian Bowley for her book *Housing and the State* (London, George Allen & Unwin, 1945), and magnificent work, now unfortunately out of print, whose equal has been rarely attempted and never achieved.

unwilling to bear. This, coupled with the cumbersome procedure required by the Acts, meant that comparatively few houses were built under them, and those that were built were an unconscionable time a-building.

Just before the First World War the housing reformers were pressing for loans to local authorities for housing purposes at 2½ per cent, that the sinking fund to amortise the capital debt should be borne by the local authority (on the ground that the houses would be a future asset), and that houses so built should be let to the poorest. The war intervened and in consequence a Bill putting these provisions into effect was lost, but the pressure for reform continued unabated throughout the war. Later the proposal for a 2½ per cent rate of interest was abandoned in favour of an arrangement whereby the Treasury would bear all losses arising from local authority housing schemes except for the product of a local penny rate. Before the war was over a Ministry of Reconstruction was set up in the hope that among other things plans could be drawn up for a massive housing drive after peace had broken out. At the same time the Tudor Walters Committee was busy laying down minimum standards for working-class houses and brought forth the first Government-sponsored Housing Manual, very advanced for its time, which had a profound influence on estate planning and house design for many years afterwards. So much so in fact that many years later in 1935 Lord Simon of Wythenshawe was quoted as saying: "It is difficult to see how this standard can be improved . . . we believe it is safe to assume that the Tudor Walters cottage may be regarded by town planners as a permanent standard."

The First World War came to an end and a Government came to power pledged to build "Homes for Heroes". Broadly speaking the intention was to build 500,000 houses for the working classes over a period of three years. This was a rate of building not achieved previously for many years, if at all, but even so it hardly measured up to the needs of the time. According to Dr Bowley the shortage of dwellings at the time of the Armistice amounted to something like 600,000, and by 1921 this deficit had risen to 805,000. And these figures made no allowance for replacing insanitary or

34

obsolescent houses and those which were pulled down for other reasons. So even at this stage we may reasonably say that the sights had not been raised sufficiently high and the programme would have been inadequate even if it had been fulfilled. In fact it was not. Dr Addison managed to get the Housing, Town Planning, etc., Act passed in July 1919 and thus imposed on local authorities the duty of surveying the needs of their districts with regard to houses and of making and carrying out plans for the building of these houses. The sense of urgency felt at the time is emphasised by the requirement that the first survey had to be carried out within three months of the passage of the Act. Ministry of Health approval was needed before the plans could be carried out and once that approval had been obtained the Treasury would bear all losses in excess of the product of a penny rate. Local authorities were to be the chosen instruments for providing working-class houses (with some help from public utility societies — these would be known now as non-profit-making housing associations), and the State would for all intents and purposes foot the bill. The dreams of the housing reformers had been realised.

Or so they thought. In fact the programme, which we have shown to have been inadequate, turned out to have been grossly over-optimistic, and in 1920 subsidies were offered to private builders as well. This took the form of a lump sum of £130 to £160 to any builder who built a house either for sale or to rent. There was a restriction on floor area of these houses but no limit on price, nor was there any restriction on who should occupy them. The subsidy was available for only one year. In the event not more than one-third of the houses attracting the subsidy were working-class dwellings.

As to the rents which local authorities could charge for dwellings built under the Act, these were to be based (until March 1927) on rents charged for comparable existing working-class houses, though allowance could be made for the better amenities of the new dwellings and the rent-paying capacity of the tenants. By March 1927 it was supposed that the high costs associated with the immediate post-war period would have subsided; rents were thereafter to be economic rents based on post-1927 costs (irrespective of when the houses were built). This is an interesting arrangement. Since the Treasury subvention would go to those authorities with the greatest losses (and thus presumably to those areas where tenants were least able to pay economic rents), the subsidies provided under this Act were, in a rough and ready way, progressive with need. And this was not to be the case again until 1972 and then under very different circumstances.

Despite the high hopes, the houses were not forthcoming. The Treasury, not for the first and certainly not for the last time, took fright and it was decided in July 1921 that the subsidy should be discontinued. Altogether 213,821 houses were provided under the Act, of these 170,090 by local authorities, 4,545 by public utilities and 39,186 by private enterprise under the lump-sum arrangements. In addition about 54,000 dwellings were provided by private enterprise without subsidy so that the total number of dwellings built since the Armistice came to just over a quarter of a million. And this, it will be remembered, came to just under half the number of houses which it was felt was needed at the time of the Armistice. After less than two years of state-subsidised provision of dwellings for the working classes, the last state was worse than the first. Let Dr Bowley complete the story:

No new policy was inaugurated until the spring of 1923. By that time building by local authorities had dwindled to an insignificant level as the permitted number of subsidised houses was completed, nor had plans been made for the future. During these two years no serious attempts at all appear to have been made to deal with the outstanding problems of building costs and supplies of skilled labour. The alarm engendered by the fact that the Treasury had nearly burnt its fingers had turned into inertia, doubtless to the relief of those who were root and branch opposed to State intervention. It was a dismal story.

It was commonly supposed at the time that it was the Addison subsidy itself that pushed house-building costs sky-high during the period immediately following the First World War. Later examination of the circumstances shows quite clearly that this was not the case and that building costs had already started to fall when the whole scheme was axed in 1921. Nor can its failure be wholly attributed to the fact

36

that the Treasury commitment was "open-ended". The Ministry of Health had power to control standards, costs and rents although it probably failed to make proper administrative provision for this to be achieved. (No further "open-ended" subsidy was offered to local housing authorities until 1967; but that subsidy was accompanied by strict cost-control by the housing cost yardstick.) Della Nevitt suggests that the penny rate local subsidy was more onerous than at first thought and that local ratepayers dug their heels in.* This may be so, but it does not account for the fact that the decision to stop building under Addison's Act was a Government decision. Had the subsidy been continued, local authority housing today would present a different and a happier picture. As it was, we can rightly condemn the decision to abandon Addison as a failure of will from which calamitous results were to flow. To the extent that the subsidy did help to put up prices during 1919-20, it is proof of the need to control resources administratively and comprehensively in times of shortage if social goals are to be achieved. And that would be difficult enough in 1973; in 1921 it was unthinkable.

After the enforced breathing space of 1921-23, there was the inevitable return to financial orthodoxy in 1923 after a change of government. Under Neville Chamberlain's Housing Act (Housing, etc., Act 1923), local authorities were to receive a subsidy of £6 a year for twenty years. Private builders could get the same subsidy or alternatively a lump sum of £75. No subsidy from the rates was required at all. Houses could attract the subsidy provided they reached a minimum size and standard and did not exceed a certain maximum size. Otherwise there were no limitations as to rent or price or who could have them. Moreover, the local authorities could build the houses only if they could persuade the Minister of Health that it would be better if they did so rather than private enterprise. So not only was there a reversal of roles between central and local government (in the matter of ultimate financial responsibility), there was also a reversal of roles between public and private enterprise (as to who should build the houses). Clearly Chamberlain was

Housing, Taxation and Subsidies, London, Thomas Nelson 1965.

37

convinced that the housing shortage was only temporary and
would soon be over and done with. This is an extraordinary
idea, the more so when one considers the evidence to the
contrary which had been mounting over the previous fifty
years. But the view that private enterprise would be able to
fulfil all needs without the encouragement of·subsidy was
widely held at the time and indeed is not yet dead, fifty years
later. In the sense that half a loaf is better than no bread, the
Chamberlain subsidy was better than nothing; none-the-less it
was a regrettable and regressive measure and represented a
victory for those who were determined that the provision of
working-class houses should not become a social service. And
the fact that the subsidy came as a lump-sum payment meant
that it went to those districts where the houses were actually
built without regard to the rent-paying capacity of the
population or the financial needs of the district itself.

Chamberlain's policy was short-lived. The Conservative
Government which came to power in 1922 gave way in 1924
to the Labour Party and the new Minister of Health,
Wheatley, brought in another Housing Act (Housing
(Financial Provisions) Act, 1924). The new subsidy was still
to be paid as a lump sum, £9 in urban areas and £12 10s. 0d.
in agricultural parishes. This is the first time that it was
recognised in the legislation that different areas might have
different needs. The authorities themselves could contribute
£4 10s. 0d. a year from the rates. The role of the authority
vis-à-vis private enterprise was once again reversed, it being no
longer required that the authority should prove its
superiority to private enterprise before being allowed to
build. Curiously the Chamberlain subsidy was not abolished,
indeed it was now made available for houses completed
before 1 October 1939, i.e. fifteen years ahead. In fact, long
before that date both the Chamberlain and the Wheatley
subsidies had been abolished and this attempt to introduce a
long-term housing programme was thus frustrated. In the
meantime, Wheatley had made his famous "gentleman's
agreement" with the building unions, the latter relaxing their
rules so that the supply of skilled workmen, the principal
bottleneck preventing an increase in the rate of house-
building, could be increased.

Before we leave Wheatley, it is worth while having a look at the rather complicated rent arrangements which came as a package with the subsidies. Rents, on average, were to be fixed in relation to the controlled rents of houses built before the First World War, in fact they were not to exceed controlled rents unless it was necessary to do so to prevent a loss after the authority had contributed £4 10s. 0d. per house per annum from the rates. This applied only to average rents; individual rents could be varied at will. This is the second occasion (Addison's Act being the first) on which rents were laid down as having to compare with controlled private rents. This was all very well, but it had already been well demonstrated that these rents were not within the reach of the poorer families in the community. Many felt that these were the very people that state-aided housing was meant to benefit. Moreover the Act did not make it clear which controlled rents were to be selected as the comparables for local authority rents. It was all rather vague.

The 1924 Labour Government was short-lived and in 1927 the succeeding Conservative administration decided to reduce the Chamberlain subsidy to £4 a house for twenty years and the Wheatley subsidy to £7 10s. 0d. a house for forty years (£11 in rural parishes). The local authority contribution was reduced to £3 15s. 0d. Two years later the Chamberlain subsidy was dropped altogether and the Wheatley subsidy would have been further reduced had not a Labour Government regained power in the summer of 1929. The Wheatley subsidy was repealed in 1933. Between them, the Chamberlain and Wheatley subsidies cost the taxpayer about £6.9 million a year from 1934 on; this according to Dr Bowley was equal in 1936 to about 1.8 per cent of the receipts from income tax, super tax and estate duties taken together, not an onerous burden. The same Acts cost the ratepayers no more than about £1.9 million in 1936 when it represented only 0.9 per cent of the total rate expenditure. With their demise ended the first attempt to establish the local authorities as suppliers of houses for ordinary working-class families in the face of a declining private enterprise. This principle was not to be re-introduced until 1946 when once again, following a worldwide cataclysm, the hearts and minds of men were full of social purpose.

Before returning to the 1930s it is worth remembering, as Dr Bowley reminds us, that during the eleven and a half years during which the Chamberlain and/or Wheatley subsidies were available, private enterprise and local authorities between them had built rather more than 2.2 million houses. This is equal to 28 per cent of all the houses existing in 1921! The last houses to be built with the aid of the Wheatley subsidy were completed in 1935. Their completion brought the total number of houses built by local authorities with the aid of Chamberlain/Wheatley subsidies to 579,800. Add to this the 170-odd thousand local authority houses built under Addison's Act and we get a total of three-quarters of a million dwellings spread over sixteen years. The highest number built under Addison in any one year was 80 thousand (1922) and the highest number under Chamberlain/ Wheatley was 103.9 thousand (1928). This cannot be regarded as an impressive achievement, although this latter figure was not to be bettered until after the Second World War, when subsidies were much more generous.

While all this was going on nothing much had been done about the slums. Although local authorities had possessed powers to deal with slums for over fifty years, the energies of local authorities (if energies is the right word) had, in the years 1919-1930, been concentrated on building new homes. This was not unreasonable; the war had ended with a massive shortage of houses and in such a situation there seemed to be little point in getting rid of any houses of any sort, however bad. It seems that during this period about eleven thousand slum dwellings had been replaced, mainly with the help of a subsidy under the Chamberlain Act which provided that the Treasury would bear half the annual loss on approved schemes. Now that the acute shortage had been eliminated, pressure began to mount for action to clear the slums. The minority Labour Government elected in 1929 decided in fulfilment of its election pledges to embark on a slum clearance programme. Arthur Greenwood, Minister of Health, introduced and secured the passage of the Housing Act, 1930, in which the Wheatley Act subsidy was continued for general needs but a new principle was introduced in regard to subsidies for slum clearance. Instead of giving a fixed amount per dwelling, the subsidy was given for each person rehoused from a slum. This amounted to £2 10s. 0d. per person in agricultural parishes and £2 5s. 0d. in urban parishes. There was also an extra £1 per house when agricultural workers were rehoused. The local authority's contribution was £3 15s. 0d. All these contribution were for forty years. There was also, for the first time, an additional subsidy for building tall flats on expensive sites. The circular accompanying the Act emphasised that a subsidy should be given only to those who needed it and only for so long as they needed it.

The Act therefore made it possible for local authorities to introduce differential rents or rent rebate schemes. Provided the accounts balanced and provided that the rents were what tenants could reasonably be expected to pay, the authority could charge what rents it thought fit. (There had been some doubt up to this time as to whether differential renting was legal; the Chamberlain and Wheatley Acts had not forbidden it but neither had they sanctioned it. Even as late as 1935 a case on this point had gone as far as the Court of Appeal.) Furthermore Greenwood intended to keep local authorities up to the mark. They were to consider the housing needs of their areas as often as occasion arose or three months after the Minister of Health had instructed them to do so. Every authority with a population of more than 20,000 was required to produce plans for dealing with slum clearance and building more houses during the next five years.

But it all came to nothing, or to be more exact, the combination of slum clearance plus building for general needs was put in abeyance because of the economy campaign (this was 1930 remember). Before it could be effectively revived, the Wheatley subsidy was concluded by the Housing (Financial Provisions) Act 1933. Thereafter local authority activity was to be concentrated on slum clearance and rehousing in a five-year programme. New houses for the working class were to be left to private enterprise, supplemented where necessary by unsubsidised building by the local authorities. The 1933 Act also encouraged borrowing from the building societies for investment in housing to let. This was to be done by local authorities guaranteeing mortgage loans which exceeded 70 per cent of valuation. In fact the building societies did not need much encouraging, they already had more money than they knew what to do with, but the scheme was not popular with the local councils and by March 1939 fewer than 22,000 loans had been guaranteed in this way.

Once again, those who had set their faces against state intervention in the housing situation had triumphed and the local authority function was reduced to what it had been prior to the First World War; with this difference, that subsidy was now available. The degree of local authority activity from now on would depend on the view that authorities themselves took of the state of housing in their areas. And as we shall discuss in a later chapter, authorities have always been prone to underestimate the number of unfit dwellings within their borders. This situation was affected but not fundamentally altered by the Housing Act, 1935 which aimed at dealing with overcrowding. Overcrowding of course has always been one of the more pressing housing evils and one which the slum clearance policies of the nineteenth century had aggravated rather than alleviated. The 1935 Act aimed to deal with overcrowding during a period of five years following the five years of slum clearance. And once overcrowding had been abolished in any area it was to become a legal offence and the local authority would have the duty of providing the additional houses where necessary. Certain subsidies were available under this Act for flats of three storeys and over on expensive sites, a discretionary subsidy not exceeding £5 per annum in special cases and a rural area subsidy of between £2 and £8 a house for forty years. All these were to be supplemented by contributions from the rates.

Now a situation had been reached where subsidies for slum clearance were put on quite a different basis from those for overcrowding. This did not make sense; people live in overcrowded homes for the same reason they live in slums, i.e. they cannot afford anything better. This was recognised in 1938 by the Housing (Financial Provisions) Act which gave a uniform subsidy of £5 10s. 0d. a year for forty years whether for slum clearance or for decrowding.

42

Up to 1935 local authorities were required to keep separate accounts for houses built under each of the Acts mentioned. The Housing Act of that year permitted them to consolidate these accounts into one housing revenue account. It was thus possible to pool all income including subsidies, and rents, and to adjust rents without reference to the actual costs of building individual dwellings. This was a real advantage and one which was to become more apparent during the years of rising costs following the Second World War. It meant a much greater flexibility in the way the housing stock could be used. But it also meant that, for instance, dwellings which had been built to increase the general supply of working-class housing could now be used as replacements for condemned slums instead of the authority having to build new ones. To quote Dr Bowley again: "This element of elasticity was a real gain; the weakness of the whole system was the inexpansibility of the supply of houses to let, and the criticisms of the new accounting system turn entirely on the point that it tended to discourage new building."

The 1935 Act also envisaged some of the Treasury's subsidies being returned in due course to the Government. Any surplus made after 1940 was to be divided between the Treasury and the local authority in proportion to their contributions towards subsidy. But before this could happen the country was fighting another world war.

Local authorities became involved in housing in the first place as part of their sanitary functions. This was logical since the authorities themselves had in many cases come into being in order to carry out sanitary duties (Urban and Rural District Councils had in the first place been known as Urban and Rural Sanitary Authorities). They were later involved in the provision of new houses as an extension of those duties. When the first great experiment in the state provision of houses was attempted in 1919, local authorities were the chosen vehicle partly because of history, partly because the authorities themselves were moving towards omni-competence, but mainly because "they were there". Many of them were unwilling to shoulder this new burden and many more, however willing they may have been, lacked the resources. Their involvement in housing affairs was no longer logical, though it may have been administratively convenient. Nor were the acts of Government consistent; over the twenty years under discussion there had been no less than eight major changes in housing policy, an average of one change every two-and-a-half years. Moreover the performance of the department of state charged with the responsibility for housing was uneven in the extreme, not least because many (fortunately not all) senior civil servants were completely out of sympathy with the policies which the Government they were paid to serve were trying to implement. Despite all the difficulties, the local authorities in England and Wales managed to build rather more than one million homes during this period. Compared with any previous time this was an impressive performance. Moreover more people had been rehoused from the slums during the five years' campaign than all the earlier slum clearance schemes put together. This was a not inconsiderable achievement, but it was not enough. The new era had opened with a campaign for "Homes for Heroes"; hundreds of thousands of the "heroes" were still living under bad or even atrocious conditions twenty years later. Rudyard Kipling's observations on the public's peacetime attitudes to Tommy Atkins were proved to be excruciatingly acute. It was, as Dr Bowley had said, a dismal story.

5 Subsidised housing 1945-1973

We have seen how, between the great wars of the twentieth century, the efforts of the housing reformers at last bore fruit and how, in the general aura of social solidarity and common purpose which seems to characterise the closing stages of a great war (but which does not long thereafter persist), housing provided by the State for ordinary working-class people became not only acceptable but positively sought as a proper objective of government policy. We have further seen how that when the bills started to come in, public interest in homes for its erstwhile heroes quickly faded; how the sheer numerical need for houses was grossly underestimated; how undue faith was placed in private enterprise for the production of houses for all social groups; how the role of local authorities was, as in previous times, dominated by the sanitary idea and how the policies of government, well-meaning as they may have been, failed to get to the root of the problem and help those most in need.

We now come to the third phase of state intervention in housing affairs, the period from the end of the Second World War to the present time. The first and most disheartening thing to note about this period is how very like the inter-war period it turned out to be. Governments and those responsible for formulating policy (they may well be different groups) appeared to have learnt little and to have forgotten nothing. And this despite a growing sophistication in social and economic affairs — Beveridge, for example, would have not been possible (nor thought necessary) in the years immediately following the First World War. True, the British people emerged from the Second World War with a greater confidence in themselves and their capabilities than at any time this century. And not without reason. They had withstood the onslaughts of an enemy equipped with the most powerful war machine the world had then seen, and they had themselves fashioned a military apparatus which itself made a significant contribution to final victory. The man in the street began to realise, perhaps for the first time, that he could influence the whole circumstance of his life. It did not greatly matter therefore that Britain had emerged from the war an impoverished nation with large areas of its cities devastated and much of its industrial equipment obsolete and fit only for the scrap heap. The rebuilding of Britain — and this included its housing — would be dealt with in the same way as a military operation; a Minister of the Crown said as much when introducing the first post-war Housing Bill. The General Election, held after victory had been achieved in Europe but before Japan had been beaten, had brought to power a Labour Government with a massive majority; this Government proceeded to set about the housing problem in a most determined way. For the time being, the Minister could confirm compulsory purchase orders "without public local inquiry or hearing" (Donnison), which was in itself an astonishingly radical departure. House-building had for all intents and purposes come to a stop during the war (some houses, maybe 200,000 in all, had been built for war workers but all other house-building had ceased), but was resumed under the provisions of the Housing (Financial and Miscellaneous Provisions) Act of 1946.

Local authority house-building was no longer to be restricted to slum clearance, and a general subsidy of £16 10s. 0d. per dwelling for sixty years (£25 10s. 0d. in agricultural districts) was to be matched by a local rate contribution of £5 10s. 0d. (£1 10s. 0d. in agricultural districts). Moreover the Minister could reduce the rate subsidy in certain circumstances and make up the difference from central funds. There were additional subsidies for flats and high-cost land and for housing associations. Local authorities were once again to be the chosen instrument for the housing drive; they could, however, pass on a small proportion of their allocations to private builders. The Minister, Aneurin Bevan, one of the ablest men ever to be put

46

in charge of the nation's housing, made it clear that local authorities had been chosen because they could be made to do as they were told: "the speculative builder, by his very nature, is not a plannable instrument". But the Labour Government, despite its enthusiasm, had undertaken no radical reappraisal of pre-war thinking and, very much as had been the case in the Addison era, relied on a combination of public subsidies coupled with rent control (reimposed in 1939) in the privately rented sector. Once again, as in 1919, the sheer size of the problem had been grossly underestimated. The "Caretaker Government" (the Government which followed the wartime coalition and which preceded the post-war Labour Government) had thought that three-quarters of a million dwellings were necessary to get rid of the shortage, perhaps a further half-million to complete slum clearance, and that something like three or four million would be built by the mid-fifties. Once again even this modest target was to prove elusive; the four millionth post-war dwelling (Great Britain) was not completed until 1962. Once again economic problems held back the drive for more houses, only this time there were additional factors such as the balance of payments, the general shortage of materials, made worse by the lack of foreign currency with which to buy them, the fuel crisis of 1947, and so on. Moreover Bevan had much else on his mind. As Minister of Health he was the architect of the National Health Service, undoubtedly the Labour Government's greatest legacy to post-war Britain; had he been able to devote his whole time to housing, things might have turned out differently. He had set himself a target of 240,000 a year but never reached it. In 1947 12,541 dwellings were completed, and 206,559 the following year. The target was thereupon reduced to 200,000 a year, but in fact for the remainder of the Government's life output did not rise much above 170,000 a year. By the end of June 1951, 913,604 permanent dwellings had been completed in Great Britain and there were 214,099 under construction.

Meanwhile, in an effort to supplement the inadequate production of new dwellings, the Housing Act, 1949, introduced a system of improvement grants whereby the

Government paid to local authorities at a fixed rate for twenty years, three-quarters of the annual loss incurred by improving or converting existing buildings. The dwellings thus provided had to have an expected life of not less than thirty years and had to conform with standards laid down. This was an extension of the kind of grant which had been made available in 1926 for agricultural cottages only; in fact very little use was made of it. The same Act, ostensibly to encourage the creation of mixed schemes and balanced communities, removed the requirement that local authorities should build only for "the working classes". It is more likely that it was becoming increasingly difficult to identify just who the "working classes" were.

But the Labour Government were running out of steam, in housing as in much else, and they had quite enough to be getting on with merely in keeping the country's economic head above water by encouraging exports, restricting home consumption (which included rationing building materials), and restraining inflation. In any case, the size of the long-term problem had not yet been appreciated, set as it was against a background of predictions of a falling population. This is worthy of note. Between the wars, the birth-rate had fallen to about half the 1914 figure. During and immediately after the Second World War the birth-rate rose to near replacement level as men in the forces were demobilised and returned home. But men who had been separated from their wives and sweethearts apparently did not want to be surrounded by too many children during the early years of their reunited bliss and the birth rate fell again thereafter. Gloomy forecasts of a declining population (with all the problems that *that* would have entailed) continued well into the 'fifties: ". . . it is at least possible that a hundred years hence our numbers will be back where they were just before the Industrial Revolution — and this despite all the improvements in health which have steadily reduced the death-rate over the last forty years."* As it turned out, nothing could have been less likely. The period following 1951 was marked by a modest but real and continuing

*Croome and Hammond, *An Economic History of Britain,* London, Christophers 1953.

improvement in the standard of living. The bearing of children was no longer as economically disastrous (or indeed as morally reprehensible) as it had been hitherto for a large section of the population; they increased and multiplied, if not exceedingly, much too much for comfort. The birth-rate which in 1951 had stood at about 15.8 per thousand (actually lower than in 1932) decreased the following year but thereafter steadily increased until it reached 18.7 in 1964. Although this figure is nothing like as high as the nineteenth-century levels (as recently as 1870 the birth-rate was 35.0), it was still quite enough to send the demographers' predictions haywire. It also upset long-term predictions of housing requirements. A falling population is an ageing population and the potential housing requirements will be less than for an increasing population of the same size. And any temporary "bulge" in the population can more readily be accommodated; it is only a matter of time before it disappears. Therefore the planners felt less keenly in 1951 the pressing need for a large and long-term house-building programme than some of their successors do in 1973.

If the Labour Government were running out of steam, the Conservatives were just beginning to raise theirs. Stunned by the unexpected loss of office in 1945, they took several years to regain self-confidence. By 1950 public support for the Government was waning and at the Conservative Party Conference that year a somewhat hesitant platform had forced upon them an undertaking to build 300,000 houses a year when next in power. This was enough. The General Election in that year reduced Labour's majority drastically and the Prime Minister (Attlee) went to the country again in 1951 and was defeated for his pains.

Thus the Conservatives came to power committed to building 300,000 dwellings a year. At the same time they were also committed to a return to free enterprise. The Housing Minister, Harold Macmillan, realised that he couldn't manage it with private enterprise alone and once again local authorities were chosen as the instrument through which government pledges would be redeemed. The Housing Act, 1952, raised all subsidies, partly to meet increased costs, partly to meet higher rates of interest (now 4¼ per cent), but mainly to ensure that the local authorities kept on building. The Exchequer subsidy was increased to £26 14s. 0d. per annum (£35 14s. 0d. in agricultural areas) with corresponding rate subsidies of £8 18s. 0d. or £2 10s. 0d. In keeping with Conservative intentions to encourage the sale of council houses, the provision in the 1936 Act that the best possible price should be obtained was repealed, to be replaced by a requirement limiting resale price, or rent within five years from the date of purchase. Greater assistance was now being given to council tenants by means of subsidy than was being given to owner-occupiers through tax-relief.

It worked. In 1952 the number of new houses built amounted to 239,922, a post-war record (for which, however, Macmillan could hardly take the credit). The next year the target was beaten decisively with 318,779 and in 1954 it rose to 347,805. Of this latter figure the local authorities had contributed 234,973, an increase of 45 per cent over 1951. Private builders had built only 90,936 but they were coming up fast; this was an increase of more than 300 per cent over 1951. 1954 represented the high point in housing production at that time, both in the total numbers built and the numbers built by local authorities. The latter fell away rapidly until by 1957 they completed fewer than they had in 1949. But by then Macmillan had gone and so had his successor, Duncan Sandys.

The Macmillan house-building drive must be considered a success, but only compared with the stated target. One can never be sure when reference is made to such figures as 300,000 a year whether the speaker is referring to England and Wales, Great Britain or the United Kingdom. Frequently government statistics flit from one to the other depending on how they want the figures to look. If one is referring to England and Wales, i.e. that part of the country for which the Minister of Housing and Local Government had responsibility, then the target was reached in 1954 but not again thereafter until ten years later. The figures for Great Britain, on the other hand, exceeded 300,000 in 1953 and did not afterwards fall below that figure except in the years 1958 to 1961 and 1963. House production for the United Kingdom topped 300,000 in 1953 and fell below that figure only in

1958 and 1959, reaching a record figure of 425,834 in 1968; this however happened during the tenure of a Government pledged to build *500,000 a year.* Macmillan had used the local authorities to redeem his party's pledges on housing and although he did not thereafter discard them completely it can be claimed that on the whole his successors, Duncan Sandys and Henry Brooke, did.

The brakes, however, had been taken off the private builder. With the coming of the Conservative Government, licences for house-building were granted freely and by 1954 building licensing was abolished altogether. Once the private builders had started it was difficult to stop them. When therefore it was judged necessary to restrict the numbers of houses being built (to restrain inflation or to prevent overloading the industry for example), it was the local authority and not the private builder as hitherto who provided the balancing factor and was singled out for cutback. And as Donnison puts it, "once the local authority building programme lost its central position among the instruments of housing policy, the tide of public opinion could rapidly turn against it." Government subsidy, which in England and Wales alone totalled about £20 million in 1949-50, shot up to £30 million in 1952-53 and to over £35 million the following year. This was a natural outcome of the increased Macmillan subsidies and the resultant rise in production. It was very easy for the Government, the Treasury and the taxpayer to take fright at this apparently limitless demand and it came as no surprise when the Government did so; much as it had done in 1921. Once again state involvement in housing was relegated to the sanitary function with the passing of the Housing Repairs and Rents Act in 1954, coupled with the Housing (Review of Contributions) Order of the same year.

Slum clearance for all intents and purposes had come to an end with the 1938 Munich crisis on the very reasonable grounds that with a major war looming ahead it was prudent to keep in being as many dwellings as possible even if they were of a low standard. For much the same sort of reason, comparatively few slums had been cleared since the war. Under the 1954 Act local authorities were required to assess the number of slum dwellings in their areas and to submit proposals for dealing with them. They could also buy slum property in advance of demolition and keep them in use (by "patching" with the aid of grants) for as long as they had to be occupied. The idea was to help those authorities which had large numbers of slum dwellings and could not hope to clear them quickly. The Act also laid down, for the first time, a uniform standard of fitness, in other words it defined, or attempted to define, what constitutes a slum. Improvement grants were to be encouraged by removing the top limit on the cost of work eligible for grant under the 1949 Act, although the maximum grant stayed at £400. The minimum expected "life" of a property so improved was reduced from thirty to fifteen years, and the increase of rent allowed to landlords was raised from 6 per cent to 8 per cent of his net expenditure.

Not long afterwards, the Housing (Review of Contributions) Order, 1954 reduced subsidies to £22 1s. 0d. in urban areas (£31 1s. 0d. in agricultural areas) and made corresponding reductions in other grants. This was a clear discouragement to local authorities to build for general needs unless they were determined to do so, and it was a portent of what was to come. The Minister, Harold Macmillan, speaking in December 1953, declared: ". . . we intend during 1954 to make a new assault on the housing problem. We are going to give a fresh impetus to slum clearance. We are going to speed up . . . improving . . . the older houses and we are going to go on building new houses, so that another million people will have a happier Christmas next year." By the following March he had already forgotten about "going on building new houses". Speaking in London, he said, "In this third phase we must return . . . to the removal of slums, and to the full routine repair and improvement of millions of sound houses. And as there are more slums than we can clear and replace in five years or so, we must do some patching . ." By the time he got to the 1954 Conservative Party Conference he had decided to reduce the local authority contribution in 1955 to 160,000. By the time 1955 arrived he had gone to the Foreign Office and Duncan Sandys was Minister.

Mr Sandys' main contribution to housing legislation

appears to have been the Housing Subsidies Act, 1956, which reduced subsidy for general needs to £10 a dwelling a year. It also abolished the requirement that local authorities must make a contribution out of the General Rate Fund, though they could still do so voluntarily and in any case had to make good any deficiency. The slum clearance subsidy and some other subsidies were retained. The act was followed by the Housing Subsidies Order, 1956, which abolished subsidy for general needs but kept it for dwellings with not more than one bedroom, i.e. for dwellings for old people or single person households.

It was also about this time that government policies were hardening towards publicly-provided housing. The Conservative Party had never, with one or two notable exceptions, been entirely convinced of the propriety of council housing, though as we have seen they had been party to a number of parliamentary measures which increased public involvement in the housing field. When they had returned to power in 1951 they would have preferred to have turned away there and then from the local authority as house builder (except perhaps for slum clearance which is unattractive to private enterprise as there is little or no profit to be made) and left it all to private enterprise. But private enterprise was not ready and in any case this policy would have been in direct conflict with public opinion. But by the mid to late 'fifties public opinion was shifting. Housing was no longer undisputed king. There were great difficulties in the immediate post-war years but everyone was agreed on fundamental policy which was to get as many houses built as possible and to see that they went to the people who needed them most. It had been an emergency situation, but one that by 1956 had been going on for ten years and one cannot go on for ever thinking in terms of emergency. Moreover, the view was gaining ground that the crude shortage of houses, at any rate, was virtually over and that a surplus (which for some reason policy-makers seem to dread) was just around the corner. This was implicit in much of Duncan Sandys' statements and was explicit in those of his successor Henry Brooke. Certainly the ten-year period had been one of great public investment in housing. Local authorities and new towns in Great Britain had in the period 1946-56 built rather more than 1.8 million permanent dwellings and in England and Wales alone had invested something like *two and three-quarter thousand million pounds* in housing, virtually all of it borrowed at rates of interest ranging between 2½ and 4¼ per cent. It was not surprising, therefore, that government spokesmen should maintain that the gap between houses and households was rapidly decreasing and that, apart from replacement, the main need was for more efficient use of existing accommodation, which a realistic rent policy would achieve. In the same year the Islington Borough Council closed its housing list because all new building was needed for slum clearance. It was the first, but certainly not the last, London borough to take this step, as a result of which 16,000 families were told "with the deepest regret" that there was no hope of a council home for them. The previous year the local authorities in England and Wales had estimated that between them they had rather more than 850,000 slums to clear. Almost everyone concerned knew that this was an underestimate since the authorities had included (in most cases, not all) only those dwelling which they wished or felt able to deal with. Yet in the first half of 1956 the clearance area resolutions submitted by local authorities covered only 21,048 slums.

The birth-rate, which had been hovering around the 15½ per thousand mark for some years, started in 1956 its upward climb which continued unbroken for the next eight years, and although there was a fall back after 1964 even by 1970 it was still higher than it had been for almost thirty years. But in 1956 policy-makers were still obsessed with a fear of a falling population; after all only a few years earlier the Economics Committee of the Royal Commission on Population had predicted that there would be a sharp *fall* in household formation during the 1950s and that a major slum clearance programme would be required to prevent a slump in the building industry. In fact between 1931 and 1951 the population of England and Wales had increased by about 10 per cent (from 39.95 millions to 43.76 millions), which was serious enough. The number of households, however, had increased by just under 29 per cent. This must have been known to the Royal Commission; presumably they dismissed it as being no more than a temporary phenomenon. And even as the Government was, in 1956, preparing to extricate itself from the housing business, a Polish tailor, whose very name was to become a synonym and a symbol for the worst abuses in private landlordism this country had ever known, was pursuing his nefarious activities and had been doing so for over two years. (Rachman died in 1962 having sold most of his residential property in 1960.)

In the privately rented sector, too, the Government were preparing to reaffirm their faith in free enterprise. At the end of 1956 Duncan Sandys introduced a Rent Bill with the aim of removing rent control for a large proportion of privately rented dwellings. It was bitterly attacked by the Opposition and just as stubbornly defended by government supporters. The details can be left to a later chapter, but it was all part of the Government's policy to return housing accommodation to the higgling of the market. (Duncan Sandys was translated to higher things before the Bill became law; it was finally piloted through the legislature by his successor Henry Brooke who if anything was more convinced than Sandys had been of the efficacy of private enterprise.)

Not surprisingly, no significant housing legislation was passed during this period. The Housing Act, 1957, was a consolidating measure bringing together the various enactments relating to local authorities' housing powers with the exception of financial matters; these were taken care of by the Housing (Financial Provisions) Act, 1958. The House Purchase and Housing Act, 1959, was designed to further the cause of owner-occupation. It encouraged building societies to lend on pre-1919 property (which they had been reluctant to do); it enabled local authorities to grant 100 per cent mortgages (instead of 90 per cent), and removed the £5,000 limit hitherto imposed. Discretionary improvement grants were continued, though the conditions attaching to them were made less onerous; in addition standard grants were introduced. These were for specified basic amenities and could be claimed by the building owner as a right, provided his interest in the property would continue for at least fifteen years and the building was likely to survive that long. The grants made under the 1949 Act had never made much headway, many local authorities having been reluctant to put public money "into landlords' pockets", as they saw it. The new standard grant procedure undoubtedly made a great many houses more tolerable to live in, but even so it failed to make the greatest impression where it was most needed, i.e. the privately rented sector. We shall go into this aspect in greater detail in a later chapter.

Housing as a branch of state activity was now well and truly in the doldrums. The Government, having been returned to power in 1959 on the hypothesis that the British people had "never had it so good", were well content to leave future housing provision to private enterprise. For some peculiar reason it was still felt that measures like the 1957 Rent Act would at last cause private enterprise to re-enter the rented housing field; "peculiar" because there was no supporting evidence for it at all. There was plenty of evidence that the private landlord was unwilling or unable to expand his activities and that builders would consider building for rent only if the owner-occupied market was saturated. (This had in fact happened in the mid-'thirties.) As for the Rent Act, its main effect was to remove the last obstacles to the sale of a large number of previously rented dwellings to owner-occupiers. Whether this was a good thing or not we can leave for the moment, but it was hardly the outcome that had been claimed for the Act by its protagonists. The Government had moreover given scant attention to the question of security of tenure and so surprisingly had a large section of the public. Owner-occupiers and council tenants, to all intents and purposes, already had it and so did most private tenants by virtue of rent control. Eviction, being cast into the cold, cold snow, belonged to the realm of Victorian melodrama, not to an orderly civilised society such as Britain's. Complacency could hardly go further. But the clouds, no larger than a man's hand, were already on the horizon. Rising population, household formation rising even faster, the demolition of cheap rented dwellings through slum clearance, reduced security because of the 1957 Rent Act, greater concentration of population in cities and thus increased competition for a diminishing supply of dwellings, the cessation of council building for general needs; all these and other factors besides were combining to bring about a housing crisis of first-class dimensions. Some inkling of what was to come was already apparent when Henry Brooke piloted through Parliament the Housing Act, 1961.

This Act restored the general needs subsidy but cast it in such a way that it was to some extent related to the financial needs of the area. At least that was the intention. The Government had been thinking in terms of a review of all housing subsidies which would result in their being based on financial rather than housing need, which up to that time had been the predominant factor in determining the allocation of council houses. Indeed a kite to that effect had been flown the previous year by Enoch Powell, who had been a Junior Minister in M.H.L.G. as well as Financial Secretary to the Treasury. There was much exhortation from ministers for local authorities to introduce differential rents and to set their rent levels "realistically" (which in practice meant as high as they could get away with). The 1961 Act brought additional pressure by introducing a two-level subsidy; either £8 a year or £24 a year (for sixty years) according to a "resource test". The "test" assumed a rental income equal to twice the gross value (for rating purposes) from all the council's dwellings; if this combined with Exchequer subsidies and other income would cover all outgoings, then the subsidy would be £8 a year, if it did not then the subsidy would be £24 a year. This was an extremely blunt instrument, just how blunt can be deduced from the reported fact that Eastbourne qualified for the £24 subsidy whereas Liverpool, with vastly greater problems, could only attract the £8 subsidy. Power was given to the Minister to reduce or abolish subsidies provided under the Act, and after ten years to reduce or withdraw subsidies already being paid under the Act. In addition, the Government hoped to encourage housing associations, first by providing subsidy (at the higher rate) and secondly by providing £25 million for loans to housing associations. This was regarded as "pump priming" following which private investment would flow into housing associations for building to let and for co-ownership.

This was a reversal in policy but was not enough to prevent

the forthcoming storm. Through the media of newspapers, radio and television, the public were becoming increasingly aware that very large numbers of their compatriots were living in intolerable conditions and that some (a small but growing number) were literally without a roof over their heads at all. This latter group was a new phenomenon. True, there had been homeless people since the beginning of recorded history, but these were largely the feckless, the eccentric, and those whom misfortune had for one reason or another left totally without resources. But now the situation had been reached where a man in full work could find himself in a situation where he could not put a roof over his family's heads. This was both new and disturbing. Then in 1963 there blew up one of those public scandals with which the British public from time to time regales itself. We may regret the media's concern with the private activities of public men but it also brought to light the activities of the notorious Rachman who, it will be remembered, was already dead and had ceased his operations three years previously. Now this scandal had nothing whatever to do with housing but during the uproar and the never-ending "revelations" the extent and depravity of Rachman's operations were uncovered. If such a state of affairs was possible (even though in London where the pressures were the most severe), then something must be very wrong indeed. Public concern was now thoroughly aroused. A Committee of Inquiry was appointed with Sir Milner Holland in the chair to look into the question of rented housing in London.

That was August 1963. The next year there would have to be a General Election and the Government clearly felt that when it came its record on housing would be seen as less than adequate. Further house-building would have to be encouraged and the local authorities brought back into the picture. The Housing Act, 1964, was one of the most comprehensive pieces of housing legislation to emerge in post-war years, certainly from a Conservative administration. It contained important provisions to encourage housing societies of a new kind. These were to provide accommodation either for letting at cost rents or on the basis of common ownership (co-ownership). A new government agency, the Housing Corporation, was set up with the general duty of promoting and assisting these new societies. The building societies were also brought in and it was hoped that the new housing societies could borrow one-third of their requirements from the Housing Corporation and two-thirds from the building societies. The Corporation was enabled to borrow £50 million (it could be increased to £100 million) from the Exchequer to finance these schemes. The Act also made it possible for old dwellings to be compulsorily improved on an area basis provided at least half the dwellings in the area lacked the basic amenities and had at least fifteen years of life left when improved. The Act further strengthened local authorities' powers of dealing with houses in multiple occupation (houses built for one family but occupied by more than one family without proper conversion). Some powers in this respect had been included in the 1961 Act, e.g. power to make management orders and to limit overcrowding. The 1964 Act enabled the local authority virtually to take over badly managed dwellings of this kind and manage them themselves for periods of five years. This was a very drastic interference with established property rights and one that would have been unlikely if not downright impossible only a few years previously.

The year also saw the fruit of the encouragement given to house-building. When the figures for 1964 were made public it was seen that the number built by public sector authorities (155,582) was better than any year since 1957. The contribution by private enterprise at 218,094 was a post-war record, so was the total number of dwellings built, which at 373,676 exceeded the previous best year, 1954, by more than twenty thousand. This came too late to save the Government. The General Election, at which housing had been a major and possibly decisive issue, resulted in a Labour administration coming into power with a very slender majority. One of the first acts of the new Government was to bring in stop-gap legislation (The Protection from Eviction Act, 1964) which made it an offence to evict without an Order of the Court. Thus it was hoped Rachman-style operations would be checked.

The new Government immediately set its sights high and aimed at a total production of 500,000 dwellings a year by 1970 and to keep it going thereafter. But the Government was dogged by economic misfortune, much of it not of its own making, almost from the moment it took office. So although the upward movement noted in 1964 continued for the next four years, the half-million target was tacitly abandoned following the devaluation in November 1967. Meanwhile the temporary measures against harassment and illegal eviction of private tenants was given permanent form in the Rent Act, 1965 (consolidated in the Rent Act, 1968). The Rent Act made harassment of a tenant a crime punishable by fine and/or imprisonment. The Act also made a serious attempt to deal with the vexed question of controlled rents. Rent control had been with us on and off (mostly on) since 1915 and by 1965 their level was unjustifiably low. The Rent Act provided for a system of rent regulation to supersede controlled rents, phased over a period. The rents were to be determined, or agreed, by a new official, the Rent Officer, whose job it would be to register the regulated or "fair" rents. If either landlord or tenant disagreed with the Rent Officer's determination they could appeal to a Rent Assessment Committee. This "fair rents" legislation aroused a good deal of opposition, some of it from the Government's own supporters on the grounds that the new rents were higher than the old. A Government Committee of Enquiry appointed in 1969 (the Francis Committee) reported in 1971 that the system of rent regulation was in general working well, though it suggested a number of amendments and modifications.

The Labour Government did not at once increase subsidies. Until 1966 it was working on a very slender majority, devoting much of its energies to the task of remaining in office. The 1966 General Election returned it to power with a good working majority and the way was clear for a substantial innovation in the method of subsidising local authority housing.

Up to 1967 (with the exception of the 1919 Addison subsidy) subsidies had always been a fixed sum payable for a certain number of years in respect of each house built.

Sometimes the local authorities were required to add to the Exchequer subvention and sometimes not. This was not a very logical and sophisticated way of going about it; not only did it take no account of differing needs in different areas but in a time of inflation any fixed sum soon became too small. For many years various pressure groups and commentators had urged the government to make money available for housing at low rates of interest. (This was, and still is, a major European method of subsidy.) It had been rejected, particularly by Conservative Governments on the grounds that it could not be done, or if that argument didn't work, that such arrangements would contain a hidden subsidy, though why that should be unacceptable was never made clear. The Housing Subsidies Act of 1967 came as near to providing low-interest loans as makes no difference. The subsidy provided under the Act in effect made up the difference between a rate of interest of 4 per cent and the rate the local authorities were actually having to pay. There were drawbacks which will be dealt with in a later chapter, but from the outset the amount of Exchequer subsidy increased substantially. Because the new subsidy was in effect a percentage grant, the Ministry of Housing took power in the Act to control the upper limit of house-building costs by means of a cost yardstick which specified the upper limits of cost for dwellings of various sizes and density. Almost from the moment the Act was passed interest rates began to rise and so of course did the level of subsidy. It was only a matter of time before pressure from the Treasury to reduce the subsidy level or abandon the idea altogether would prevail.

Meanwhile forces were at work which would once again bring about a change of emphasis from new building to improving the existing stock, a return in effect to the sanitary idea. The Minister's own Committee, the Central Housing Advisory Committee, set up a sub-committee early in 1965 to look into "objective criteria" for the purposes of slum clearance, disrepair and so on. The sub-committee (the Denington Committee) reported the next year making a number of recommendations, though it declined to raise the standard at which a dwelling is considered "fit", apparently on the grounds that the country couldn't afford it. This may have been reasonable but it was not "objective". The Committee recommended compulsory improvement and repair of existing dwellings and also made some assessment of the number of slums (771,440 in England and Wales).

After the devaluation of 1967, the Minister, Mr Anthony Greenwood, announced that there would be a shift of emphasis towards rehabilitation and followed this up with a White Paper (*Old Houses into New Homes*). The Government proposed that the levels of improvement grants, standard and discretionary, should be raised and that a new General Improvement Area scheme should replace the improvement area provisions of the 1964 Act. Perhaps the most interesting feature of the White Paper was the inclusion of the results of a National House Condition Survey which had been carried out by experienced public health inspectors working to a common brief. The survey disclosed that the estimated number of slums in England and Wales at 1.836 million was more than twice that shown in the Denington Report. And they were more widespread than had previously been thought. Moreover, about 4.5 million of those dwellings not classified as units needed substantial repair or lacked amenities. The White Paper proposals were enacted in the Housing Act, 1969, and thereafter house production figures fell away while the number of improvement grants made available rose sharply.

Public concern regarding bad housing conditions which had become temporarily intense at the time of the Profumo scandal subsided again to its former complacent level until late in 1966, when there appeared on television a play by Jeremy Sandford with the title *Cathy Come Home*. Sandford had created a rumpus five years earlier over the pitiful condition of the London homeless in Newington Lodge. ("Families in Need of a Home", — *The Observer*, 17 September 1961) The first showing of his TV play passed without too much comment, but the second brought public indignation to the boil. Acres of newsprint and hours of television time were devoted to the plight of the homeless. Greenwood made his ministry officials see the play over again, and Des Wilson launched a National Campaign for the Homeless under the code name SHELTER. For years the whole question of homelessness had been surrounded by callous public indifference, now overnight it was a matter of national concern, widespread and deep. That is, until the media turned its attention to other things and the public found other causes to distract its attention. In little more than three years a new government would come to power modelled on the concept of Selsdon Man, dedicated to ridding the country of its lame ducks and determined to root out the soggy morass of subsidised incompetence. Cathy could go hang.

The new Government felt that the time had come for a radical change in housing policy. Owner-occupation was to be encouraged in every possible way, council houses were to be sold wherever possible or if not their rents were to be raised to "fair" rent levels. The Housing Finance Act, 1972, one of the most bitterly contested measures since the war, provided that all existing subsidies to local authorities should be abolished and replaced by other, less generous arrangements. Local authorities were to lose their previously unchallenged freedom to set their own rent levels; these in future were to be based on "fair" rents with a procedure similar to, but not identical with, that obtaining for regulated rents in the private sector. There were to be compulsory rent rebates for council tenants and rent allowances for private tenants who could not afford the higher rents demanded. But the existing benefits afforded to owner-occupiers through tax relief on mortgage interest were to remain. *The Times* called this "a conspicuous omission", and well it might. At one stage seventeen local authorities declared that they would not operate the Act, but one by one resistance crumbled away in face of the severe penalties for non-compliance contained in the Act itself. In the end only one authority, Clay Cross U.D.C., stood out, but in the end after investigations by the District Auditor, and the appointment of a Housing Commissioner, the Council had to resign.

At the beginning of this chapter the point was made that housing policy since the Second World War followed very much the same pattern as that in the inter-war period. This is tragically true. In both eras enthusiasm was the characteristic of the immediate post-war period. Both were followed by

economic difficulties caused by the aftermath of the war.
These in turn were followed by reappraisal and cutback. In
both periods there was a return to the local authority as a
general provider of housing; in both cases, following a few
years of comparatively high output, society felt it had done
enough and relegated the local authorities to the sanitary
functions of slum clearance and installing baths in worn-out
dwellings. "It was a dismal story", wrote Marian Bowley of
the period 1923-33, and it is a dismal story today. Despite
official reassurances we can be certain that there are as many
unfit dwellings as there were when housing became a local
authority duty. We know that there are more people
homeless than at any time this century. We can be sure that,
because of the dramatic rise in land and house prices, fewer
families than ever can aspire to owning a modern home. It is
clear that precipitate decontrol of rents in 1957 in conditions
of acute scarcity (a scarcity not recognised by the
Government of the day) led to abuses, harassment and misery
on a scale not equalled this century; Rachman and Cathy
were in their separate ways the direct result. We know that
the "prejudice against landlords, tenants [and] other groups
of the population" noted by Milner Holland still persists.
nowhere more so than in the case of council tenants and only
slightly less so in the case of private tenants — an extension,
if you like, of guilt by association. It was this prejudice, a
feeling that council tenants were some kind of pampered
parasites, that led to the 1972 Housing Finance Act. This, to
put it mildly, was a pity, because some reform was much
overdue, but the aura of prejudice prevented on both sides of
the political fence a dispassionate and objective consideration
of the issues involved.

There was failure, too, to develop the "common
approach" urged by Milner Holland; changes in direction
have been as much a feature of post-war as of inter-war
housing policy. There have been no less than eleven major
Housing Acts in the past twenty-seven years. But the greatest
failure of all was the failure of political will, the will to build
the houses, deal with the slums, provide for the homeless, to
protect the weak and the vulnerable, to achieve in short the
commonly accepted goal of housing policy which is to

provide a separate decent home for every household in need of one. In spite of the achievements of individual local authorities, some of which have been very considerable indeed, we are driven once again to the conclusion that housing in the twentieth century has turned out to be a great British failure.

6 New towns and expanded towns

Up to now we have been considering the provision of housing within established communities. We now turn to another aspect of state intervention, this time by the establishment by government decree of complete, more or less self-contained, new communities, financed by the Exchequer. We are referring to the new towns, which for some reason are considered to be a British invention, and the expanding towns.

There is nothing particularly new in the new town concept. From time to time throughout his history man has brought into being new towns and cities for a variety of reasons and in a number of ways, frequently in search of some Utopian ideal. Early in the nineteenth century, Robert Owen established his community at New Lanark as a practical example of the theories he had expounded in a book he had published in or around 1816. Owen, for all his radicalism, was not acting completely altruistically since he expected improved output from the mill around which his village was based. Owen's experiment has been described as an early and well-intentioned form of paternalism; so it was, and not necessarily the worse for that, but like many a man in advance of his time his ideas were much ridiculed despite their merits and his influence on contemporary and future thinking was negligible.

During the rest of the nineteenth century and the early twentieth century, there were numerous other attempts, almost all promoted by industrialists for the better accommodation of their workers. Early among these were the railway towns, Wolverton in 1838 onwards, and Crewe and Swindon developed during the 1840s. In each case the railway company concerned undertook not only the building of workmen's dwellings but also of what would now be called community facilities: schools, reading rooms, libraries, public baths and occasionally churches.

Then there was Saltaire, developed by Sir Titus Salt during the 1850s, again as a piece of industrial philanthropy to provide accommodation for this workers at a new site not far from Bradford. Salt's enterprise in establishing Saltaire, and the standard of the housing he provided, have from time to time been much praised and much derided. The dwellings have little to commend them seen from a mid-twentieth-century standpoint, but they were reasonable enough at the time of building and had other nineteenth-century employers similarly felt the weight of social responsibility bearing upon them, England might have been a better place in which to live.

On a different scale and certainly to a much higher standard was Port Sunlight, built by the first Viscount Leverhulme in the last decades of the nineteenth century. Leverhulme, apart from being a considerable manufacturer of soap, was one of the great housing reformers who did so much to draw public attention to the evils of bad housing around the turn of the century. It was common enough to take a fairly crude view of working-class life at that time (and not only then — "too good for the likes of them" is an attitude which lives with us still); clearly Leverhulme did not share it. He thought that work-people should not only be housed, but be comfortable into the bargain and should live "in semi-detached houses, with gardens back and front, in which they will be able to know more of the science of life than they can do in a back slum". His work at Port Sunlight bore the impress of his thinking: not only did he build at what was then the incredibly low density of eight to the acre, the planning of the dwellings was much in advance of what had up to that time been considered necessary; they had bathrooms for instance without apparently it being necessary to prevent the tenants from putting coal in the baths.

Again as a result of their factory being moved out from a central urban area, the Cadbury family built Bournville in the last years of the nineteenth century. Bournville, which was not confined to Cadbury's workers, was also developed at low density, though on the whole the housing was less ambitious. But its particular merit was Cadbury's insistence that there should be a 4 per cent return on building capital, his intention being to encourage local authorities to do likewise. There seems little doubt that Bournville was one of the most successful of these quasi-industrial housing developments, and though in later years it tended to lose its identity as it was engulfed by the advancing Birmingham suburban tide, it is still a remarkable example of its kind: "the practical precursor of the garden suburb of almost any town, anywhere, in the twentieth century", as Professor Tarn puts it. The village was handed over to the separately endowed Bournville Village Trust in 1900; by the time the Second World War began about 2,600 dwellings had been built on the estate, including bungalows for pensioners and flats for single women. Since the war almost as many dwellings again have been built, quite apart from development by the COPEC Housing Society and Self-Build Associations. Cadbury himself was also prominent in the early housing reform movement but, unlike Leverhulme, he had a greater interest in town planning evidenced by his work for the Garden Cities Association, later to become the Town and Country Planning Association.

All these, and others like them, were however based on the needs of a particular employer who required housing for his work-force within easy reach of his factory. Whatever other benefits accrued (and they were considerable) were secondary to this central consideration. However, towards the end of the last century a new movement was emerging, mainly as a revolt from the urban situation. For the best part of a century, the British had been able to observe, many of them at first hand, what it was like to live in the congested, insanitary, urban sprawl which appeared to be an inevitable concomitant of industrial advance. They had been able to see what it was like and they did not like what they saw. What they wanted above all else was to get out and return to a more spacious and (as they saw it) a more healthy way of life. But there lay the dilemma. The countryside, attractive as it might be for its own sake, could not, except for the few, afford them employment; for the great majority only the despised towns could do that. It was, as it were, like two magnets pulling in opposite directions. Ebenezer Howard, who followed the rather unlikely calling of a court reporter, conceived the third "magnet" — town - country — which would combine the merits of both and would of course nullify the "pull" of the other two. His famous book, *Tomorrow, a Peaceful Path to Real Reform,* published in 1898, spelt out the essence of his proposals, the garden city, a self-contained community, developed at low density, where people could live and work and satisfy their everyday needs. Howard went on to develop Letchworth Garden City in 1903 and Welwyn Garden City in 1919. Much of his argument was naïve, some of his proposals were impossible of achievement, and would not have been beneficial anyway. Like the other anti-urbanists of the time, he shared Ruskin's distrust of the whole nineteenth-century way of life, and Morris's dislike of the ugliness of the city; unlike Ruskin and Morris he had a genuine alternative to offer. However unsophisticated that alternative may have been, it was to form the basis of a movement which has since become influential not only in this country but throughout the world.

The developments at Letchworth and Welwyn, interesting as they may have been, made no more than a minimal contribution to housing and environmental needs, and the whole movement might well have fizzled out had it not been for the onset of the Second World War. Just before the war the Government appointed a Royal Commission on the Distribution of the Industrial Population. Its report, the Barlow Report, laid stress on what by then were the obvious strategic disadvantages of the concentration of industry in relatively few densely populated areas. The report went on to suggest that the remedy might be found in the enlargement of some small towns or the creation of new ones. Action on the report had to be shelved until the war was over, although Abercrombie in his Greater London Plan of 1944 had put forward proposals for ten satellite new towns outside the Green Belt.

Only two months after the end of the war with Japan, a New Towns Committee was set up under the chairmanship of

Lord Reith, whose many attributes included a formidable administrative ability. The Committee had the following terms of reference:

> To consider the general questions of the establishment, development, organisation and administration that will arise in the promotion of New Towns in furtherance of a policy of Planned decentralisation from congested urban areas; and in accordance therewith to suggest guiding principles on which such Towns should be established and developed as self-contained and balanced communities for work and living.

By July 1946, only nine months after its constitution, the Committee had issued not one but three reports which between them contained the recommendations which were, in the main, included in the New Towns Act, 1946, which received the Royal Assent on 1 August. If the Attlee Government intended to treat housing like a military operation they showed equal determination and dispatch in bringing into being the legislative framework on which the whole post-war new town movement was based. Designation orders for the first new towns soon followed, that for Stevenage being made only a month after the Act had become law. Apart from Stevenage, the Towns included in the first batch were Crawley, Harlow, Hemel Hempstead, Aycliffe and East Kilbride. Aycliffe was intended to service the Aycliffe Industrial Estate, Co. Durham, and East Kilbride to relieve congestion in Glasgow. The others were needed to decentralise industry and population from London. Later designations included Basildon, Bracknell, Hatfield and Welwyn Garden City (to serve London), Corby, Peterlee, Cwmbran, and Glenrothes. Thus within the lifetime of the Attlee Government the New Towns Committee had been set up and had reported, the New Towns Act had been drafted and passed, and no less than fourteen new towns with a total area of 71,164 acres had been designated. And all this despite last-ditch opposition to the designation orders (which involve liability to compulsory purchase) at Stevenage, Hemel Hempstead and Crawley. The litigation was taken all the way up the judicial ladder to the House of Lords which confirmed the reversal by the Court of Appeal of a High Court decision in favour of the objectors. All this was time-consuming and unnecessary, as Lewis Keeble puts it: "Filibustering attempts to frustrate the will of Parliament on technicalities are seldom edifying and the time taken up by litigation in these cases sadly hampered the bold attempt to tackle speedily one of the most urgent problems of post-war development which the passing of the New Towns Act represented." Notwithstanding, the successful establishment of the first wave of new towns must be seen as an administrative achievement of a very high order and one seldom equalled by any government department.

The development corporations appointed by the Minister to carry out the development of the new towns found the going less easy. Sir Ernest Gowers as Chairman of the Harlow Development Corporation added to his already considerable reputation for using plain words when he wrote in the Corporation report in 1950:

> Although the Corporation is given by statute the task of building the New Town, it is subject to all existing authorities who have any control over the various activities that go to building a town. In this respect its position hardly differs from that of a private developer. The County Council are responsible for roads and surface water drainage, education and certain health services. The District Council's building by-laws must be observed and that Council have statutory powers in respect of sewerage, open spaces, and sometimes water. The Parish Council are the street lighting authority. The Ministry of Health (now the Ministry of Housing and Local Government) exercise supervision over the planning and cost of houses and their approval is required to all water and sewerage schemes. The Board of Trade control the location of industry. The Ministries of Labour and Works have their hand on labour and materials.

> This multiplication of controls may be inevitable in present circumstances. To some extent it certainly is. For instance, the Corporation must be closely concerned with the provision, siting and design of schools, but no one would suggest that any authority but the Education Authority should carry the ultimate responsibility for education. Yet it may be doubted whether this great array

of independent authorities or its consequences to the taxpayer are generally realised; there are few who see the picture as a whole. The Crawley Development Corporation referred to this subject in their Annual Report for 1948-49, and gave, in Appendix E, two lists, one of the "consultations and approvals required for the execution of plans" and the other of "authorities whose plans and projects have to be co-ordinated with those of the Corporation". Of the contents of these formidable catalogues the Crawley Corporation said with restraint, "they consume a great deal of time and effort". The Harlow Corporation would be more disposed to say that they create machinery which is in some respects cumbrous almost past belief and which produces in profusion officials doing one after another work that one official could well have been trusted to do by himself. Development Corporations have too many masters.

They have, moreover, their own particular master, the Ministry of Town and Country Planning (now the Ministry of Housing and Local Government). It is, of course, right and proper that the Ministry should exercise supervisory powers over Development Corporations. The Corporations are spending public money, and a Minister must be able to satisfy Parliament that the money is being spent wisely. The Act that created Development Corporations expressly provided that certain of their activities need approval by the Minister. But from the fact that it placed on statutory Corporations the direct responsibility for building new towns, Parliament must be presumed to have intended that the degree of Departmental control must be different from what it would have been if the Department had been directly responsible for the enterprise. Control cannot, of course, be exercised wholly by the Minister himself; it must be mostly delegated to his officials. The Corporation wishes to put on record that, in its opinion, its progress has been unnecessarily delayed and its expenses unnecessarily swollen by prolonged scrutiny on the part of Ministry officials of matters of detail which might reasonably have been left to the Corporation's discretion. As has been recorded in this report, the Corporation's proposals for the development of part of the Mark Hall neighbourhood were both with the Ministry for nearly five months before being approved and the Corporation has only just received approval (9th May, 1950) of a plan for development of the East Industrial Estate submitted to the Ministry on the 1st December, 1949. Delays like these can cost money in two ways. So far as they may be caused by examination of detail of no great importance they mean that the time of Departmental staff is being wasted, and so far as they impose an unnecessarily long gap between the completion of a plan and starting to carry it out, they mean that staff which is ready to get on with the job cannot do so except by anticipating approval, and so risking a waste of time and labour if approval should eventually not be given. In the two cases referred to, the five months' thought devoted by the officials of the Ministry to each project ended in acceptance of both, subject to slight modifications which effected a reduction of some £3,000 in programmes estimated to cost nearly two million pounds.

The Corporation recognises, of course, that there are two sides to this question. The problem of how much control it is proper for a Government Department to exercise over a statutory board is exceedingly difficult, and no generally accepted solution of it has yet been found. Just as there have been occasions when the Corporation felt that officials of the Minister were unwarrantably interfering with what was the Corporation's proper business, so, no doubt, there have been others when those officials felt that the Corporation was claiming a degree of independence inconsistent with their own responsibilities.

What can hardly be questioned is that the tangled thicket of controls and overlapping duties depicted in the Crawley Corporation's Appendix contains much that serves no useful purpose, and needs to be drastically pruned if Development Corporations are to be given a chance to build new towns in reasonable time and at reasonable cost.*

The burden of this much-quoted extract is that there is too

Quoted in Lewis Keeble's *Principles and Practice of Town and Country Planning*, Estates Gazette, 1974.

Housing: the great British failure

much control for control's sake, something to which some government departments seem particularly prone and which the years have done little to alleviate. In fact from 1950 any development in a new town requiring the Minister's consent no longer needed approval by the local planning authority.

After the designation of Corby on 1 April 1950, with one exception no further new towns were to be designated until 1961, a gap of over eleven years. The exception was the new town of Cumbernauld designated at the end of 1955. Cumbernauld for a number of years seemed to personify the success of the British new towns movement. It is the one new town above all the others where students and observers of the planning scene seem to make for; foreign planning experts in particular would arrive at Heathrow, change planes and fly off to Scotland, passing en route half a dozen developments from which they might have learned just as much. Cumbernauld was in fact a brilliant design, breaking away from the low-density, neighbourhood unit concept, and has no doubt merited the praise which has been lavished on it, though whether it will be regarded so reverently in twenty or thirty years' time remains to be seen.

Then followed Skelmersdale (1961), Livingstone (1962), Dawley (1963 but later incorporated in Telford in 1968), Redditch, Runcorn and Washington (1964) followed by Irvine in 1966. These were still to be comparatively small towns; none up to this time was intended to grow much beyond 130,000 population and some were very much smaller, Peterlee for example with a target of 28-30,000 which would no doubt have pleased Ebenezer Howard no end. The third wave from 1967 onwards was a different matter altogether. Milton Keynes (designated 1967) was expected to grow from about 40,000 to nearly a quarter of a million; Peterborough from 81,000 to 187,000; Telford from 73,000 to about a quarter of a million; Warrington (1968) from 122,300 to about 225,000. It seems reasonable to suppose that as more and more experience has been gained in the creation of these new communities, the larger target populations have appeared not only feasible but desirable. The merits of the arguments for and against this trend one must leave to the planners; in the end what will matter is

74

whether the larger new towns are attractive places in which
to live. Clearly Howard's town-country "magnet" has been
left far behind. It is of course possible to argue that in the
case of say Peterborough, Northampton and Warrington, and
maybe some others, what is happening is a major expansion
of an existing town, expanding towns rather than new towns,
and that the new town procedure is being used mainly
because it is more convenient.

New towns are developed by development corporations
whose members are nominated by the Minister (now the
Secretary of State for the Environment). They fall, therefore,
well within the category of *ad hoc* bodies, whose
multiplication has been such a feature of the post-war
administrative world. Their powers are wide, they may "do
anything necessary or expedient for the purposes of the New
Town or for purposes incidental thereto". They employ
professional and technical staff of all kinds, many of them of
high calibre. And the 1946 Act provided that when they had
finished their job they were to be wound up and the
undertakings transferred to a local authority within which
the designated area of the new town lies. The New Towns
Act, 1959, altered these arrangements by setting up a
Commission for the New Towns (October 1961) which was
to take over and administer the assets of the development
corporations after they had been wound up. The reason for
this departure was not clear. Presumably the original
arrangements recognised that development corporations are
not democratically elected bodies and that it was both logical
and desirable for local authorities to be the natural inheritors
of the developed town. But the Commission for the New
Towns is also an *ad hoc* body to which similar objections can
be made on the grounds of its undemocratic nature. Or
perhaps the Government of the day were wary of so much
land and property passing into the hands of any local
authority. Crawley, Hatfield, Hemel Hempstead and Welwyn
Garden City alone have been transferred to the Commission.

With the coming of the Labour Government in 1964 the
policy was changed once again, the Prime Minister declaring
that:

The present Government have always felt that the idea of

handing over new town assets to a Commission for the new towns was wrong . . . at the right time we shall change the law and take powers to dissolve the Commission . . . The local authorities, the statutory housing authorities, should eventually be responsible for managing all publicly-owned housing when a new town is fully developed. Non-housing assets . . . raise special problems which are very complex . . .*

The Commission is still in existence, possibly because the "special problems" are even more "complex" than Mr Wilson or his successor thought. At the time of writing, however, no further new town has been transferred to the Commission.

Housing is clearly a major responsibility of a new town and from the beginning it has been subsidised in much the same way as local authority housing. For example under the 1967 Housing Subsidies Act, a development corporation received the same basic subsidy as a local authority plus an additional grant for ten years, the size of which depended on the number of years the corporation had been building. New town housing is now subject to the Housing Finance Act, 1972, in much the same way as local authority housing.

One of the major difficulties encountered in the development of new towns has been to keep house-building and industrial development in step. To some extent this is a chicken-and-egg situation, the development corporation being reluctant to build houses that cannot be occupied within a reasonable time and industry being equally reluctant to come unless it can be assured that the houses are there. Houses standing empty for any length of time are frequently a matter of much local criticism quite apart from being a financial loss to the corporation. Nevertheless, despite the difficulties some success is from time to time achieved in this direction. For example in a Parliamentary Answer in March 1969 the Minister for Planning and Land announced that, in the years 1965 to 1968, 22,100 houses had been built on land made available in new towns and that during the same period the net increase in jobs in factories in the same areas was 22,600.

We may at this point consider the overall effectiveness of

*Mr Wilson at Stevenage, July 1967.

new towns as part of state action to increase the supply of housing accommodation. By the end of 1972 the twenty-two new towns in England and Wales had themselves provided 154,889 dwellings. In addition during the same period the local authorities within the new town areas had built 26,958 with a further 32,317 provided by other agencies. The number of dwellings provided directly by the new towns since 1947 amounted therefore to less than six months' total output nationwide. This by itself is hardly breathtaking, though one must remember that the development corporations have been engaged in creating whole new communities, infrastructure and all, and have not been confined solely to building houses to rent. Moreover the corporations themselves have become less active in house-building: from the dates of designation until the end of 1971 they had built 75 per cent of all dwellings provided in their areas; by 1972 this proportion had dropped to less than 50 per cent.

The stated objectives of the new towns policy was to redistribute people and jobs from the congested areas by the creation of new communities of limited size. The new communities have been created and may on that account alone be worth the capital investment of nearly £844 million (England and Wales — the figure for Great Britain is £1,055 million). Whether the other objectives have been achieved is open to question. The number of dwellings provided within the new towns since designation amounts to no more than 1.1 per cent of the country's total stock. Their population since designation has risen by 611,230 (in England and Wales to the end of 1972). Some of this increase would probably have come about naturally in any case, but ignoring that possibility we can see that the additional population accommodated amounts to 1.23 per cent of the total population of England and Wales. At the most, therefore, one person in eighty-one has been affected by the creation of the new towns.

As for industry, since designation 1,526 factories totalling 43,404,692 square feet have been provided in the new towns. This sounds like an impressive figure, but although no comparable figures for the country as a whole appear to exist, it is worth considering that this area amounts to just under 1,000 acres or just over 1½ square miles, which as a proportion of the total industrial capacity in the country as a whole must be very small indeed. And, of the area quoted above, 65 per cent has been provided in the eight new towns forming the London ring, 12½ per cent of it in Basildon alone.

We will not here concern ourselves with whether or not the British new towns have proved successful in administrative, social or economic terms. What we can say with certainty is that as an aspect of state intervention to provide new homes, the new towns have proved no more successful than their local authority counterparts. This is not to be taken as failure, since the new town authorities have by and large done what they set out to do. But the areas which were supposed to be affected by all this activity and all this expenditure appear not to have benefited very much and one can say that from our point of view the operation has been a failure.

Before we leave the subject of the new towns we should mention briefly the contribution made by expanding towns. By 1949, when the first eight new towns were well under way, the Ministry of Town and Country Planning turned its attention to the possibility of bringing about further decentralisation from London and other large centres by expanding small towns already in existence. As in the case of the new towns, the expanded towns were to be self-contained communities in which the migrant population would work as well as find housing accommodation. The scale of the operation would, however, not be sufficiently large to justify the establishment of development corporations. Broadly speaking, the effect of the proposals, which were incorporated in the Town Development Act, 1952, would be to bring together the large, congested area with the small town which might wish to improve the facilities and opportunities for its inhabitants but which lacked the financial or administrative resources to bring this about. The two towns would enter into an agreement whereby overspill population and industry would move out together from the larger authority (the "exporting" authority) into housing and industrial accommodation provided in the area of the smaller authority (the "receiving" authority). On the face of it, the proposal had a good deal to commend it; the infrastructure in the smaller town would already exist and though it might have to be expanded, this could be done much more quickly and cheaply than by the designation of a new town, subject of course to any restraints that threshold theory might impose. The smaller town would receive a much-needed shot in the arm and the injection of new industry and population would make it a more worthwhile place in which to live and work.

That was the theory; in practice the operation of the expanded towns policy has been distinctly disappointing. Not all the smaller towns wishing to accept overspill are capable of providing the sites nor the services necessary for the expansion. Not all the smaller towns having the potential for expansion wish to have anything to do with it. The receiving authority wants the incoming industry more than it wants the overspill population; the exporting authority will find it easier to move people than industry. The essence of the matter is that expansion comes about largely as a result of haggling between two authorities without much regard to the planning issues involved.

By the end of June 1972, sixty-eight Town Development Act agreements had been entered into, nearly half of them connected with London. The total number of dwellings for rent to be provided came to 163,495 of which 78,908 had been completed. Thus over a period of about twenty years the Town Development Act had brought into being about as many dwellings as are normally built, in the country as a whole, in about three months. Whether or not the Town Development Act has brought to the larger cities the hoped-for relief from congestion is not the purpose of this book to discover. It does, however, seem reasonable to conclude that, in the matter of providing housing, the expanding towns policy has proved no more successful than the new towns movement. In strictly housing terms it is a failure.

7 Municipal housing

There are now getting on for 6 million council dwellings in Great Britain or round about 30 per cent of the total housing stock. Of these an insignificant number were built before the First World War, about 1.13 million between the wars, and the rest since the Second World War. On the whole they have been built to a good standard, the major influences in space and standards having been the Tudor Walters Committee of 1918, the Dudley Committee of 1944 and the Parker Morris Report of 1961. Although the latter report was intended to apply to both public and private housing sectors, its provisions were not made mandatory in the public sector until 1967 for the new towns and 1969 for local authorities, and then only so far as space and heating are concerned. It has never been mandatory in the private sector and indeed right up to this day a large proportion of privately-built owner-occupied houses do not conform to Parker Morris. It is fair to say therefore that in some respects most council housing is superior to what is available in the private sector and certainly in the privately-rented sector, although obviously there will be exceptions especially at the luxury end of the market. Moreover nearly all council housing design has had to be approved by the appropriate government department as a necessary prerequisite of obtaining subsidy and loan sanction. Despite this record a good deal of public sector housing is monotonous to look at and sometimes downright drab; it is not easy to account for this, though a number of reasons may suggest themselves. There may have been, particularly in the early days, undue reliance on standard designs published by the Ministry of Health, or perhaps the explanation may be found in the fact that many

80

smaller authorities felt unable or unwilling to employ professional architects. Then again there has been unwillingness to provide the little flourishes so beloved in the private sector and which tend to set one house apart from another but which public authorities will eschew, especially in the search for economy. Moreover, there was undoubtedly in the early days in some authorities a deliberate attempt to make council houses look "less eligible", possible to dissuade would-be tenants, perhaps as a hangover from a Poor Law attitude of mind. This is particularly the case of dwellings built for rehousing from slum clearance. Horrifying tales of coals in the bath or other even more unmentionable practices (not always apocryphal) may have generated the feeling that it was necessary for dwellings to be sturdy rather than attractive. Whatever the reasons, the fact of monotony remains, though to be fair to the local authorities some of their developments are as good and as attractive as anything in the country and perhaps as anything in Europe as well. These regrettably are the exceptions and it is still true, as a generalisation, that in most parts of the country you can recognise a council estate when you see it without having to be told.

When the Addison subsidy was introduced in 1919 it was intended that local authorities would, for the time being at any rate, emerge as an alternative provider of working-class housing, quite apart from their role as clearers of slums. Private enterprise would not, for some years perhaps, be able or even willing to resume its traditional role as the source of working-class dwellings, particularly as there was at that time a great range of alternative, more profitable work for it to do. During the twenties therefore it was as general suppliers of houses to those especially in need of it that the local authorities as agents of the State intervened to increase the supply. A large proportion therefore (nearly two-thirds) of all council dwellings built between the wars had three bedrooms, the traditional family size house. In the main local authorities did not see themselves as agencies making special provisions for very small or large households and this is reflected in the small proportion of one- and four-bedroom dwellings built during the period 1919-39 — 4.3 per cent and 3.7 per cent respectively. Rather more two-bedroom accommodation (17.5 per cent) was provided, three-quarters of it in the form of two-storey houses. Less than 100,000 flats were built in this period. These accounted for only 8.5 per cent of all inter-war dwellings, and then one suspects mainly as rehousing from the slums in situations where it was necessary to rehouse as many families as possible on the cleared sites.

⌐ For some years after the Second World War much the same situation obtained, though differences were beginning to appear. During the period 1945-64 the three-bedroom house still predominated, accounting for 52.6 per cent of the total. The proportion of two-bedroom accommodation rose to 30.6 per cent and that of one-bedroom dwellings to 13.3 per cent. The latter represented quite a dramatic increase; for every such unit built during the twenty inter-war years, more than five were provided during the twenty post-war years. This was due partly to a growing recognition of the increase in single-person households and the need to provide small, cheap accommodation for elderly couples, and partly to the fact that for a period at the end of the 'fifties subsidy was concentrated on this kind of house-building. Dwellings for larger families were still few and far between; only 2.4 per cent of council dwellings built during this period had four or more bedrooms. To put it mildly this was (and is) unfortunate as it limits severely local authority capacity to deal with the larger families whose housing predicament can be particularly severe.

⌠The standards of these post-war dwellings were high, particularly those built immediately after the war before the Treasury stepped in and forced the spending departments to trim the local authorities' sails. The average floor area (including outbuildings) of three-bedroom houses rose from 1,026 in 1946 to 1,055 sq. ft. in 1949 but falling thereafter, particularly following the return of a Conservative Government in 1951. In that year the floor area for this kind of dwelling was 1,032 sq. ft., the next year it had fallen to 947 sq. ft. continuing this decline each year until by 1959 it had reached 897 sq. ft. This is not as retrograde as it sounds. The 1961 Parker Morris Report recommended the following areas

82

for dwellings to accommodate five persons (the usual capacity of a three-bedroom dwelling):

	sq. ft.
three-storey house	1,010
two-storey centre terrace	910
two-storey semi or end terrace	880
maisonette	
flat	850
single-storey house	810

These of course are minima, but as is usual with limits of this kind they have come to be regarded as upper limits. (Although Parker Morris space standards were not compulsory until 1969, many authorities had been building to these standards some years previously.)

The growing shortage of building land, coupled with the requirements of slum clearance, also led local authorities to go in for flat construction in a big way. Over half a million of the dwellings built during 1945 to 1964 were flats, representing 28.78 per cent of the total. Prefabrication may also have had something to do with it (most prefabricated systems were more competitive in high-rise than in low), but the era of the tall prefabricated block of flats really belongs in the post-1964 period. But the large (four or more bedroom) dwelling was still being neglected, taking up no more than 2.36 per cent of the dwellings provided in this period.

The period under consideration saw the resumption of slum clearance in the mid-'fifties and the move towards prefabrication in the 'sixties. It also marked the end of references to housing for the "working classes" in 1949, and though this was intended as an attempt to secure a wider social "mix" on council estates, one suspects that with growing affluence, thinly and unevenly spread as it was, it was becoming increasingly difficult to distinguish between who was working-class and who was not. This is all to the good, at least to those who share with the author the goal of a more equal and just society; in practice it made very little difference, particularly when local authorities came to concentrate more and more on slum clearance and to rehousing people from the slums. After all people in Social Category A-B are pretty thin on the ground in a slum clearance area.

When we come to the last period, i.e. 1964 to the present time, we find that at last the predominance of the three-bedroom dwelling has come to an end, the proportion of these having dropped to 35.5 per cent. Once again the proportion of one-bedroom dwelling rose, this time to 28.8 per cent which meant that as many dwellings of this kind were built in the eight years 1964-72 as in the previous twenty years. Proportionally more two-bedroom accommodation too was provided, accounting for 32.7 per cent of the total; not so the four- or more bedroom house which remained static at 2.6 per cent.

Of all the dwellings built during this period more than half (54 per cent) were in the form of flats, many of them built in some form of prefabricated construction. For a number of years, prefabricated systems, most of them using large concrete slabs, had been developed and used on the Continent. They had proved particularly successful in France and Scandinavia as well as some Eastern European countries. The Government at home were faced with a dilemma which expressed in its simplest form was that the annual production of dwellings needed to be raised from round about the 300,000 mark to half a million. But the labour necessary to build these houses in traditional forms of construction would not be forthcoming. Clearly some recourse to factory-style construction was called for and the early 'sixties saw many large British building firms either taking out patents or licences on foreign systems or developing their own. The analogy with the motor-car was frequently pressed into service. After all, had motor vehicle building remained in the handmade-by-craftsmen era, its development as mass transportation would not have occurred (whether that would have been a blessing or not is outside the scope of this book). If mass production methods could be applied to housing, not only would costs come tumbling down (so the argument ran) but the much-desired increase in output would be achieved. Not only that but construction time would be reduced and the quality of workmanship would be improved by removing much of the work to the more disciplined environment of the factory. There was a massive response from industry anxious to cut themselves in to this new and largely untapped market. At one time there were somewhere between 300 and 400 systems under development, most of which were never to get beyond that stage. Had this state of affairs continued it would of course have made nonsense of the whole idea which logically required no more than perhaps four or five systems each producing large numbers of dwellings. Moreover the idea of prefabrication would have to be sold to the local authorities partly because of the unattractive appearance of the immediate post-war examples and the troubles they experienced with corrosion in some long-life aluminium bungalows (which had made it necessary to get rid of them prematurely). The Government set up the National Building Agency in 1964 to appraise the various systems and generally enable the local authority client to see the wood despite the trees. Curiously no financial incentives were introduced to encourage system building, apart from the high-rise subsidy which of course applied to traditional and industrialised building alike. This is in contrast with the period at the end of the war when the government of the day subsidised prefabricated dwellings in the hope of achieving economy in the use of traditional materials and a greater output.

From the start local authorities did not give system building a chance. Industrialised methods, which involve very heavy capital investment, need large orders and long runs in order to become economic; they also require the minimum of departures from a standard design. In too many cases local authorities were prepared to concede neither. In those pre-Banwell days many authorities were still requiring open competitive tenders. These were already outdated when dealing with traditional building, but in the context of industrialised methods they were patently absurd. And those responsible for commissioning building work (not infre-quently these were architects who should have known better) more often than not demanded variations in standard designs which nullified the advantages of system building both in cost and speed of erection; it is not unreasonable to accuse them of being more concerned to erect monuments to themselves than to get the best result in the shortest possible time and at the lowest cost.

None-the-less during this period, say 1964-67, system building was making headway. In 1964 system building was used in 21 per cent of public sector housing; by 1967 this had risen to 42 per cent. By 1968 rather more than 40 per cent of two-storey dwellings were system-built and nearly two-thirds of high-rise flats. Cost-wise system building was competitive only in high-rise flats, a situation which persisted until 1968 when there were signs that it was becoming more economical for all types of dwelling. But in that year an event was to take place which was to deal industrialised house-building a blow from which it has not yet recovered.

Early on the morning of Thursday 16 May 1968, the tenant of Flat 90, Ronan Point, Canning Town struck a match to light the gas for her morning pot of tea. In so doing she set light to escaping gas which caused an explosion resulting in the displacement of certain external load-bearing panels from which the block had been constructed, and the progressive collapse of that corner of the building. The dust never completely settled. Public confidence in system building was thoroughly shaken, the use of industrialised methods for building high-rise flats received a set-back from which it has not recovered (and may never recover), and Councillor Ronan has, innocently and reluctantly, secured a permanent place in the history of housing.

There were naturally enough considerable repercussions. If this could happen at Ronan Point it could happen elsewhere; at the time the Ministry stated that local authorities had identified 56 blocks containing 2,724 flats as possibly requiring strengthening so as to resist explosion and collapse. The cost of strengthening work was very high. At the time Newham, which had five other blocks similar to Ronan Point, estimated that this would cost £130,000 per block (£1,182 per dwelling), or almost 30 per cent of the original cost of construction. And at a conference in 1969 the Surveyor from Felling U.D.C. (population 38,000) stated that his authority had 5 blocks each of 16 storeys with a total of 400 dwellings, that they were losing rent at the rate of £1,600 a week (the blocks had been evacuated) and were faced with a bill for strengthening amounting to £160,000. The Government, had it acted with respect for the usual canons of responsibility (it had after all exerted considerable pressure on local authorities to adopt system building), would have accepted full liability for meeting all the costs connected with this affair; in the event it offered first of all 40 per cent of the cost of strengthening and then, after some haggling, increased it to 50 per cent.

Nor was that all. The opponents of high-rise living, and they were many ranging from sociologists to the more doctrinaire anti-urbanists, now had a field day. Not only were these unloved monstrosities socially disreputable, they were now demonstrated beyond argument as being potentially unsafe. This was too much. The number of flats being built in high-rise blocks (five or more storeys) by industrialised methods had reached over 20,000 in 1967. It dropped to 14,000 the next year, to 5,500 in 1969, to 1,500 in 1970 and to a mere 752 in 1971 when this kind of building virtually ceased. Ronan Point has now been rebuilt and has been reoccupied; at the time of the disaster several tenants expressed their confidence in the building by saying they would return. In the event only one family moved back, although Newham Council gave all of them an opportunity to do so. But many factories producing system building had to close or turn to the manufacture of other things, bringing to a close an unhappy chapter in a British housing story which had opened with such high hopes only a few years previously. System building continues to be used for low-rise developments and is seemingly competitive with traditional forms of construction. At the same time public sector housing which reached peak figures in 1968 has diminished year by year, until in 1972 it could do no better than 122,000 in England and Wales, the lowest annual total since 1963. There appears to be some correlation between the industrialised building fiasco and the decline in local authority housing output.

We may reasonably ask why local authorities had turned to high-rise flats as a housing method. They have provided, in round figures, 400,000 flats in high buildings. Many, but by no means all, have been system built. This is a major departure in British social life and one requiring adjustments not easily made in the short run. The dwellings thus provided have been built to a high standard, frequently have good views (on the upper floors particularly), have access to sun and air to a degree frequently denied to houses on the ground, offer tenants a degree of privacy not previously found in working-class housing, tend to save on land (though not to the degree one might think) and, in the case of system building at least, can be built more quickly, thus reducing the unproductive period between site purchase and the time the dwellings are occupied and the rents and subsidies start to come in. They may possess other virtues, e.g. they are frequently built nearer to urban centres than low-rise estates, thus shortening the times of journeys to work and visits to shops, entertainments and so forth.

Against this they are inordinately expensive. Just why this should be so in Britain is not clear, as it is an experience not shared by many other countries including the U.S.A. where it is the rule that multi-storey construction is cheaper than low-rise. It has always been something of a mystery to the author just why it is possible to transport building materials (including large components for system-built dwellings) long distances, maybe hundreds of miles, in a horizontal direction comparatively cheaply but as soon as it is necessary to move them perhaps no more than two hundred feet vertically costs soar in the same direction. It may not in fact go on and on increasing. At a certain level, which could vary with circumstances, the increase could level off so that for example it might be no more expensive to build on the fortieth floor than on the twenty-fifth. Another point which seems almost always to be ignored is that a tall block of flats is virtually a street standing on its end. That being so, the costs of the vertical services and communications ought not to be charged to the individual flats but rather dealt with as part of the immediate environment.

High-rise living is held to have other drawbacks, medical and social, some of which will be real, others imagined; this is not the place to go into this aspect in any detail. The buildings themselves are frequently unattractive and environmentally disruptive. They do not save much land; at least success has been claimed for a number of low-rise schemes which have provided almost as many accommodation units as would have been the case had they been built high-rise. One real disadvantage may be encountered in blocks of flats where the lift service is less than adequate. Unfortunately lifts seem always to be a target for economy, particularly when the tenders come in too high. This is a ghastly mistake. A good lift service is vital, and in the case of very tall blocks it may be the only means of communication with the upper floors. (Try pushing a pram up twenty-four flights of stairs.) Put another way, a breakdown in the lift service in a tall block may be the equivalent, in horizontal terms, of street closures involving a detour on foot of *several miles.* Some of these objections are valid, others have been promoted by an anti-urbanist school which tends to ignore the virtues and advantages of living in cities. Men after all came together in cities in order to enhance the quality of life, and to seek to escape from the city appears to be a nineteenth/twentieth-century aberration.

Whatever the disadvantages of these high dwellings, some people seem to like them. A survey undertaken by Proplan for Wates in 1966 found that the majority of tenants were satisfied with their high-rise homes and that most of the tenants would be as satisfied living at high level as at low. Research undertaken by M.H.L.G. in 1969 into Estate Satisfaction on Six Estates found that it was the general character of the estate that was crucial, not the building form. Pearl Jephcott reported similar findings in her study *Homes in High Flats* published in 1971. Despite the Ministry and other findings, it has been official policy since 1968 to discourage high-rise building by manipulation of the housing cost yardstick (of which more later).

THE TENANTS

So much for the dwellings themselves. What about the people who occupy them? It should not be forgotten that when subsidised council housing was introduced in 1919 the

Housing: the great British failure

intention was to bridge the gap between private enterprise
(the traditional supplier of rented houses) and the immediate
needs. In other words, local authorities should cater for
general needs and not only for the poorest families. This is
important for two reasons:

(*a*) Families should not be precluded because they had
adequate income. ("They have no right to be in council
houses.")

(*b*) It explains why many of the families most in need have
not been accommodated by local authorities.

This policy was pursued during the 'twenties and again from
1945 to 1956, and 1961 to 1970. Thus excluding the Second
World War, during the forty-eight years of subsidised housing,
local authorities have been permitted and sometimes
encouraged to cater for any family who needed a home to
rent for thirty-four years. There are not therefore any
statutory limitations on the kind of persons who can occupy
council houses. It has, however, been laid down that in
selecting their tenants local authorities must give a reasonable
preference to persons who are occupying insanitary or
overcrowded houses, have large families, or are living under
unsatisfactory housing conditions.

Authorities in fact move in different ways towards the
problem of selecting who shall live in their houses. In some
small authorities selection is still on the recommendation of a
local councillor, a situation which may and frequently does
lend itself to abuse. Others, again a minority, still deal out
their housing on a "first-come first-served basis"; this may be
satisfactory provided there is no shortage and no other
special local factors to be taken into account. Others again
divide their applicants into groups from which from time to
time they select individuals according to the priority
accorded to the group in question. But the majority of
housing authorities operate on a "points" system in which
points are awarded for overcrowding, lack of amenities,
sharing of accommodation, health factors, residence in the
locality, length of time on the waiting list. This system is an
attempt to deal with widely differing claims on an objective
basis. It is exceedingly difficult to devise and not always
intelligible to the applicant. It cannot deal satisfactorily with

90

less objective factors which rely on individual judgment of merit. If the system is to be acceptable, it should always be made known publicly. An applicant will accumulate points over a period of time and sooner or later (later in too many cases) he will be considered as eligible for the award of a tenancy of a house.

It is sometimes held that it can be detected whether or not the local authorities have been doing their job properly by examining the categories of people who are actually occupying their houses, the purposes of public housing being fulfilled if local authority tenants are the poorest households or those with the largest families or the largest proportion of elderly, retired or chronically sick people. Quite apart from the fact that such concentrations would be wholly undesirable from the social point of view, we have already seen that, for a substantial proportion of the time publicly provided housing has been in existence, it has been public policy to make council housing available to those in greatest housing need, which may not be the same thing as greatest economic need. Even so, when we examine recent figures (these are obtained, except where otherwise stated, from the Family Expenditure Survey, 1971), we find that almost 30 per cent of local authority tenants are retired or unemployed (compared with 26.8 per cent of all households), and 57 per cent are in manual occupations (compared with 43.6 per cent of all households). On the other hand only 3.8 per cent of council tenants are self-employed (compared with 8.1 per cent of all households), 4.9 per cent are in clerical occupations (as against 6.6 per cent) and 4.5 per cent are in professional, technical, managerial or teaching professions (as compared with 15.0 per cent). Taking the broad view therefore, it may be said that local authority dwellings tend to be occupied by the kind of person that in the popular mind council housing was intended for. But younger people tend not to get council houses. In 1971 the proportion who were also under thirty years of age was about 10 per cent, compared with 14 per cent with all households. (To express it another way, 23 per cent of heads of households under thirty were in council accommodation compared with 31.4 per cent of all households.) Other age groups showed little difference between those in council houses and those holding other tenures, the proportion in council houses being very slightly higher.

HOW PUBLIC HOUSING IS PAID FOR

General

No work on housing is complete without some account of the way public housing is financed. The difficulty facing the present writer is that there has just (1972) been a major change in housing finance legislation and no one really knows yet how the new arrangements will work out. Certain main principles persist, however.

The housing operations of a local authority are brought to account in a housing revenue account. The money flowing into this account comes mainly from rents and subsidies and the money flowing out goes to meet loan charges, repairs, maintenance and management. (There are other factors, but these are the main ones and the only ones that need bother us here.)

Rents

In the beginning, i.e. during the period following the First World War, local authorities had to set their rents by reference to what was being charged as controlled rents for working-class dwellings in the locality. In later years the only requirement has been that the rents shall have been reasonable, a nice question-begging piece of language which has been interpreted very much according to the subjective judgment of those responsible for setting the rents. Since 1936, however, local authorities have been able to "pool" rents (about which more in a moment), and since in the short run both expenses and expenditure have been fixed, and since the housing account had to balance (and not overbalance), rents in many authorities have been set at a level which was sufficient, with subsidies, to meet expenses and no more. Indeed, authorities were not allowed to make a profit on their housing operations; this is one of the facts that makes it so unfair to accuse local authorities of charging

92

"absurdly" low rents. Authorities have also been able to hold down their rent by "pooling", which in effect means averaging out their rents over their whole housing stock, old and new, and thus enabling them to hold down the rent of recent, expensive dwellings by increasing the rent of older dwellings built at a lower cost. Although the tenants of the older dwellings have to pay more than the historic costs of their houses would justify, they still pay very much less than market rents while at the same time helping to keep down the rents of dwellings being currently produced. This is an exceedingly valuable aspect of local housing and has led incidentally to the situation where at least a quarter and probably a third of local authority tenants are not being subsidised at all in relation to the actual cost of the dwelling they occupy, a fact that is frequently and conveniently forgotten by critics of subsidised council housing.

According to statistics released by the I.M.T.A., average council house rents in April 1972 came to £2.75 a week, and though this is obviously a low figure it nevertheless represented an increase of nearly 45 per cent over the corresponding figure four years earlier. This average figure concealed, as averages frequently do, a wide range of rents charged by individual authorities, for example the average rent charged for three-bedroom houses varied from £8.30 (City of London) to £1.21 (Flaxton R.D.C.). Flaxton Council was charging in 1972 an average rent of no more than £0.55 for its one-bedroom houses completed before the war. Even so, the figure of £2.25 at April 1972 included the statutory increase of 50p which at that time had been levied by about 40 per cent of all authorities under the provisions of the Housing Finance Act, 1972. The remaining 60 per cent of authorities had opted to increase their rents by £1 in October 1972, or with ministerial consent proposed to levy a smaller increase or, in the case of a few authorities, had resolved not to apply the rent increase provisions of the Housing Finance Act at all. What these figures do emphasise, in no uncertain way, is the very great advantages secured by local authorities and their tenants by their ability to "pool" their housing costs and rents. The larger the authority, the greater the advantage, particularly if the authority is one which in the earlier days took its housing obligations seriously and built large numbers of dwellings. This is a point to be taken very seriously into account by those who wish to disperse local authority housing assets either by selling off to individuals for owner-occupation or by transferring them to groups of housing associations.

In the county boroughs, which have on their books about 47 per cent of all council dwellings outside London, rents in 1970 accounted for about 73 per cent of their total income which is a slightly smaller proportion than had been the case a few years before. This reflects the effect on the housing accounts of the increased Exchequer subsidies payable under the 1967 Act. The county borough figures are fairly representative of all classes of authority outside London which means that over the country as a whole (London excluded) an increase in rent of about 30 per cent would have eliminated the need for subsidy altogether as far as existing dwellings are concerned. It would of course at the same time have reduced the ability of authorities to build new dwellings at corresponding low rents and in some areas would have inhibited it altogether.

In any discussion on housing finance, much is usually made of the percentage of family income that it is thought "right" for families to spend on rent or equivalent housing costs. Figures of 20 per cent and even 25 per cent are frequently mentioned in this respect, showing much confusion of mind. These high proportions represent the maxima that building societies will usually allow families to incur for mortgage commitments and even then they usually discount any income except that earned by the head of the household. But as inflation continues and incomes increase, the proportion of income thus devoted to housing falls; in practice owner-occupiers do not pay much more than 10 per cent of their incomes except in the early years of a mortgage. And these people are acquiring a highly valuable asset and one whose value will continue to increase, whereas tenants acquire no asset at all. The author is very firmly of the opinion that there is no "right" proportion of income that tenants should be expected to pay as rent. On the other hand he feels that anyone who pays any more than 10 per cent is being hard done by. Whether that is a correct opinion or not, we can see from Table 1 that in 1971 local authority tenants overall were paying about 8¼ per cent of household income in rent. In the lower income ranges this proportion was much higher and did not fall below 10 per cent until household income reached a level of £35 a week.

(The incomes of families in local authority and in privately rented accommodation was raised in Parliament in November 1970 by the then Secretary of State for the Environment. Mr Walker's statement is discussed in Appendix 1 under the title of 'Families on Low Incomes'.)

Subsidies

Subsidies payable by the Exchequer have already been discussed in chapters 3 to 6. All that we need to remember here is that from 1919-21 the Treasury bore practically the whole loss on council housing, but because of the very high prices of the time they quickly recanted and thereafter right up to 1967 government subsidy took the form of a fixed sum payable annually for forty or sixty years. The sum might and did vary considerably from time to time according to the current government wish to encourage or discourage council building, but it remained a fixed sum which once granted the local authority could not increase and which (until 1972) the Government did not in practice withdraw. Now there is some justice in allocating a fixed sum as subsidy so long as building costs and rents and rates of interest are stable. Over the inter-war period building costs fell, certainly from 1921 to 1935 when they started increasing again as a result of economic recovery and coming rearmament. Since the Second World War however, prices have steadily increased, more rapidly at some times and less rapidly at others, but the increase has been continuous and sustained. The effect of this is to reduce the value of subsidy as time goes by, and authorities on the whole were able to continue building only because of pooling already mentioned. But interest rates, which had been low (3½ per cent) since 1934 and which fell to 2½ per cent in 1946, started to rise in the mid-'fifties and have gone on rising ever since. Now the level of the rate of interest has a profound effect on local authority housing

TABLE 1 – *Weekly income of household*

	Under £10	£10-15	£15-20	£20-25	£25-30	£30-35	£35-40	£40-45	£45-50	£50-60	£60-80	Over £80	All
Average weekly income (£s)	7.89	12.40	17.55	22.52	27.49	32.50	37.45	42.52	47.42	54.69	68.14	112.26	38.48
Average weekly rent paid by tenants of local authority dwellings (£s)	2.28	2.73	2.85	3.08	3.10	3.30	3.45	3.45	3.56	3.63	3.82	4.07	3.18
Average weekly rent of local authority dwellings as percentage of average weekly income	28.9	22.0	16.2	13.7	11.3	10.2	9.2	8.1	7.5	6.6	5.6	3.6	8.26

Source: Family Expenditure Survey, Report for 1971.

finance. Virtually all council housing is paid for with borrowed money. The cost of land and building does not therefore enter directly into the housing revenue account (which deals with costs year by year) but loan charges do. (Loan charges mean payments of interest on the money borrowed and payments (in whatever form) which reduce (i.e. "pay-off") the amount owed.)

As rates of interest have risen, so has the proportion of housing expenditure devoted to loan charges. This proportion, which was about 55 per cent at the beginning of the 'sixties, had risen to about 76 per cent by 1972. (The general effect of interest rates is discussed in the author's note, Appendix 2.)

Local authorities, writers and commentators had therefore for some years pressed the Government to make loan money available at low and stable rates of interest so as to bring some stability to the housing revenue account. Such arrangements are commonly made in other European countries as the Government's contribution to low housing costs. In Britain it was held, at any rate up to 1965, that such arrangements were (*a*) impossible, (*b*) inequitable, and (*c*) constituted a "hidden" subsidy (this was clearly not true — the effect of a reduced rate is obviously capable of being calculated and made known arithmetically), although comparable arrangements had been available for many years to reduce effectively the rate of interest paid by owner-occupiers on their mortgages.

In 1966 the then Minister of Housing (Mr Anthony Greenwood) introduced just such a scheme which was embodied in the Housing Subsidies Act, 1967. This did not make loans available at low rates but it did, by means of variable subsidy, make up the difference between the rate of interest the local authorities were having to pay and a rate of 4 per cent.

(Strictly speaking, this is not quite true: in any year the Government, after consulting the local authorities, fixed a "representative rate of interest" considered to be representative of the rates at which local authorities could actually have borrowed money the previous year. From this they calculated the amount of subsidy required to keep money borrowed for current building down to 4 per cent and applied this subsidy to the dwelling to be paid throughout the sixty-year loan period. This of course made no allowance for subsequent rise or fall in interest rates, the theoretical assumption being that the authority had taken out loans for the sixty-year period. They would in fact be unlikely to do so even if they could get them, especially when rates are high. The new subsidy arrangements moreover made no provision for the refinancing of previous loans taken out at lower rates of interest, when they fell due.)

From the start the new form of subsidy ran into trouble. Interest rates, partly because of the world monetary situation and partly because of difficulties with the balance of payments, rose even more steeply. The crunch came when, after only a few months, the pound was devalued in November 1967 and, as a result of Treasury intransigence, the house-building programme was cut and a massive switch of resources from building to improvement made a central feature of government policy. There was another side to this coin. The Ministry had always exercised some control over house-building costs but this was an aspect of public policy to prevent excessive spending by local authorities; up to 1967 the Treasury's own liability was not directly affected by the cost level. But the new form of subsidy represented in effect a percentage grant, the higher the cost, the higher the subsidy. No spending Department is going to countenance such an "open-ended" subsidy without taking powers to control cost levels fairly closely; in the 1967 subsidy this took the form of a "Housing Cost Yardstick" which laid down the maximum costs the Department would permit for dwellings of different sizes and built to different densities. The yardstick is dealt with in some detail in Appendix 3; what is important here is that it introduced a further element of central control over local authority housing operations. It was one which the Department were not slow to use. Clearly in an inflationary situation it will be necessary to revise such a yardstick from time to time and in fact the White Paper setting out the yardstick principle contained an undertaking to revise its costs levels annually. In practice this did not happen; the first revision took place in April 1969 and although there have been subsequent revisions they have never kept pace with rising building costs and they have become less and less realistic with the passage of time. It has in consequence become more and more possible to cut local authorities housing programmes by the simple expedient of doing nothing, i.e. by not raising the yardstick levels. This inhibition of local authority housing activity by administrative (in)action had been a feature of central control for many years; the yardstick procedure just made it that much easier.

The 1967 subsidy was abolished in October 1972 by the Housing Finance Act but the cost yardstick was retained. The new forms of subsidy still require some form of cost control and the yardstick or something like it is likely to remain. Provided the yardstick levels are revised from time to time so as to take into account changing circumstances, it seems a useful discipline and one which authorities ought to accept. As it is, it seems to be an inhibiting factor more than anything else and one need not be surprised that the Association of Municipal Corporations, for example, are now (1973) calling for its abolition.

From 1919 up to 1961 local authorities have been required themselves to make a contribution from the rates towards their housing operations. Under the 1919 Act this liability was limited to the product of a penny rate (the amount that the authority could raise if they levied a rate of one penny on each pound of rateable value of all the property in its area). Subsequent legislation introduced the principle that the local authority contribution should stand at some fraction of the amount contributed by the Treasury by way of Exchequer subsidies. This fraction varied from time to time, but the necessity to contribute from the rates was abolished in 1961. Local authorities could still contribute from the rates if they wished to and many of them did, especially in London where very high costs still made it necessary for a high rate-borne subsidy if rents were to be held down to an acceptable level. Moreover housing authorities had to balance their accounts each year and if there was any deficiency it had to be made good out of the rates. The whole basis of rate-borne subsidy was altered, in

Housing: the great British failure

common with other factors, by the Housing Finance Act of
1972.

Repairs, maintenance and management
As a matter of prudence as well as necessity, local authorities
make proper arrangements to keep their houses in repair. The
amount set aside for this purpose varies from year to year
and from authority to authority, but in 1970 it worked out
at about £20 per dwelling, outside London. London repairs
contributions were almost double that figure. Supervision
and management charges are also borne by the housing
revenue account. In 1970 these varied from about £8.50 per
dwelling in urban districts to about £30 in London.

Housing Finance Act, 1972 (See also Appendix 7)
The whole business of rents and subsidies was fundamentally
altered by this Act, an extremely controversial measure
which had a rough passage through Parliament and which
aroused deep antagonism in many local authorities up and
down the country, even to the extent of some authorities
announcing that they would refuse to operate its provisions.
(The author wishes to say here and now that although he
fully understands and appreciates the very deep feelings
which led to this situation, he is of the opinion that
opposition taken to these lengths was wrong both as tactics
and as strategy. Nothing is gained in the long run — and
probably not in the short run either — by a lawfully
constituted authority refusing to obey the law.)

Briefly, the Act's provision may be summarised as follows:
1. Local authority freedom to fix their own rent levels has
been abolished and in its place there has been introduced a
variant of the fair rents procedure now operating in part of
the privately rented sector under the Rent Acts, 1965/68.
Under these arrangements rents will in the first place be
determined by the local authority and then amended or
confirmed as the case may be by a Rent Scrutiny Board
whose members will be drawn from the same panel as the
Rent Assessment Committees who hear appeals from the

Rent Officer in the private sector. The Rent Scrutiny Board's functions will however be administrative, not appellate, their decision is final and there is no appeal to them nor from them. On the other hand, if they substitute a rent of their own for the figure proposed by the local authority, they must give reasons and these must be placed on deposit at the authority's office, in other words made public. At this stage the local authority may make representations (only in writing) to the Board and what good that may do them is a matter for cynical conjecture. 2. All previous Exchequer subsidies were immediately abolished and in their place was substituted a temporary residual subsidy which in effect was the previous subsidies reduced in 1972/3 by £20 a dwelling, and if there is any left by a further £20 in 1973/4. After that, if there is still any of the previous subsidy left (in most cases there won't be), it will keep on reducing until it is all gone.

There is further a temporary transition subsidy whose purpose is to help an authority whose rent income increases more slowly than the residual subsidy is phased out. However, the Borough Treasurer of Hemel Hempstead, the magnificent Henry Aughton, tells us to forget about the transition subsidy as few if any authorities will get it. So we will forget it. The third temporary subsidy is the operational deficit subsidy. This, broadly speaking, is half of what the authority had been contributing to the housing revenue account out of the rates. The authority has to make an equivalent contribution out of the rates. If granted in 1972/3 the subsidy goes on until 1981/2 unless for reasons specified in the Act it is reduced or eliminated before then. Of the new permanent subsidies the most important is probably the rising costs subsidy. For the years 1972/3 and 1973/4 this will cover a proportion of the rise in costs. The first year's rise will attract a 90 per cent Exchequer grant for ten years, and the second year's rise will attract an 85 per cent grant for nine years, and so on until it reduces to 75 per cent in year four and each following year. A rate fund contribution makes up the difference. What will be allowed for the purpose of this subsidy will be called "reckonable expenditure" and what will or will not be allowed as reckonable expenditure is to be determined by the Secretary of State.

Every local authority is to introduce a rent rebate scheme as a concomitant of the progression to "fair rents". The cost of rebates is to be borne by the authority's general rate fund in the first instance and a subsidy, the rent rebate subsidy, will be payable by the Government to that fund on the assumption that the rebate scheme is the model scheme included in the legislation. If an authority wishes to introduce a more generous rebate scheme it can do so, but must bear the additional cost itself. The amount of subsidy (which is payable to the rate fund not the housing revenue account) will be 90 per cent in the first year, 85 per cent in the second, and so on down to 75 per cent, the difference being borne by the rates. The whole costs of administering the rebate scheme is to be borne by the authority itself.

Rent allowances are also to be available to tenants in the privately rented sector. These are paid as cash allowances which will be on identical terms with the rent rebates allowed by the authority for its own houses. The cost of these allowances will fall on the general rate fund and will be met by an Exchequer grant of 100 per cent for the first four years and then 80 per cent thereafter. But again the whole cost of administration falls on the local authority.

Next there is the slum clearance subsidy. This is a 75 per cent grant payable to the authority's general rate fund for at least fifteen years; it is generally welcomed. There are one or two other subsidies which need not concern us now.

At first glance all this looks very generous, particularly when contained in legislation the aim of which, in part, is to reduce the amount of Exchequer liability towards housing. There is therefore a snag and this is it. The local authorities will continue to increase their rents as part of the "fair rents" arrangements. In many places the housing revenue account will come into balance. As soon as it does, subsidies will cease to be payable, not all at once obviously, but in the following order as the surpluses materialise:

(*i*)   transition subsidy   (and associated rate fund contribution)

(*ii*)   rising costs subsidy   ditto

(*iii*) operational deficit subsidy   ditto
(*iv*) rent rebate contribution

If there is still any surplus left it goes to the Secretary of State who will recover from any contribution made from central funds towards rent allowances in the private sector. If after all that there is still anything left, the Government will keep half and return the other half to the local authority.

This is a brief account of the Act. Anyone who wishes to get to know the finer details should read one of the many legal books on the subject. He will find it hard going.

The Act has been the subject of much criticism both from within and without the local authority world, not least because of the default provision whereby a Housing Commissioner appointed by the Secretary of State may take over the housing functions of any authority failing to comply with the Act. This has already happened. The point has already been made that the "fair rents" procedures for council tenants are not comparable with "fair rents" in the private sector, and it is not surprising that it is the new rent assessment procedures that have been most roundly condemned. On the whole the author is inclined to wait and see. Clearly the previous arrangements were far from satisfactory; there were after all something like seventy different subsidies payable under eighteen different Acts and their effects on the authority's housing revenue account depended largely on historical accident. Whether in order to put this right it was necessary to introduce such a detailed, complicated and fiddling piece of legislation is another question which only time will answer. Even if the Act turns out to be fair and workable (and that is a very big "if" indeed), one cannot escape the feeling that it could be more or less the right Act introduced for the wrong reasons. For whatever may have been in the minds of those responsible for bringing forward these complicated provisions, there can be little doubt that those who voted for them in Parliament felt a distaste for local authority housing, that council tenants were on the whole worthless parasites who had had it easy for far too long and who ought to be clobbered hard enough to drive them out of rented housing altogether, whereve: possible. It can be argued that it was a highly political and vindictive piece of legislation; no one who had any hand whatever in bringing it to the statute-book will ever have the right to accuse another of "bringing politics into housing".

As we have seen, local authorities have brought into being between five and six million houses, on the whole well designed, well built and maintained, and until 1972 let at astonishingly low rents. How then can it be held that public rented housing is a failure? The nub of the answer lies in the preceding paragraph. Since subsidised rented housing first became a public responsibility there have been those root and branch opposed to it. Not infrequently the opposition has come from those whose public duty it was to promote public housing. Consider the following quotation:

> Subsidies of any kind are apt to produce unexpected results, and I believe that the solution of the whole housing problem depends appreciably upon the building industry being freed from all the entanglements involved in State financial assistance . . . The subsidising of house building has had about as much justification as the Rents and Mortgage Restriction by Statute. Thoroughly uneconomic, the former has interfered with the Building Industry in such a way as to raise the costs of building, whereas the latter has led to gross profiteering by tenants, considerable injustice to owners, and has seriously complicated the whole housing problem. By modifications of the principle and the amounts of subsidy of Local Authorities and others, the injurious effect of the Government intervention has been gradually reduced; but the entire cessation of the subsidy, the removal of restrictions, and the restoration of freedom once more for the free play of economic forces are, in the public interest, devoutly to be desired.

These words were written around 1927, by a man who had been Director of Housing at the Ministry of Health (Sir J. Walker Smith), a man whose public duty it had been to *encourage* subsidised local authority housing. (Sir Walker Smith was writing an introduction to a book by B. S. Townroe entitled *The Slum Problem,* published by Longman in 1928 — elsewhere in the same book the slum dweller is referred to as "a valid sub-species of homo sapiens".)

From the beginning local authority housing has had to face a barrage of just such hostility, not only from public officials (though that has happened far too often), not only from politicians, but from private landlords and tenants, owner-occupiers, not to mention those whose self-appointed task it seems to be to denigrate public activity and expenditure of any kind whatsoever. (Well perhaps not *any* kind, for even these extremists are probably in favour of policemen and fire-brigades.) Such feelings have from time to time manifested themselves in physical barriers which some communities have insisted on to shield themselves from council tenants on adjoining estates. The most famous of these is probably the Cutteslowe Walls at Oxford which were the subject of a book by Peter Collison (*The Cutteslowe Walls,* London, Faber 1963). Built in 1934, they were seven feet high (with revolving spikes on top), knocked down twice, rebuilt twice and demolished finally (one hopes) in 1959. The council tenant in short was, and is, considered an inferior being for whom inferior and segregated housing should be provided if any is to be provided at all. For an excellent account of these attitudes of mind read *Honourable Estates* by James Tucker (London, Gollancz 1966). Such attitudes have been often provoked by the behaviour of some of the tenants themselves. It is all very well to discount the horror stories prevalent in the 'twenties of tenants who kept coal in the bath; there is no doubt that some tenants did keep coal in the bath and if this had been the worst manifestation of anti-social behaviour things might have turned out better. We cannot dodge the issue that in some cases council house tenants will have low standards, some will be feckless and improvident, some will lack, in the words of the Cullingworth Report (*Council Housing, Purposes, Procedures and Priorities,* H.M.S.O. 1969), "the social skills required to obtain and keep good housing in the private sector".

But even those who do possess "the social skills to obtain housing" in the private sector are increasingly finding it impossible to do so. What chance then do the less adequate stand? With the private sector visibly diminishing before our eyes day by day, local authorities are the only hope for the homeless, the inadequate, the socially disadvantaged of every kind, fatherless families, families with one or both parents mentally ill or retarded. Yet these are precisely the families that so many local authorities have gone out of their way to avoid. Local authorities still have a duty, under the 1957 Housing Act, to give preference to persons who are occupying insanitary or overcrowded houses, or are living under unsatisfactory housing conditions. A duty in short to give preference to those whose mode of life exacerbates the very problems that local authority housing management finds so tiresome. Without suggesting any simple-minded connection between better housing and better social behaviour, one cannot avoid pointing out that intolerable housing conditions will certainly make that behaviour worse. The duty to house such families is clear and unmistakable, it is also one that far too many authorities have sought to avoid. It is not a problem that will go away if you pretend not to see it. Such families will no doubt frequently misuse good housing if it is made available to them; they will keep coal in the bath (or whatever the 1970s equivalent is) — they will not learn not to keep coal in the bath until the opportunity to use the bath for its proper purpose is there for them to choose. In some cases it may take years, it may take a lifetime; it has been truly said that the education of our children starts a hundred years before they are born.

Local authorities, with their unique combination of housing powers and provision of personal social services, are especially well placed to deal with problems of this kind; on the whole they have failed to meet them. Where they have been unable to dodge rehousing (e.g. under slum clearance) they have more often than not tucked the offending families away on as remote a corner of their estates as could be found and left them as far as possible to their own devices. On the other hand local authorities have over the years shown preference for the "deserving" tenant, i.e. those who will be able to pay the rent (and will actually do so), will keep their houses neat and tidy, will tend their gardens, will not chop down the fences for firewood, will not keep pets without permission, will not quarrel with their neighbours, will exercise sufficient control over their children to prevent them from being a nuisance to anybody, and who, one is tempted to add, will maintain at all times a proper and respectful attitude towards the housing manager and his staff and anyone else whom authority may see fit to supervise and control them. All this is good and fine, it means that the majority of those living in council houses will be ordinary, decent people well able to manage their own affairs. And this, without any doubt, applies to the vast majority of those who seek to become council tenants. But it also means that while ostensibly giving preference to those most in social or financial need, the local authorities have in fact been providing for those who are a number of steps up the social ladder.

This has not prevented a growing public hostility towards council tenants as a group. That such attitude still persist is clear from the allowance for "stigma" that valuation officers make when assessing the rateable value of council housing or indeed allowances for "stigma" that are currently being made by the local authorities themselves when assessing "fair rents" under the 1972 Act. This has been stimulated by a growing denigration of the very idea of tenancy itself as if to want to rent a house is in some peculiar way immoral. And this has spilled over from council tenancies to tenancies in the private sector, a sort of "guilt by association". This has been aided and abetted by propaganda, partly political in origin, aimed at promoting the idea that anyone worth his salt will eschew the very idea of tenancy and will wish to become an owner-occupier. Owner-occupation as a tenure has many virtues and brings with it its own very considerable rewards as we shall see in a later chapter; morally it is neutral and is neither better nor worse than any other form of tenure. But moral, economic and social pressure has been such that great encouragement has been given to local authorities to sell their houses to the sitting tenants. The result has been an increase in the annual number of such sales from about 2,000-2,500 in the 1950s to almost 25,000 in 1972. It has been the subject of much bitter argument inside Parliament and outside it. The Conservative Party has vigorously pursued a campaign for the sale of council houses; the Labour Party has been just as anxious to limit it. The point has already been made that much of the argument is irrelevant. The occupier of the house does not change his spots or become morally superior when he stops paying rent and starts repaying a mortgage. If the local authority is to continue to be able to discharge the housing duties laid on it by Parliament, it will have to replace the house sold, and at a much higher price. Management problems are made worse by having little islands of owner-occupation pepper-potted all over their estates, and the advantages of rent pooling are reduced as the size of the housing stock is reduced (but such advantages are to be lost under the Housing Finance Act anyway). There is no doubt that those tenants who wish to buy are motivated by the financial advantages conferred by ownership in an inflationary situation, coupled with the give-away prices being charged by many authorities. (In theory local authorities may offer a discount of not more than 20 per cent off market price; in fact this seems to lead to a very low price level. Not far from where the author lives a local authority has been selling its houses at just over £3,400 each; similar houses in the private sector would fetch not less than £9,000. This looks like a discount of 62 per cent — for stigma?)

Nor is there any great advantage to the local authority. The author was greatly impressed by one very well-known local authority Treasurer who described himself as a "blue-nosed Tory", much in favour of selling council houses. The political situation changed in his borough and at last this Treasurer actually had an opportunity to sell some houses. He looked further into it and in the end he came to the conclusion that there was no advantage to the local authority in selling except possibly for a very narrow "band" of housing built in the early 'sixties. Older housing was much cheaper and therefore profitable, more recent housing was much dearer and the authority would suffer from loss of subsidy and repayment of the loan capital. One may debate whether this was a typical Treasurer operating in a typical situation; one could be forgiven for concluding that the demand that local authorities should divest themselves of their housing assets is in part at any rate politically inspired. It is a great pity that so much heat has been generated by this issue when so often in fact it does not greatly matter one way or the other. For the house continues to exist, the former tenant continues to live in it (for the time being at any rate), the taxpayer gains because of the withdrawal of subsidy; he then goes on to lose five or six times as much because the occupier will now be claiming tax relief on his mortgage interest or else an option mortgage subsidy. It would be a great advantage to housing if the protagonists would forget the whole thing.

CONCLUSION

We find that up to October 1972 local authorities had provided getting on for six million dwellings and had let them at low rents. The contribution to human happiness over the past fifty years must have been enormous, and for all their shortcomings local authorities have left a legacy of immense value for the coming generation. And yet, as a solution of the basic housing problems facing this country, council housing must be deemed a failure. In simple terms it is a failure to reach those most in need; a failure to recognise the paramount importance of good housing in promoting the welfare of the individual and the nation. We see it in the half-hearted and inadequate policies adopted by the local authorities themselves, we see it in the failure of successive governments to ensure that the authorities carry out the duties that the legislature has placed upon them, we see it in the use by central government of housing as a pawn in the regulation of the economy, we see it above all in the confusion of mind prevalent in central and local government alike as to the place of publicly provided housing in society and the manner in which it should carry out that role. Since state-aided housing began in 1919 there have been fundamental changes in policy every five years or less. This means that on average housing policies have not outlived by any great margin the parliament that brought them into being. Couple with this the vagaries of local politics (which may or may not be party political) and we can begin to wonder how on earth the local authorities have achieved as much as they have. We can agree with Milner Holland that "housing has for too long been the sport of politics". We can question the choice of local authorities as the vehicle for the execution of national housing policy. We can argue, and later in this book it will be argued, that housing should be taken out of the hands of the local authorities altogether and placed in the charge of some national organisation that is at least one stage removed from the political process. It seems to the author that in no other way can the long-held and frequently stated objectives of public housing policy be achieved.

8 Private renting

As we have seen, the national stock of housing is made up of three main types: (*i*) houses owned by private owners and let to tenants mainly but not entirely on weekly tenancies, (*ii*) houses owned by their occupiers, and (*iii*) houses owned by local authorities and let to selected tenants.

It has not always been so. Prior to 1914 something like 90 per cent of dwellings were privately owned and let to tenants. During the last fifty years the outstanding changes in the make-up of the national stock of houses have lain in the parallel growth of municipal houses and of owner-occupied houses on the one hand, and the decline of houses privately owned and let to tenants on the other. For the purpose in hand one can ignore the dwellings provided by housing associations and trusts; welcome as their operations are, one can see no evidence that their contribution is likely to be a large one within the foreseeable future.

The decline in the number of dwellings privately let has been in evidence since the turn of the century and has been continuous since 1919. Many of them have been demolished under slum-clearance schemes and this process must continue if the built environment is to come within measurable distance of what twentieth-century living requires. Although successive governments have endeavoured to encourage private renting, whether by modification of rent control (1957, 1965) or by granting subsidies to private tenants (1972), or by other means, the building of such houses has been negligible when compared with the numbers built for owner-occupation. For a few years between the wars, in the late 1930s, a number of new dwellings came on to the rented market; this appeared to be the result of the saturation of the owner-occupied market rather than any deliberate change of policy. Certainly this type of building has not been resumed on any scale since 1945. Government encouragement of building for private renting has not met with success, despite a good deal of misplaced political optimism, and we have now arrived at the situation where this tenure represents less than 14 per cent of the national stock.

How and why has this come about? It is clear that houses as an object for the investment of private capital have lost the widespread attraction which they had in the nineteenth century. There are other investments which are without doubt safer and which give a better return — the expression "as safe as houses" has long become an historically interesting anachronism. Other kinds of investment moreover involve less attention to time-consuming detail such as housing management demands. Rent control, as we shall see, has not played the decisive role in this decline that its antagonists frequently assert. The decay of the privately rented sector can be attributed to a combination of the following factors:

1. *Constraints imposed on private landlords by the State.* These have been numerous and frequently onerous. One can cite particularly the public health legislation of 1875 which made house-building more expensive. Rent control, though not a primary cause, must have been a contributory factor, particularly since 1945.

2. *The lack of appropriate financing institutions.* During the nineteenth century lenders were willing to keep their money out on mortgage; frequently these were trustee funds administered by solicitors. This source has now dried up and alternative sources have not developed. Banks will not as a rule lend sufficiently long, and even where building societies are willing to lend, their terms are not usually acceptable to aspiring landlords.

3. *Competition from owner-occupation financed by building societies.* This has been formidable since the 1930s. An owner-occupier is prepared to invest his money (i.e. the deposit) without receiving interest; he puts his money into the house and gets a tax-free real income (the occupation of the house) instead of a money income. Moreover as

owner-occupiers do not pay tax on the rental value of their houses they can outbid the private landlord on the price of land; the owner-occupier can in short afford to pay more for his housing (taking tax-relief into account) than a private landlord letting to a tenant with comparable income. Since 1945, there has been the additional lure of a capital gain and many householders have become owner-occupiers, partly because they had no choice, partly because it gave security, but mainly because they have seen, with inflation, the value of privately-owned dwellings increasing year by year. The prospect of this capital gain has in many cases been a decisive factor in the decision to buy; the fact that such a gain has been (and is) largely illusory, since any house they buy will be at least as expensive as the one they sell, does not seem to have weighed heavily with prospective owner-occupiers. Such an attitude moreover has been encouraged by politicians of all shades by the assertion that "buying a house is the best investment a householder can ever make". So it is, but the massive inflation since 1970 has not proved profitable for the great majority of owner-occupiers. (Where houses have been bought as an investment, i.e. bought and resold without being occupied, the gain has been considerable, but would be considered less reputable if only it were more widely understood.)

4. *The tax position of landlords.* A house is considered by the taxing authority to last for ever and landlords cannot write down their investment. Even payments into a sinking fund to replace the dwelling when it is obsolete cannot be treated as a cost. This also applies to any new equipment installed as an improvement, although such equipment may in fact have quite a short life. The tax position of landlords is in other respects inimical to their interests and is considered by many to be iniquitous. Without going quite that far there is no doubt that landlords have been discriminated against quite unfairly and that this has led to severe distortions in the housing market. Worked examples of these distortions have been made frequently and with varying degrees of sophistication; the example quoted here was presented by the Borough Treasurer, Hemel Hempstead (Henry Aughton), to the Annual Rating Conference at Brighton in 1971. Mr

Aughton assumed that a house cost £4,000 (but this was 1971!) and was financed by borrowing the full amount at 8½ per cent for thirty years in the case of a private landlord or an owner-occupier and sixty years by a local authority. A rent of £10 a week would give the private landlord no profit at all, a local authority could charge £7.35 a week without subsidy (in practice it would be less because of rent pooling), whereas an occupier could buy at a cost of £6.33 a week including repairs. This disparity clearly has implications of great difficulty in the application of any system of "fair rents" and was foreseen by the Milner Holland Committee which pointed out that tax is an additional cost for the private landlord, a reduction in cost for an owner-occupier, but does not affect the local authority either way.

5. *The attraction of other forms of investment.* Since 1878 manufacturers have been permitted to depreciate their plant and machinery and the tax advantages of doing so have made investment in industry more attractive. Moreover, developments in national financial institutions have made it possible to invest in a more lucrative manner, with greater liquidity, than could the former private lender putting his money out on mortgage to the private landlord.

Rent control, on the other hand, cannot be held to be primarily to blame, From about the 1880s onwards less money was forthcoming to finance house-building to let and this trend became very marked during the first two decades of this century. The number of houses built in 1903 in the United Kingdom was something of the order of 150,000. In each of the years following, the number declined inexorably year by year until by 1914 it had fallen to about 48,000. (These figures include Southern Ireland which at that time was still part of the United Kingdom.) (See figures 1 and 2 on pp. 116-117.) This decline must have reflected a falling-off of demand for house-building by private landlords; neither owner-occupation nor council housing were yet significant. But rent control was not introduced until 1915. Furthermore, the private landlord did not flourish in the years between the wars despite the fact that (*a*) new houses were not subject to control, (*b*) rents were for most of this period controlled at about their free market level, and (*c*) there was no suggestion during this period that rent control would be extended, only reduced, i.e. there was no real element of political uncertainty. What rent control does do is to turn housing into a fixed yield investment. It is true that in later years the yield has been unconscionably low and may even have attained a negative value, but all this happened a long time after the rot set in. On the other hand since 1945 rent control and its inevitable concomitant, security of tenure, have without question made it impossible for landlords to maintain their property properly, let alone improve it. (It does not of course follow that higher rents would have led to privately-let housing being properly maintained and improved — most landlords would, in the manner of conventional entrepreneurs, have sought to maximise their profits by the simple process of not carrying out repairs.) And any attempt at decontrol must, in conditions of scarcity, lead to abuse. The last major attempt at decontrol was made in 1957; by 1959 Rachman and others like him were in full cry.

Clearly then, houses privately let will play a continuously decreasing part in our future housing, since few if any are being built, but large numbers of them are being demolished under slum clearance or are being sold for owner-occupation. This reduction will be gradual and unless some drastic measures are taken meantime, the existence of these houses will affect the housing situation for some years ahead. For the most part they were built before 1914 (at least 80 per cent) — either small houses lacking the amenities now considered essential or larger houses once occupied by a single family but now occupied by several families without the changes in structure of equipment called for by this change of user. It follows that with very few exceptions they are not splendid houses. The 1967 Housing Condition Survey revealed that 70 per cent needed repairs costing more than £125, 46 per cent had no internal W.C., 39 per cent no fixed bath, 53 per cent no H. & C. at three points, while no less than 57 per cent lacked one or more of the standard amenities. There are still two and a half million of these houses and over one-third of them are unfit (to put it another way, two-thirds of all unfit dwellings are privately rented). In the interests of the tenants and of society as a whole it is vital

115

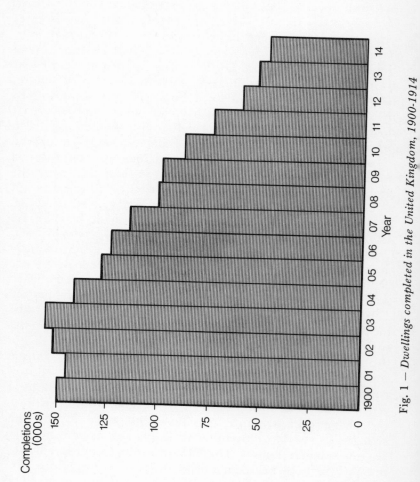

Fig. 1 — *Dwellings completed in the United Kingdom, 1900-1914*

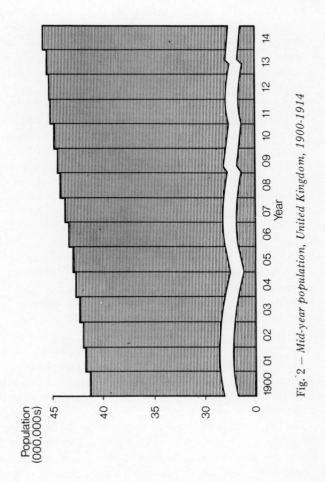

Fig. 2 – *Mid-year population, United Kingdom, 1900-1914*

that as many of these dwellings as possible should be saved and brought up to standard, but it seems that this is unlikely to happen as long as they remain in private hands. For many years society has hamstrung the private landlord and encouraged other tenures. It has not made up its mind whether it wants a privately rented sector or not, to the great detriment of the houses involved and the people living in them.

Renting one's house is a traditional form of tenure and one that until comparatively recent times was considered eminently respectable. For reasons perhaps not unconnected with subsidised public housing, private renting appears in recent years to have taken on a faintly soiled if not immoral image as if there is something reprehensible about wishing to rent (or perhaps about not wanting to buy — we shall discuss this in the next chapter). This, to put it mildly, is a pity. Renting makes a lot of sense to a lot of people, particularly to the young and mobile still building their careers. It makes economic sense, too, since the cost of providing the dwelling can be spread over several generations instead of one generation or less as is the case with a building society mortgage; admittedly this is less likely to be significant when interest rates are high. The private landlord moreover, whatever his shortcomings, brought an element of variety and choice to the housing scene which other forms of tenure have so far been unable to achieve. But he requires an economic environment with a narrow range; stable costs, which are unlikely to increase or decrease significantly over a long period of time, coupled with low and stable interest rates. Both aspects are significant: no investor is going to put his money into rented housing if he thinks that costs are going to fall in, say, five years' time. The later houses will clearly undercut those built previously. The reverse situation will obtain if an investor thinks costs are going to rise. As for interest rates, there appears to be a crossover point which the author calculates at between 4 and 5 per cent, under which it is more profitable from the occupier's point of view to rent, and above which it is cheaper to buy, assuming in each case costs are stable. These situations have not existed in any great degree since before the First World War.

If it is felt that there is still a place for the private landlord in the British scene, then consideration should be given as to how this can be secured. If not, means should be devised for him to quit the scene with decency, dignity and some degree of justice. The following offer themselves as possible solutions:

1. Do away with all controls and restraints and remedy the landlord's anomalous tax position. Investment in housing to rent could then be allowed to sink or swim. This would be in accord with recent policy of requiring all lame ducks to stand on their own feet; it seems to have little else to commend it. The last major attempt at decontrol (1957) resulted in a marked *decrease* in the number of houses privately let. Moreover, such a proposal would not only be politically precarious, it could be held to be ethically suspect in that it would be analogous to keeping a man bound hand and foot for half a century and then asking him to stand up unaided.

2. Recognise that the private landlord has a part to play and back this up with direct cash subsidies. To some extent the rent allowances given under the 1972 Housing Finance Act are doing just this; they are however based on so-called fair rents which are bound by the nature of the case to be something of a compromise and which will almost certainly prove to be insufficient to keep the private landlord in business. There does not seem to be any valid reason why, if the case for subsidies in this sector is accepted, they should not take the form of payments made direct to the landlord for keeping rented housing in being. It would almost certainly be fairer to make such payments to a limited number of landlords than to raise rents to the level where most tenants need subsidy and then make cash rent allowances to the majority of them.

3. Release all controls as in (1) but make it obligatory first to offer the dwelling to the sitting tenant at a reasonable price. This would do nothing to check the polarisation of tenures into two major groups, which many (the author not included) hold to be financially and socially dangerous. It would beg the question as to what, under the circumstances, is a "reasonable" price. There are other obvious difficulties including the matter of unoccupied dwellings and, more

seriously, the position of the poorer tenant who might be unable to buy and at the same time unable to pay a market rent.

4. Require local authorities to acquire, compulsorily if need be, all privately rented dwellings and administer them as part of their housing stock. When municipalisation was last in the air it was not a practical proposition, mainly because of the sheer numbers involved. On the practical level, it is now a possibility; local authorities have the expertise, the manpower and the administrative muscle. It would require massive government subvention. It would be highly unpopular with some authorities. Some landlords and most tenants would, I think, welcome it. As with (3), polarisation of tenures would be encouraged. Whether local authorities, in view of their record, would administer the additional stock with sensitivity and justice is another matter. Probably most would and some would not.

5. Set up government-sponsored housing associations at either national or regional level to take over these dwellings. The housing corporation, suitably reinforced could undertake the initial organisation. Again much money would be needed. The organisational problems would be considerable, but not, at first sight, insuperable. In the long run it would mean setting up organisations parallel with local authorities but with less expertise and capacity, and what would be the point of that?

6. Set up, compulsorily, government-sponsored co-ownership societies on the housing corporation model. This, as far as the tenants are concerned, would be akin to renting and yet would give them a stake in the property without requiring much in the way of an initial deposit. Status and income might be a problem for the less affluent occupant but should not prove insuperable as mortgages are given to the society not to the individual. Increases in capital value (if any — remember these are old houses) would accrue to the society and ultimately to the occupants. Administration of this kind of society is not easy and would probably be more difficult in the circumstances. Whether the administrative expertise could be found from among the tenants is debatable, but if it could then, of the solutions offered here, this seems to be the

least objectionable. Any solution will in fact be difficult, which is not surprising since the problem has been a long time in the making.

Currently, hope is being pinned on the concept of "fair rents" first introduced by Richard Crossman in the 1965 Rent Act (since consolidated in the Rent Act, 1968). The 1957 Rent Act had reduced the area of protection (security of tenure at fixed rents) to cover dwellings of low rateable value and only for as long as they remained occupied by the then tenant or his successor. Crossman's purpose was to restore protection to the great majority of private housing to let. (Rachmanism was still fresh in the public mind when Crossman had introduced the Protection from Eviction Act in 1964, a temporary measure designed to hold the field until permanent legislation could be introduced.) This protection applied to tenancies of dwellings with a rateable value not exceeding £400 in Greater London or £200 elsewhere with certain exceptions, a major one of these being furnished apartments. Within these limits tenancies not still controlled in the 1957 Act (now consolidated in the 1968 Act) and tenancies which pass out of control as time went on were subject to rent regulation. Regulated rents are those registered as such by a new official, the Rent Officer. Either the tenant, the landlord or both may apply to the Rent Officer for a particular rent to be registered or for the Rent Officer to fix a fair rent. If either party objects to the Rent Officer's decision they may appeal to a Rent Assessment Committee. There is no appeal from a Rent Assessment Committee except on a point of law. The formula by which both Rent Officer and Rent Assessment Committee have to work is contained in Section 46 of the 1968 Act, which states that regard shall be had to all the circumstances, other than personal circumstances, and in particular to the age, character and locality of the dwelling, and its state of repair. No allowance is to be made for scarcity; the Rent Officer (or Rent Assessment Committee) has to assume that "the number of people seeking to become tenants of similar dwelling-houses is not substantially greater than the number of such dwelling-houses in the locality which are available for letting on such terms." This in theory is nonsense. If there were no scarcity there would be no need for regulated rents and no need for Rent Officers. Scarcity value must therefore be a matter for highly subjective judgement, as also must be the interpretation of the term "substantially greater". Nonetheless, a Committee appointed to review and report on the operation of regulation under the Rent Act (The Committee on the Rent Acts, otherwise known as the Francis Committee) reported in 1971 that by and large the system was working well. It can be argued that any system, however bad, can be made to work well provided its operators have sufficient determination; on the other hand it can be held that the system has its merits. Obviously Crossman was in a dilemma in 1965. He clearly could not go back to pre-1957 rents which were even more nonsensical than any system of "fair rents" could be. On the other hand neither he, nor the Government, nor indeed the public at large, were ready to face the circumstances of unrestricted market rents. "Fair rents" are therefore a compromise, and on the whole it seems an acceptable compromise at that. The findings of the Francis Committee produced strong and mixed reactions ranging from "one of the great State Papers of our time" (Mr Julian Amery — Minister of Housing and Construction) on the one hand to a description as "a Landlord's charter" on the other. Whatever the validity of the latter charge may be, there is no doubt that the majority of the Committee were impressed by the evidence submitted by private landlords (and their associations) and in particular by the well-known Freshwater Group of Companies, prominent in the privately rented field, especially in London (see special article in the *Sunday Times* Review of 18 November 1970). But to describe this Report as a "great State Paper" is very clearly overdoing it.

The provisions of the 1968 Rent Act have been modified by the Housing Finance Act of 1972, particularly in the matter of progression towards "fair rents".

The Rent Officer, who in many ways is the king-pin of this system of rent-fixing, is a new breed of public servant. He is appointed by the Clerk to the local authority but he is not a local government officer. Although his function is mainly that of valuation, most Rent Officers are not trained valuers, many of them coming from local and central government, the police force and a few from H.M. Forces. They may be dismissed only by the Clerk of the local authority with the consent of, or by the direction of, the Secretary of State.

Rent Assessment Committees consist of a lawyer, a valuer and a lay member, appointed by the President of the Panel for the area. In England the Secretary of State appoints the Panel Presidents and Vice-Presidents from among members who are appointed by the Lord Chancellor. There are parallel arrangements for Wales and Scotland.

Nothing in the "fair rents" system seems likely to arrest the decline in the numbers of privately rented dwellings. A number of companies, operating principally in London, are operating profitably within the scope of the Act, on the principle of "maximising rental potential". But the great majority of landlords are more likely to be interested only in securing vacant possession so that they may sell at the best price and be rid of the obligations of private renting once and for all.

The nineteenth-century landlord seems to have been an exceptional creature brought into being by nineteenth-century conditions. Changes operating in the last quarter of that century were already militating against his continued existence. The celebrated housing reformer Alderman W. Thompson of Richmond felt constrained to write as early as 1903 that "private enterprise, undirected and uncontrolled had failed" to provide adequate housing for the working classes and it seems likely that, in British conditions at any rate, the private landlord could not long survive the turn of the century. Perhaps in these latter days the provision of dwellings for renting is no longer an appropriate activity for private enterprise. Those with an obsessional objection to municipal rented housing will endeavour to use any argument for the private landlord's survival. But whatever his merits may have been (and it seems unlikely that they were ever considerable), the private landlord seems destined to perish sooner rather than later. And all attempts to delay his demise seem likely to end in failure, a word which we have heard all too often already in this account of British housing but from which there appears to be no escape.

9 Owner occupation

Nearly half the dwelling houses in the United Kingdom (more than half if you are thinking of only England and Wales) are owned by the people who live in them. This form of tenure is called owner-occupation and is commonly held to be "a good thing". As a form of tenure it is not a particularly modern development, but its widespread appeal is a twentieth-century phenomenon which had its roots in the development of building societies in the nineteenth century. The early societies were "terminating" building societies, in which a number of people got together, each paying a regular weekly amount into the society's funds. When enough money had been paid in, the society bought a house and allotted it to one of their members, frequently by ballot. The lucky occupier went on paying his subscription, as did the other members, and again, when funds were large enough, a second house was purchased and so on. When all the members had been housed, the society, having achieved its aim, was wound up, or terminated, hence the name.

The philosophy of self-help was widely accepted in those early Victorian days, but despite the good intentions of their members, many of the early societies ran into difficulties, some caused by default by members who may have fallen on hard times through sickness or unemployment, others through sheer maladministration by the societies' officers who were frequently untrained and even more frequently unpaid. Other difficulties were occasioned by the very long period some members had to wait before having the chance of getting a house. Many of these gave up in despair before their turn was reached; they forfeited their right to a house but also upset the arrangements for other members of the society.

What clearly was needed was some arrangement whereby money could be borrowed from investors who were not themselves interested in buying a house, at any rate not through the society. When this stage had been reached, which was about the middle of the century, there was no reason why a society could not go on lending out money which had been repaid by previous borrowers, or additional money lent to the society by new lenders. In such circumstances a society could go on operating indefinitely and so could earn the title of "permanent", the use of which persists right up to the present day. In those days money was lent out on mortgage, commonly for periods of between five and fifteen years, rather shorter than is usual today.

By 1890 the societies had nearly £50 million out on mortgage and, despite some setbacks later that decade, this figure had reached almost £60 million by 1911. Even so, by the time the First World War had broken out not more than 10 per cent of houses in Britain were owned by their occupiers and it was still very unusual indeed for working-class families to own their own homes. Nor is the reason difficult to seek. What a mortgagor needs more than anything else is a secure job that pays well (and unless his employer will pay him when he is ill he needs good health as well). High wages, security of employment and even good health (though that was improving) were not notable features of nineteenth-century working-class life.

The great period of expansion in building society activity came between the wars. The societies had already, despite some spectacular frauds (which were in fact few and far between) shown themselves to be trustworthy organisations, well able to manage their affairs in accordance with good business principles. They had moreover increased their funds during the First World War and when peace came they were well placed to extend their activities. After a slow start in 1919 expansion came quickly, especially in the mid-'twenties when private house-building was encouraged by subsidies available under Chamberlain's Housing Act of 1923. (Under this Act a private builder could get a lump sum subsidy of £75 and in addition local authorities could add a subsidy from the rates; they could also guarantee building society mortgages which exceeded the then usual 70 per cent of valuation on houses which cost less than £1,500.) Over the inter-war period the societies' total investment grew by more than 13 per cent each year on average, and even the depression years failed to halt this growth. From 1928 to 1937 the number of borrowers increased from 554,000 to 1,392,000 and the amount out on mortgage from £227 million to £636 million. The amount advanced in 1928 was £58.7 million; by 1937 this had increased to £136.9 million. This dramatic rise was helped by a downward movement in building costs each year up to 1934; then increasing demand made itself felt and costs increased each year until the outbreak of the Second World War. However, even in 1939 the cost of house-building was still less than it had been in 1924. These variations in costs did not appear to be reflected in the size of individual mortgages taken out by house-owners. These had averaged £425 in 1928, had increased each year until 1931 when they reached £471, from 1932 to 1935 they remained steady at £446, increasing again to £463 by 1937. Between the wars private enterprise built something like 2.88 million dwellings, mostly for owner-occupation. Of these 430 thousand were subsidised, mainly under Chamberlain's Act.

The great expansion in house-building, hitherto unparalleled in this country, is held by many to have been a major factor in Britain's comparatively rapid emergence from the Depression. For house-building not only employs labour on a considerable scale, it also uses a wide range of materials which are the products of numerous and diverse industries. Not only that, it stimulates the demand for furniture and furnishings of all kinds, gas and electrical equipment and so on. And for the first time both house and furniture could be paid for on instalments. The author recently came across an old copy of the *Sunday Express* in the bottom of a drawer; it was dated 13 February 1938 and carried a number of advertisements for new houses. Nearly all of these advertisements show the weekly sum required to buy the house; quite a number of them quote only this and do not mention the cost of the house at all. Some could be secured for as little as £5 deposit and the weekly repayments range from about 13s. to £1. This of course was 1938 when rising costs coupled with a near-saturation of the potential market were making houses more difficult to sell; it was during this period that the only revival of the rented market since 1914 was evidenced.

If the advertisements are anything to go by, the houses were of good quality. Wimpey's claimed that their houses had cavity walls and close-boarded roofs ("no middleman's profits"), and Wates were insisting that every one of their houses carried the certificate of the National Housebuilders' Registration Council (cost from 17s. 9d. weekly including rates and insurance). Those were very definitely the days, provided you could afford the repayments and had a secure job.

By 1939 this boom was falling off and had there been no war it seems likely that there could have been a widespread return to private renting which in those days was still considered to be a respectable way of paying for your accommodation. For some years after the Second World War building society activity was on a comparatively low level mainly due to the restrictions on private building for sale. After 1952 however there was a rapid rise which has continued, with some check, right up to the present day. By 1945 about 26 per cent of all dwellings were owner-occupied. This increased to about 40 per cent by 1965 and today (1973) it stands at just under 50 per cent in the United Kingdom or about 52½ per cent in England and Wales.

It is interesting and possibly profitable to speculate how this considerable change in tenure patterns came about. The growth of owner-occupation has taken place largely at the expense of private renting. This is at first blush surprising when you consider that the renter pays for housing as he uses it, whereas the owner buys a lifetime of housing in advance. (Not quite true of course; many of them buy it over twenty or twenty-five years. The fact remains that over a comparatively short period the owner will buy housing which will last his lifetime and very likely someone else's as well.) There must be other factors at work. Two much quoted American writers, North and Ring, list a number of compelling reasons apart from "basic instinct and desire".

127

These include independence, adventure, peace of mind, creative instinct and security. Those who do not aspire to home ownership may be persons who "have neither socially nor economically ripened to undertake the duties and responsibilities which home ownership necessitates". Maybe so, but that cannot be all. It is clear that the desire to own one's home is widespread and it certainly provides the freedom to pursue one's life in one's own style. When putting forward this argument, however, the protagonists often compare the owner-occupier's undoubted freedom with the petty restrictions frequently imposed by the less imaginative local authorities, in short they are hardly comparing like with like.

But more than that, home ownership is an investment, a hedge against inflation, and in addition holds for many the attraction of a sizeable capital gain. That this gain will be largely illusory, at least for so long as they need housing, does not seem to weigh heavily in their minds. The prospect is there, and that is enough. Illusory or not, the gain is available for use whenever the owner sells, and although he may have to pay a similarly inflated price for his next house, he nevertheless has a substantial sum of cash in hand to put down as a deposit on a better house and this "gearing" is permitting owners already on the ladder to live in a better quality house than would be the case if there were less or no inflation. John Willis, former Director of SHELTER, claimed at a conference in November 1972 that a man earning £645 p.a. in 1956 could have bought a house valued £2,300 and by selling and rebuying in 1963 and 1970 he could be living in a house which he had bought for £4,208 and which might be worth £10,260 by 1972 and earning (assuming constant inflation) £1,683 p.a. And if one took a similar example based on a man with the *same* loan advance (£4,208) and earning the *same* income (£1,683), one could start again with a house costing £4,208 (100 per cent advance) in 1972 and by 1993 could have a house costing £45,518 which seven years later could be sold for more than £73,000. (All based on inflation at 7 per cent p.a. compound.) Such are the consequences of house-price inflation. Such gains are massive and are a principal reason why people go in for house-buying;

but the gains are illusory in the sense that it is an improvement in the quality of his house that the owner-occupier obtains rather than an improvement in his bank balance (which in the circumstances quoted may in fact suffer a reverse.) It should be clearly understood that such "benefits" are available only to those already on the owner-occupation ladder and in possession of a reasonably modern house. For those not so fortunately situated inflation is making it less and less possible to buy a house of their own or indeed to secure adequate accommodation of any kind.

A second major attraction is security of tenure. An owner-occupier, provided he keeps up with his mortgage repayments, cannot be turned out; this is not the case with private renting. The great majority of private landlords are not potential Rachmans but they are quite capable of resorting to any legal means, and maybe some illegal ones, to secure vacant possession if it is really in their financial interests to do so, particularly if the tenants concerned are not too sure of their rights. Even with council rented property the tenant feels himself at the mercy of what may be a politically-motivated bureaucratic authority, particularly if he has committed the cardinal sin of improving his position and thereby earning more money than it is considered meet and right for a council tenant to have. The operation of the 1972 Housing Finance Act will do nothing to reduce this apprehension. On the other hand councils now have to get a County Court Order before they can evict; until recently under the provisions of the Small Tenements Recovery Act of 1838 they could secure an eviction order without even having to give reasons.

But the third, and to the author's mind the major, cause of the massive switch in tenure patterns (not necessarily tenure *preferences*) is that buying is so often the only way to get a house at all. No one in their right mind is going to invest in housing to let in present-day circumstances (except possibly at the luxury end of the market) and probably not in any foreseeable circumstances at all. Landlords of existing rented property will in most cases sell off as soon as they can get possession and so it is hardly worth the householder's while to look for privately-rented accommodation; it isn't there to be had. And sitting tenants, lured by the twin possibilities of greater security and the chance of making a profit, will often, if and when the opportunity presents itself, buy from their landlords. The landlords will almost certainly sell at a lower price than they could get with vacant possession because they could not get full market value anyway; they will rid themselves of an encumbrance and can put their money into something more profitable. Thus it is not surprising that following the Rent Act of 1957, an Act which was declared to be the sure means of reviving the ailing private rented sector, the number of houses going *out* of private renting (mostly into owner-occupation) increased dramatically by perhaps as many as 100,000 a year. That this should have happened is obvious and the fact that control over rent levels and security of tenure was relinquished in this way under conditions of great scarcity is indicative of the way that political prejudice can take precedence over rational thinking.

Nor should it be thought that owner-occupiers, who without doubt are the brightest jewels in any Conservative Chancellor's crown, have achieved their dominance of the housing market unaided. They have in fact received very considerable Exchequer assistance over the years, (*a*) because they are permitted to avoid tax of that part of their income which goes to pay interest on house mortgages, and (*b*) because since 1963 they have not been required to pay tax on the stream of services which their investment in house property produces. To take these in order, let it be understood that tax relief on mortgage interest payments *is* a subsidy; tax forgone has to be raised elsewhere and so falls as a burden on the general body of taxpayers. And a reduction in tax paid is just as much a subsidy as a payment made direct to the householder and sent through the post. Either way it costs the Exchequer money. Such relief has been on a considerable scale, for example it amounted in 1962-3 to £75 million, by 1967-8 it came to £180 million (Exchequer subsidies to public sector housing that year amounted to £94 million) and by 1969-70 it reached £224 million (public sector subsidies were £163 million). The next year tax relief came to almost £300 million and there can be no doubt whatever that had public sector subsidies increased at anything like this rate there would have been an outcry at this gross misuse of public funds. Needless to say there are still those, mainly house purchasers, who are still convinced that tax relief is not a subsidy but rather a matter of fiscal justice. No student of housing finance or for that matter any competent writer or commentator on housing still pretends that this is the case, however, so perhaps there is no need to labour the point here. The fact remains that at least twice as much of the taxpayer's money is devoted to subsidising owner-occupation as is spent on subsidies to public sector housing, and to bring it down to individual cases the government subsidy per mortgaged house is about £60 a year at least and is rising rapidly, whereas the Exchequer subsidy to council housing is not more than £40 a year per house and is falling as a result of the operation of the Housing Finance Act, 1972.

This is not to argue that subsidies to owner-occupation are not a good thing, and aid by means of tax relief has some advantages, not the least of which is the fact that the occupier gets most help at the beginning of the mortgage (when most interest is being paid), which is the time he needs it most. But one must also realise that this kind of aid is indiscriminate and regressive, it makes no allowance for the financial situation of those being helped; the more affluent the purchaser, the more expensive will be his dwelling and the higher will be the aid he gets from the Government. And because of surtax, the relief to the higher paid will be higher still. *The Times* called the failure to include tax relief in the Government's 1972 reforms a "conspicuous omission", and well it might. Henry Aughton called it "a subsidy to bricks and mortar crying to heaven for reform". To quote further from *The Times:* ". . . there remains the anomaly that a government which advertises its bold and radical approach to questions of public finance and its intention of ensuring that everyone stands on his own feet if he has any, makes no mention in its opening statement on housing of that third of public subvention that is of least assistance to the needy". One can agree with Henry Aughton that these are words on which it is impossible to improve. But that was 1971 and to be fair to the present Government (1973) it has shown a

Housing: the great British failure

willingness to learn from experience to the extent that it has been prepared to backtrack on almost every aspect of its stated policy. In that case it is possible, though in the author's opinion not very likely, that it will have second thoughts on this matter as well.

As for Schedule A, this tax was introduced long ago partly as a measure to tax the income of landlords (who were then predominant in housing) and partly to ensure that an owner gets taxed on the income which his investment in property represents. For if a man invests £9,000 in shares or bonds he will get an income which will be taxed and until recently at a higher rate than would have been the case had it been earned income. The man who invests £9,000 in a house similarly gets an income through the stream of satisfactions that his occupation represents though not in money terms. Or to look at it another way, he would have, say, £500 a year more disposable income than a man who had to pay £500 a year to rent a similar property. Schedule A tax was therefore based on the annual value of the property as assessed for rating purposes. During the period between the wars house-owners were already benefiting because of the under-valuation of property built during that period, and this advantage increased after the Second World War as assessments got further and further behind because of inflation. The pretence was dropped in 1963 when, amid general rejoicing, Schedule A was dropped altogether. According to the Treasury it was estimated that the cost of doing away with this tax cost £35 million in 1963-64 and £48 million in a full year. After making allowances for the increase in the number of owner-occupied houses since then and also for the increase in the assessments for annual value which have also taken place since then, it is clear that the current cost of not having this tax is a large figure which could be as high as £200 million a year.

The abolition of Schedule A benefited all owners, but tax relief on interest payments benefits only those who are paying tax. The option mortgage scheme, introduced in 1967, sought to remedy this position by giving a would-be mortgagor the option of either getting tax relief or of getting a loan at a reduced rate of interest without tax relief. The

132

amount of option mortgage subsidy (i.e. the difference between the going rate for building society mortgages and the reduced rate applied under the scheme) was calculated so as to put the non-taxpayer in roughly speaking the same position as the taxpayer getting full tax relief. The scheme is described in greater detail later in this chapter, but one can comment that not only did it bring a great measure of justice between one category of house-owner and another but it also, at a stroke, disposed of the myth that tax relief is not a subsidy.

Whether or not owner-occupation would have reached its present level without the assistance outlined above is, to say the least, arguable. In marginal cases it may be that the tax relief element was decisive, but in the majority of cases it seems likely that the other pressures and attractions previously mentioned would have been enough in themselves to have maintained the drive towards home ownership. There are of course drawbacks, for example the cost of maintenance which must figure to some extent in any landlord's calculation is frequently underestimated by owner occupiers and even more frequently ignored altogether. In fact such costs can be considerable, just how considerable one can gather from the evidence about maintenance costs that landlords individually and collectively produce from time to time to show how iniquitous are their current levels of rent income. Often an owner-occupier will feel able to do much maintenance work himself and indeed if you see a neighbour at weekends at the top of a ladder with a paint brush in his hand you can be sure that he is an owner-occupier. There is nothing wrong with a man putting his time and effort into improving his home environment, but there is a limit to what he can do. Although it seems not to have been followed up, there was a good suggestion put forward by Stanley Alderson in his book *Britain in the Sixties — Housing* (Harmondsworth, Penguin 1962) to the effect that owner-occupiers should be required to take out insurance against the necessity for major repairs. Recent suggestions in a government White Paper that grants should be make available in certain circumstances towards repairs only (as distinct from repairs coupled with improvement, which is already the case) seem to reinforce the point. One can think of the great period of home buying which happened in the 'twenties and 'thirties. Many of those who bought at that time are now coming up to retiring age and so, unfortunately, are some of the houses they bought then. At the very time these houses need substantial expenditure to keep them in good condition, some of their owners are least able to afford it. Or to put it another way, to a pensioner a leaky roof can spell disaster.

Nor should it be forgotten that not all are owner-occupiers by choice. Often it is the only way for a family to get a home whatever their personal preferences may be. It may in fact be difficult to find out just what these preferences are, since what people want is conditioned to a great extent by what they already know or have experienced. In 1964, for example, the Government Social Survey found that, outside London, 76 per cent of owner-occupiers seeking to move wanted to buy, but 16 per cent of them said they would prefer to rent. Of those renting their accommodation, 86 per cent of local authority tenants and 72 per cent of private tenants said that they would want to rent. That of course was ten years ago, before the really massive inflation in house prices had set in. Even so house prices were rising rapidly; the prices of new houses increased by 41 per cent between 1959 and 1964 and 40 per cent between 1964 and 1969. Whether rising price levels of this order encourage owner-occupation or whether they inhibit it by pricing a large section of the population out of the market is a matter of some debate. What seems to be fairly certain is that there are a large number of householders who, given a choice and assuming a sufficiency of dwellings, would just as soon rent as buy.

If it is true that a proportion of householders have been forced into buying, it follows that not all owner-occupied dwellings are splendid houses. According to the House Condition Survey, 1971, there are 9,062,000 owner-occupied dwellings in England and Wales. Of these, 3,087,000 (34.1 per cent) were built before 1919 and therefore must be at least sixty years old and a high proportion will be very much older than this. Approximately 355,000 (3.9 per cent) of all owner-occupied dwellings are unfit, i.e. slums. Or to put it another and more telling way, of all the unfit dwellings in the country, 28.5 per cent are owner-occupied. And nearly two-thirds of all owner-occupied dwellings needed repairs costing between £100 and £1,000 or more. Owner-occupied houses needed less expensive repairs than privately rented dwellings, which is what one might expect, but they needed more expensive repairs than local authority/new town houses, which clearly says something for the standard of maintenance and repair of dwellings in the public sector.

Notwithstanding anything said in the previous paragraph, there is no doubt that the privately-owned sector includes houses of a high standard which is no more than one would expect. Nearly six million of them have been built since 1919 and thus in the British mind rate as "modern" houses. About 3.37 million have been built since 1945 and will generally be good houses with modern amenities, though it is worth remembering that in, say, Germany, houses built at this time will be regarded as old dwellings in need of rehabilitation and improvement. There is no doubt that, political propaganda apart, house-ownership brings with it many advantages among which pride of ownership may properly be counted. There seems no reason why it should not be encouraged *for those who can afford it.* As we shall see this proportion is not likely to increase at anything like the rate experienced in the late 'fifties and 'sixties, and there are grounds for thinking that the market for this kind of tenure is fast approaching saturation. But before we come to that conclusion let us look at the various ways by which men (and women) may achieve home ownership.

1. *Purchase outright.* There is nothing particularly complicated about this, all one needs is sufficient money. The would-be purchaser finds what he wants and then, either directly or through an agent, makes an offer which is maybe less than the asking price. If buyer and seller agree, the matter is placed in the hands of their respective solicitors who between them draw up, first a contract which places an obligation on the seller to sell and on the buyer to buy, and second, the conveyance which is the legal document which transfers the property from one person to another. Ten per cent of the purchase price is usually paid when the contract is

signed and the balance "on completion", which is usually on or near the date when the parties sign the conveyance. The conveyance, together with the investigations as to title and other searches made by the solicitors, are called the deeds and are the purchaser's proof that he owns the property. In this respect they rather resemble the log book of a car and there has been some move in recent years to simplify the conveyancing procedure on these lines, a proposal which on the whole has been resisted by the legal profession.

Or, of course, the prospective purchaser may wish to have a house built to his own requirements. In this case he buys first a piece of land by means of contract and conveyance as outlined in the previous paragraph. He then, if he is wise, finds himself a competent architect to design the house; the architect will usually attend to the business of getting other professional advice (if necessary) and also selecting a builder to do the work. There is then a contract drawn up between the builder and the owner (called the "building owner") and in due time, and about fifty variation orders later, the house gets finished. (A variation order is an instruction from the architect to the builder to alter in some way the plans or specification for the building; the building owner, not the architect, pays any additional cost and it has been said that it is worth any building owner's while to send his architect on a holiday abroad for the duration of the contract, an exaggeration which contains a germ of truth.) The building contract usually contains some provision for the payment of damages by the builder if he does not complete the building on time (the so-called "penalty clause"). Such provisions are not usually worth the paper they are written on and penalties are very seldom exacted.

Before leaving the subject it is worth bearing in mind the existence of the National House Builders Registration Council which was set up before the war to exercise some control of the standards of house-building. The great majority of house-builders are now registered with the Council which inspects the building during construction and on completion issues a certificate that the house has been built to its standards. The certificate also carries with it a guarantee that defects subsequently arising during a specified period will be put right without cost to the owner. There is no doubt that the existence and operations of the Council have resulted in improved building standards, particularly as the Council has the ultimate sanction of removing recalcitrant contractors from their register, a sanction which on one or two occasions they have actually used. And as most building societies require new dwellings to be guaranteed by the Council as a condition of granting a mortgage, to be removed from the register is tantamount to being put out of the house-building business altogether.

2. *Purchase with the assistance of a building society loan.* In this case the purchaser, having selected the house he wishes to buy, approaches a building society in the hope that they will lend him sufficient money to buy the house. Assuming that the property is one on which the society are prepared to make an advance, i.e. it is not too old or too expensive and that the applicant's income is such that they feel he can afford the repayments, they will then arrange for a survey, usually carried out by an independent surveyor. The applicant pays the fee for this, but the report of the survey belongs to the building society and is usually not disclosed to the applicant. One may feel that there is something unfair about this, but it is well-established practice which, despite pressure to the contrary, is unlikely to change. The building societies make the point that the report from the surveyor is a valuation, not a structural survey, although of course the structural condition of the property will affect the value the surveyor is likely to put on it. When this has been satisfactorily completed the building society will usually (assuming they have not run out of funds) make the applicant an offer which in normal cases will be 80 per cent either of the purchase price or the valuation, whichever is the lower figure. After that the purchase proceeds in much the same way as described above under "purchasing outright". The purchaser has, however, to sign an additional document, the mortgage, which is the building society's security for the loan. The mortgage provides for the regular payment of interest and in most cases, the money loaned. If the buyer defaults, i.e. fails to make his payments in the manner agreed, or if he in some other way fails to adhere to the terms of the

loan, the society may "foreclose" i.e. demand their money back. If the buyer is in a position to do so he can then repay the loan and that is the end of the matter. He is, of course, almost never in a position to do so and if he cannot obtain another mortgage elsewhere the building society have the right to sell the house and keep whatever money is owing to them, plus their expenses in connection with the sale, after which they will hand over what is left to the former owner. If on the other hand the buyer keeps his side of the bargain and pays off all he owes, the mortgage then ceases and the building society will hand to him the deeds of the property, which they have been entitled to retain so long as the mortgage was in existence. Please note that the house does not become the property of the buyer at this stage, it has been "his" all along, and he has been responsible for insuring it, keeping it in repair, paying rates and taxes on it and in fact bearing all the liabilities that the ownership of property brings with it. If the owner wishes to sell before the mortgage is paid off he is free to do so, but of course he must make arrangements for the outstanding debt to be paid to the society.

Building societies will in certain cases lend more than 80 per cent. One way is for the buyer to get a guarantee from an insurance company for the repayment of any sum advanced in excess of 80 per cent. In this way, for the price of a single premium, which is usually quite small, the buyer can get 90 per cent or even 95 per cent of the value of modern property, which must however be below a certain price, which varies from time to time. Building societies will sometimes lend money on a house which is still being built or even one which is to be built for the purchaser, subject to valuation, and will even in some cases make instalment payments to the builder as the work proceeds. In such cases the buyer pays only interest until the full amount has been advanced, when repayments commence in the ordinary way. Moreover societies can, under the option mortgage indemnity scheme, advance 100 per cent on the valuation figure of modern properties. Repayments can be made in a number of different ways. The most usual of these is:

(i) The annuity method. Under this method the purchaser

pays a fixed annual amount, usually in monthly stages, and this remains the same throughout the term of the mortgage, provided that the rate of interest does not change. The annual amount paid (the "annuity") consists partly of interest and partly of repayments of capital. Because the borrower owes most in the early years of the mortgage, the proportion of his annuity which goes to pay interest is high during that period and the amount paid off the debt is comparatively low (see Appendix 2 on interest rates). It is not until the later years of the mortgage that the purchaser begins to reduce his debt substantially. For example even when the rate of interest is only 8 per cent (that is considered low now, but only a few years ago it would have been thought unconscionably high) and the term of the mortgage is twenty-five years, the owner still owes, after ten years, £801 for every £1,000 he borrowed in the first place; even at the fifteenth year he still owes £627 for every £1,000 borrowed. Repayments of capital do not account for as much as half of his annual repayments until somewhere between the seventeenth and eighteenth year. As interest rates rise, interest payments account for more and more of the sums paid in the earlier years of a mortgage, so much so that when rates are really high it is not worth while trying to reduce the amount paid each year by extending the term of the mortgage. If during the term of the mortgage the rate of interest changes, then the society may vary the amount of the annual repayments. Sometimes, in order to assist borrowers, instead of raising the amount of the repayments, the societies will extend the period over which the debt has to be repaid. With high interest rates however, there is less and less room for this kind of manoeuvre and most borrowers can expect to pay more if interest rates rise, which now seems to be happening every few months.

(ii) The "endowment" method. With this kind of mortgage the borrower pays only interest during the term. The borrower also takes out an endowment assurance policy with a yield equal to or higher than the amount borrowed. The borrower has to pay interest on the money borrowed *and* premiums on the assurance policy as well. It is thus a more expensive way of borrowing money, but the benefits are

139

considerable. The borrower gets tax relief not only on the interest payments but on part of the assurance policy premiums as well. If as is usual the policy is "with profits", he gets an additional bonus either at the end of the term or if he decides to sell meantime. When the policy matures the proceeds of the policy are paid by the insurance company direct to the building society who then discharge the mortgage in the same way as in an annuity mortgage. This form of mortgage is usually recommended if the borrower can afford it. It does of course carry with it the additional protection that the mortgage is automatically repaid (through the endowment policy) if the borrower dies at any time during the term of mortgage.

(iii) Fixed instalment mortgages and standing mortgages. These are comparatively unusual. In the case of a fixed-instalment mortgage the borrower undertakes to repay a fixed amount of capital each year; in addition he has to pay interest on the unpaid balance. The amount he pays each year will therefore vary, being higher at the beginning of the mortgage and lower at the end. (See Appendix 2 on interest rates.) Standing mortgages are those in which only interest is paid, there being no arrangement in the agreement for the regular repayment of any part of the debt. This arrangement will suit a borrower who has definite expectations of a certain sum of money in X years' time; it does not as a rule find favour with building societies who like to have some of their money back so that they can re-lend it.

(iv) Local authority mortgages. Local authorities have power to lend money for house purchase under the provisions of the Small Dwellings Acquisition Acts, 1889-1923 (not now much used) or Section 43 of the Housing (Financial Provisions) Act, 1958. The rate of interest is generally somewhat higher than the current building society rate, but some loans carry the advantage (at least it is an advantage when interest rates are low) of keeping the rate of interest the same throughout the mortgage term. Local authorities are frequently willing to lend money to purchasers and on properties not favoured by building societies; they thus fulfil a social purpose as well as a financial one. The amount available to local authorities for lending in this way is from

140

time to time restricted by the Government and so their performance in this field tends to be somewhat erratic.

(v) Option mortgage. If the borrower thinks it is to his advantage, he may forgo the entitlement to tax relief on his interest payments and opt instead to be charged a lower rate of interest. The difference between such a mortgage and the usual rates is made up by the Government and paid direct to the lender as a subsidy. The scheme came into operation on 1 April 1968 and can be applied to any of the types of loan mentioned above. Since January 1970 the amount of subsidy has been on a sliding scale depending on the normal rate of interest. This is set out in Table 16, Appendix 4. When the scheme was first introduced it was felt that the option mortgage would be of benefit only to people not paying tax at the standard rate. With rising interest rates however, it seems likely that any borrower would benefit by going for an option mortgage unless he pays supertax. Appendix 4 may assist understanding of the point; the tables it contains are calculated on the assumption that the normal rate of interest is 8½ per cent (in the hope that the present high rates of interest are only a temporary feature). It will be seen that although a tax relief mortgage works out cheaper in the earlier years of the term, this advantage gradually disappears and overall there is slight advantage in having an option mortgage. Also, because of the way annuity payments are calculated, the option borrower pays off his capital debt more quickly, and always owes less than the borrower of equivalent amounts on normal tax relief terms.

The dramatic rise in home ownership which took place between the wars and which continued, though less spectacularly since 1945, has brought comfortable modern housing within the reach of a large section of the population. It has never, however, been a possibility for the lower-paid sections of the community. The author calculated in 1964 that the purchase of new or modern homes was within the reach of not more than 40 per cent of all householders. If the calculations were based on, say, 1971 prices and wages we should find that the average cost of a house, new or existing, would be in the order of £6,200, and assuming that the building societies were willing to advance up to three times the householder's annual income, this would require an income of at least £40 a week. From the Family Expenditure Survey for 1971 we know 80 per cent of heads of households had incomes of less than £40 a week and we can say that in these circumstances house purchase is restricted to 20 per cent of households. This is not the whole story of course. Many householders with less than £40 bought houses in 1971, but many, if not most, of these had a house to sell; they were already on the ladder. In short, the man receiving the average wage cannot now afford to buy the average house and probably not any house at all.

The position has in fact worsened in the last two to three years by an unprecedented rise in house prices. Following the trend of recent years the prices of houses rose by about 6½ per cent in 1970. But prices rose by double this amount in the first six months of 1971 and continued to increase so that by the end of that year prices of new and not-so-new houses stood at about 22 per cent up on what they had been twelve months earlier. According to the Nationwide Building Society, these increases were greater than any recorded for any year in the 1950s and 1960s. Nor did it end there. The rise accelerated during the first half of 1972 (17 per cent) and even more during the second half of that year, so that taking the year as a whole the prices of new houses rose by 47 per cent and existing houses by 40 per cent (Nationwide Building Society: Occasional Bulletin 115). According to Nationwide the rate of increase started to ease off during the last quarter of 1972, but even then it was running at 8 per cent for new houses and 5 per cent for existing houses (over the three months), which only a year or two earlier would have been considered excessive for the whole year.

Why did this come about? A number of conflicting theories have inevitably been put forward. As this is not a text book on economics we can do no more than consider them very briefly.

1. *Increases in the price of land.* This is a view very widely held and is frequently expressed as landowners "holding the nation to ransom". Put in this crude way it is nonsense. The demand for houses in the short run is concentrated almost entirely on houses already in existence for which the land has

already been bought, often very many years ago. But in any case high land prices are the result of, not the cause of, high house prices; what a man buys is a house and land together, and land costs represent no more than the balancing factor between what it costs to build a house and what the ultimate purchaser is prepared to pay for it.

2. *Increases in the supply of money.* This is the "monetarist" theory of inflation which, loosely stated, suggests that since the Government have aimed at an expansionist policy so as to hasten recovery from the 1971 recession, the money supply has been increased by something like 30 per cent per annum. As an explanation of the 1971/72 house price inflation this seems unlikely; monetary measures take some time, perhaps eighteen months to two years, to bite. One would find it difficult to accept that the monetary policy adopted in 1971 started to bite even before it was put into effect. Whether or not monetary policy affects house prices in the long run is another matter which need not concern us here.

3. *The activities of the building societies.* Building societies get their money by borrowing and in order to maintain an even flow they must keep their rates of interest "competitive", i.e. more attractive than other forms of short-term investment, otherwise the money does not come in. If, as seemed to be the case in 1970 and 1971, the building societies keep their rates unnecessarily high in relation to other short-term market rates more money will flow into their coffers. But in order that such money shall earn its keep they *must* lend it out again and principally this will be in the form of lending for house purchase, which is after all why they are in business. Mortgages were therefore plentiful and easy to get during 1971/72 and since the housing market is overwhelmingly stock-dominated additional new houses to soak up the additional purchasing power were not, *and could not have been,* forthcoming (in fact private house completions were falling during this period). As building societies lost their differential advantage *vis-à-vis* other short-term rates, people turned to alternative forms of investment and the inflow slackened off in or about the third quarter of 1972, so much so that the *Daily Mail* on 21 August could carry an article by Raymond Rogers entitled

143

Housing: the great British failure

"Bang goes the Boom" and the *Sunday Times* Insight Team could at least ask "Goodbye to Gazumping?" (Gazumping was a word brought into common use during the period of peak house-price inflation; roughly, it means that a seller would back out of an agreement to sell without warning, apology or compensation — an equivalent in racing terms would, one supposes, be "welshing".) This was premature, in fact the third quarter of 1972 brought with it the highest rate of price increases yet recorded: 16 per cent for new houses and 12 per cent for existing houses, according to Nationwide. But this was almost the end of this boom; the next three months recorded increases of "only" 5 to 8 per cent (in fact these would have been considered high for a period of twelve months only a year or two before).

4. *The failure of planning authorities to "release" land.* This has been a favourite government excuse over the past two or three years. But planning authorities do not "release" land, only landowners do that, and planning authorities cannot grant permission for land to be used for housing until and unless someone applies for it. But in the short run, and it is very much the short run we are concerned with here, the conditions in (1) above apply and the failure on anybody's part to "release" land will not have much effect. In fact it seems likely that the stream of planning permissions was outstripping the construction of houses during this period, even in the south-east where the pressure was highest. No doubt other factors can be advanced, but these are enough to be going on with.

The very considerable increase in prices which happened during the period we have been considering led, predictably, to demands that the Government should "nationalise or control the price of land", should "exercise control over Building Society lending policy", partly, it seems by the setting up of a stabilisation fund into which building societies would put excess funds when money is plentiful and from which they could draw when money is tight, should "control the price of houses, new and existing", and so on. Even if all or any of these would work, which to put it mildly is not proven, it cannot be emphasised too often that house-price

144

inflation is a symptom of the failure of policy in other directions. Let us consider the following:

1. There has been a serious attempt to solve the housing problem, quantitatively and qualitatively, through owner-occupation. This has not worked, despite very considerable propaganda denigrating first council renting and then renting of any kind, until as near as makes no difference, it is now thought somehow immoral to want to rent at all. But owner-occupation cannot help the less affluent or those who for one reason or another cannot expect a regular substantial income. At the present time the average wage cannot buy the average house and it seems likely that not more than 20 per cent of householders could afford owner-occupation unless they are in it already.

2. There seems to be strong evidence that the market for building society mortgages must be near to saturation. This was happening in 1938-39 and it seems to be happening now with money chasing existing properties rather than new ones.

3. When a product is in short supply you try first of all to increase production and if that doesn't work you look for interchangeable alternatives. For three years the Government has restricted and discouraged supply in the very area where state action would have been most effective (i.e. the public sector) and would have helped those most in need of it. It would also bring nearer the day, admittedly still far off, when there is a sufficiency of good quality houses for all who need them. By restricting the supply of public sector housing the Government have ensured that the shortage of dwellings remains and have thus indirectly encouraged house-price inflation.

4. Even before the shortage of decent houses comes to an end the position will be reached where a house depreciates in value from the day it is first occupied, much as say a motor car does now. When that stage is reached owner-occupation will become much less attractive as the householder will not only be denied the prospect of a capital gain, however ephemeral, but he will actually have to set money aside to compensate for the money he will lose when he sells or when the house wears out. It may still be true in those conditions that house purchase "is the best investment a man can ever

make", but if it is, then it will be seen to be so on its own merits and not as a source of unearned increment.

5. The present privileged position of the owner-occupier should be brought to an end. He pays no tax on the cost of borrowing which pays for the acquisition of his asset (a tenant pays tax on the money out of which he pays the rent), he pays no tax on the stream of satisfactions which ownership of this asset will bring (nor does the tenant, but he does not acquire an asset), he pays on historic costs (under the so-called fair rents system a tenant is called upon to pay current costs), and he is complimented on his sturdy independence (whereas the tenant is derided). As a first step Schedule A tax or something like it should be reintroduced. This is probably preferable to abolishing tax relief as it would include all current house-owners, whereas not more than about half of current house-owners have loans outstanding and are paying interest on them. Such a proposal would no doubt be regarded as iniquitous by house-owners and it may be that there are now so many of them that it might be difficult or even impossible for it to be brought about. That of course does not stop it being a proper course to advocate. If this move were accompanied by a massive increase in the supply of public sector dwellings so that great inroads could be made into remaining shortages, and if it could be made possible to move easily from one sector to the other and back again, not only would house prices be stabilised, not only would it aid mobility and social "mixing", but we should be in a position where the householder could have a real choice between renting and buying. "Freedom of choice" has been a housing catchphrase for many years; such policies might conceivably make this freedom a reality.

To own one's home has been possible on any scale for not more than fifty years and it has come about mainly through the activities of building societies. It has received great political encouragement for blatant political reasons, but these do not greatly matter so long as they do not blind us to its drawbacks. It ought to be possible for anyone who wishes to do so to own his home provided he can afford it; equally it should be possible for anyone who wishes to do so to rent. Much has been made of the subsidies paid by the Exchequer to rented housing but little or no complaint is made of the massive government aid to owner-occupation. And yet if it is right for the tenant to stand on his own feet, what objection can there be to asking the owner-occupier to do likewise?

For the purposes of this book the case against owner-occupation rests on the fact that it has not solved or even helped to solve the major housing problems of the less affluent, nor is it possible for it to do so. This is not a failure of owner-occupation *per se,* within its own limits house ownership has been a great success. It is a failure of policy on the part of those who, for reasons which will not bear close examination, encourage owner-occupation at the expense of other tenures.

10 Housing associations and societies

As we have seen, housing tenure is rapidly becoming polarised into two main groups, subsidised council housing on the one hand and privately-built owner-occupied houses on the other. Such polarisation is held to be detrimental to the wellbeing not only of householders but frequently of society at large as well. The present Government (1973) put it fairly plainly in the White Paper "Widening the Choice: The Next Steps in Housing" (Cmnd 5280): "The Government believes that the trend towards a municipal monopoly of rented housing is *unhealthy in itself*". (My italics — Author) Just why it is unhealthy the White Paper did not say; perhaps the Government felt that it was so self-evident that no reasonable man would wish to doubt it for a moment. That there is lack of choice, no one will deny, though frequently the wrong conclusions are drawn from it. More often than not those who cannot afford to buy have no choice at all. They live in miserable and unhealthy surroundings, but they are not people who reject municipal housing; almost certainly they are people who cannot get municipal housing. In this context an expansion of "monopolistic" council housing would widen their choice, not diminish it. Even when they can afford to buy, some would still prefer to rent, and here again an expansion of the rented sector, public or otherwise, would be beneficial.

The only other agency through such expansion might come is what is loosely known as the voluntary housing movement. It is a movement whose members collectively like to think of themselves as "housing's third arm", an ungainly simile which does not in any case indicate the contribution they could make towards better housing. They do, however, constitute one of the visible alternatives to owner-occupation on the one hand and municipal renting on the other, and as such they have played a useful, if minor, role and could, given the right conditions, expand into a numerically significant house-providing agency.

Housing associations (the term is being used loosely here; there is a distinction in fact between housing associations and housing societies to which we shall come in a moment) have a long and on the whole honourable history, having been involved in the social housing field before even the local authorities. Shaftesbury's society — the Society for Improving the Condition of the Labouring Classes — was an early example which indeed still lives on through the Peabody Trust. So was the Metropolitan Association for Improving the Dwellings of the Industrious Classes which was formed by the Rector of Spitalfields in 1841. This latter was in theory a commercial organisation which, however, was limited by the terms of its charter to a dividend of 5 per cent and thus may be more properly regarded as philanthropic. Later came the well-endowed charitable trusts such as Peabody (1862), Guinness (1889), Sutton (1900), and Samuel Lewis (1906) as well as Bournville and Rowntree which have been mentioned in a previous chapter. Some of these operated on a comparatively large scale. For example by 1914 Peabody owned 6,400 dwellings, which was more than twice the number built by the London Metropolitan Borough Councils up to that time. Housing associations, or public utility societies as they were then called, were recognised as bona fide house-providing agencies and they have been eligible for local authority assistance and government subsidy from 1919 onwards.

Between the wars housing associations, partly it seems because there was still a sizeable rented sector in being and (more likely) because too much was expected of local authorities in their new-found role of universal providers, failed to expand on the scale of local authorities or private builders. When, later in this period, it became obvious that municipal housing was not the prelude to the millennium, interest in housing association work tended to revive. Just how many dwellings associations produced between the wars is difficult to say as no reliable figures appear to exist, but it must have been a tiny fraction of the total output.

After the Second World War housing associations concentrated mainly on providing accommodation for special groups (e.g. elderly or single or disabled people) and in one or two other spheres such as industrial housing associations or self-build associations. In doing so they could obtain loans or Exchequer subsidies through local authorities who could also add a subsidy from the rates if they felt like it. (Very few have done so.) The local authority frequently attached conditions to their assistance which housing associations on the whole resented but accepted as part of the price they had to pay for dependence on public assistance.

An attempt to break away from this situation was made in 1961 when the Government provided £25 million for England and Wales (£3 million for Scotland the next year) as loan capital for building houses to rent without profit and without subsidy. The rate of interest charged was similar to that being charged to local authorities. By 1963 all the money had been taken up, mostly by new societies set up for the purpose by the National Federation of Housing Societies, and the end result was about 7,000 new dwellings. When the scheme was first mooted it was hoped that the rents for the proposed dwellings would work out between £4 and £6 a week, which proved to be highly optimistic. The scheme was expanded in 1964 and was put in the charge of a new government agency, The Housing Corporation, which had imposed on it the duty of promoting housing "societies" (a term which now took on a new meaning, not to be confused with the way it had been used prior to 1964) which would provide "cost rent" accommodation or "co-ownership" dwellings. The latter was a comparatively new concept as far as Britain was concerned, in that all the occupants owned jointly all the society's accommodation. There were obvious advantages to this kind of arrangement; collectively the group could have the advantages of owner-occupation including tax-relief or option mortgage arrangements and a share in capital appreciation. Both kinds of society can borrow money from the building societies and the Housing Corporation. This at first was on a two-thirds/one-third basis,

150

but is now half and half. Because of increasing costs and rising interest rates cost rent has proved a non-starter, the potential rent levels being quite unacceptable.

DEFINITIONS

A housing association was defined in the Housing Act, 1936 (re-enacted in Section 189(1) of the Housing Act, 1957) as meaning:

> . . . a society, body of trustees or company established for the purpose of, or amongst whose objects or powers are included those of constructing, improving or managing or facilitating or encouraging the construction or improvement of, houses, being a society, body of trustees or company who do not trade for profit or whose constitution or rules prohibit the issue of any capital with interest or dividend exceeding the rate for the time being prescribed by the Treasury, whether with or without differentiation as between share and loan capital;

and a Housing Trust:

> . . . means a corporation or body of persons which by the terms of its constituent instrument, is required to devote the whole of its funds, including any surplus which may arise from its operations, to the provision of houses for persons the majority of whom are in fact members of the working classes, and to other purposes incidental thereto.

A housing society is defined in Section 1(7) of the Housing Act, 1964 as:

> . . . a society —
>
> (a) which is registered under the Industrial and Provident Societies Act, 1893 (now 1965); and
>
> (b) which does not trade for profit: and
>
> (c) which is established for the purpose of, or amongst whose objects or powers are included those of constructing, improving or managing houses, being —
>
>> (i) houses to be kept available for letting, or
>>
>> (ii) where the rules of the society restrict membership of the society to persons entitled (whether

as tenants or otherwise) to occupy a house provided or managed by the society, houses for occupation by members of the society, whether or not the purposes or objects of the society include any of the supplementary purposes or objects mentioned in subsection (8) of this section, so however that the expression shall not include a society which, in addition to the purposes or objects mentioned in paragraph (a) above, has any purposes or objects not mentioned in the said subsection (8).

And subsection (8) defines the supplementary purposes or objects as:

(a) providing land or buildings for purposes connected with the requirements of the persons occupying the houses provided or managed by the society,

(b) encouraging the formation of other housing societies,

(c) giving advice on the formation and running of such societies.

The reader will note that groups formed through the aegis of the National Federation of Housing Societies are now called housing associations, whereas those set up through the Housing Corporation are called housing societies. To make it worse a housing society is (or was) a housing association for the purposes of exemption from rent control. And if you find that confusing, the author assures you that you are not the only one.

HOUSING ASSOCIATIONS

The most usual forms of housing associations and societies are:

1. *Charitable housing associations.* These are the ones which cater for special groups, being persons in "necessitous" circumstances. This is a relative term but includes elderly people, disabled people, ex-prisoners, drug addicts, deserted mothers and others who need housing, often desperately, but cannot get help from the local authority and cannot afford anything else. The associations may, but need not, be

registered with the Charity Commissioners. Registration relieves them from paying income tax and the need to make annual returns to the Charity Commissioners. Even without registration, the association may, and probably will, be a charity in law. This kind of association is a very usual branch of voluntary activity and obviously has a great deal to commend it. It demands a great deal of voluntary time and effort for which no payment is made and one can only praise those who set up and operate this kind of association. They seldom get the recognition they deserve. Why it should be necessary for pressing need of this kind to be dealt with voluntarily, or to put it another way, why cannot the recognised organs of the State deal with this kind of need, is another question; nothing, however, can detract from the great work these associations carry on. The author refuses to say, even in the context of this book, that this kind of housing activity is a failure; the only pity is that there is not more of it.

2. *General housing associations.* Or as they are sometimes called, general family housing associations. The dwellings provided by this kind of association are for those in need of housing but who are not "necessitous" on the one hand and not eligible for council accommodation on the other. This is quite a wide range and it can include all kinds of work-people and lower paid technical, professional and teaching households. The dwellings are usually provided by conversion with the aid of improvements grants, though in certain circumstances they may undertake new building attracting subsidy.

3. *Self-build associations.* There are not many of these about. They have something in common with the terminating building societies mentioned in the last chapter. They are a group of people (ten to sixty) who get together to provide themselves with houses but instead of putting up money (or rather, as well as putting up money), they do the work themselves. Because the labour is free the initial cost is low and yet the house when completed is just as valuable as one built professionally. It helps to have, as members of the association, electricians, plasterers, bricklayers, plumbers and so on as well as those who are prepared to do the heavy

labouring work. If you can get an architect and a solicitor so much the better, though this might prove difficult. Like the terminating building society, it is a long-term project and members must accept that they might have to wait perhaps two or three years before they get a house. They must of course also be prepared to carry on working after their own house is finished. Once it is all done the houses become the individual property of the members of the association which is then wound up.

4. *Cooperative housing associations.* These are formed of people who get together to build or buy property which they then proceed to manage themselves. Any tenant must be a member of the association. The tenant pays a non-profit rent and as he occupies by virtue of an agreement or lease he has the security of tenure associated with owner-occupation without having had to get an individual mortgage. The property belongs to the association in perpetuity, so there is no question of a tenant taking with him any share of the appreciated value of the premises when he goes.

5. *Co-ownership associations* on the other hand have members who collectively own the premises which are not vested in some legal entity distinct from the tenants. Because of this every occupier must be a member, and every member must be an occupier. By this means they can get an option mortgage for the purchase of the premises or, if they prefer, they can get an ordinary mortgage and claim tax relief as individuals. When a member leaves he can take a proportion of the increased value (if any) of the premises with him together with most of what he has paid off the capital value during his occupation. This makes it very much akin to individual owner-occupation. The advantages of this kind of arrangement can be clearly seen when a group of people wish to buy a large house or a block of flats for division and occupation among themselves. Since there is no subsidy and since the association is unlikely to get finance more cheaply than the members would get as individuals from a building society, its advantages for building ordinary houses are less obvious, although of course the original occupants can have some say in the way they are designed and built.

HOUSING SOCIETIES

There are two kinds of these:

1. *Cost-rent societies.* These are formed by people who get together to make housing accommodation available for other people. They are restricted to building new accommodation and the rents are based solely on the cost of providing, managing and maintaining the dwellings, without subsidy and without profit. In practice they have not proved successful, mainly because the rents would have been much too high. Prior to the passing of the 1964 Housing Act, it was claimed that rents would work out at between £4 and £7 a week. These were quite high figures for 1964, but even so the calculations on which they were based had been made several years earlier and no allowance had been made in the meantime for inflation and rising interest rates. The whole concept is a classic illustration of why it is virtually impossible for private landlords to make any useful contribution towards new housing or for that matter stay in business with older property. Whoever was advising the Government on this business was clearly desperately clinging to the notion that unsubsidised private renting was still viable. The author is told that it is still a common practice for a cost-rent society to get the building into being in the first place and then turn over the property to the tenants by means of subsidiary co-ownership societies. There must be some advantage in doing this, one supposes, though it is not easy to see what it is. Possibly there could be some merit in keeping a cost-rent society in being to provide the initiative and expertise to get things going; this tends to be lacking in co-ownership arrangements.

2. *Co-ownership societies.* These are virtually the same as co-ownership associations except they are set up through the agency of the Housing Corporation and have to conform to its rules. They, unlike co-ownership associations, are concerned only with providing new dwellings.

The contribution made by housing associations and societies towards providing better housing, welcome as it is, has been numerically insignificant, the figure for 1972 in England and Wales being 7,252 out of a total production of

319,150 (2.27 per cent). Nor is there any indication at present that this contribution is likely to increase significantly in the foreseeable future. The present Government (1973) wishes to see a considerable expansion in voluntary housing movement to compensate for the decline in the private sector which, at last, it recognises as irreversible. Their White Paper mentioned above (Cmnd 5280) proposes that the Housing Corporation shall be strengthened so that it will play a leading role in the expansion of voluntary housing. The Housing Finance Act of 1972 made it possible for the Corporation to lend to all kinds of associations and not only the societies set up under the 1961/64 legislation. All this is fine, but one feels that it is fostered more by a dislike of municipal housing than any real feeling that the voluntary movement can play a significant role. Another suggestion, put forward this time by the Co-operative Party, would place whole council estates in the hands of tenants' co-operatives. But the wide-scale adoption of such a proposal would place a heavy strain on such voluntary expertise as exists, which is already extremely thin on the ground. Listen again to Henry Aughton:

> Above all, the mechanism of rent pooling realises for the benefit of later, more expensive houses the accruing value of earlier houses. This is an immense advantage which would be cast away if, as some thoughtless critics propound, this monopoly ownership of rented property were to be broken up by the selling off of blocks of property to housing associations or some other sort of specially set up bodies which, with technical and professional expertise recruited from we know not where, would somehow, in some way not specified, do what we have been doing but do it better.*

There in a nutshell and in clear and simple terms upon which it is impossible to improve, is the case against the dispersal of public sector housing, whether to individual purchasers, to housing associations or anyone else. It also demonstrates beyond a peradventure that voluntary housing can never provide mass housing as cheaply and efficiently as public

*Paper presented to the Annual Rating Conference, 1971.

bodies specifically charged with the job of promoting low-cost housing.

The great majority of housing associations in this country are far too small. Sample surveys carried out by the Centre for Urban and Regional Studies suggested that 18 per cent of the respondent associations had no houses at all and that of the rest just under half had less than 20 accommodation units each. A further third had 20-99 units and only 14 per cent had 100 or more. (100 houses is only a small street.) And yet that 14 per cent had provided more than 90 per cent of the dwellings owned by all associations in the sample. Well under one-fifth employed full-time staff and though some had part-time staff more than two-fifths were run on a purely voluntary basis. The "traditional" type of housing association is much dependent on local authority co-operation and assistance. The attitude of the local authorities varies widely, but many feel that the associations compete with them for land and other scarce resources, that they lack expertise and that they are an unnecessary duplication of the local authorities' own efforts. Some authorities, particularly the large ones, nevertheless welcome the operation of housing associations in providing for special needs with which the authority cannot, or for some reason does not want to, deal. (See Appendix 6 on social housing in Europe.)

And there we must leave it. The contribution of housing associations in providing for general needs has been miniscule and is unlikely to expand except at the expense of the public sector. To this extent it must be added to the long list of failures which is characteristic of twentieth-century British housing. But in saying that we must exclude the valuable work done in charity (in the best sense of the word) for those least able to help themselves. No one can say that that in itself is a failure; what we may deplore is the failure to make it more widespread.

II The slums and overcrowding

A slum is a dwelling that is not fit to live in. This may seem to be a useful, straightforward definition, but that is not the case. It is of next to no use at all ... It is useless mainly because it involves too much in the way of subjective judgement. By what standard is the dwelling unfit? For whom is it unfit? Who sets the criteria and who applies them? If you took the view that a slum is more easily recognised than described, you would be nearer the mark. The early housing legislators certainly thought so for they did not go so far as to define insanitary dwellings, believing that the officials responsible for making the representations about unfit housing would know what they were talking about, which some might think was being over-optimistic.

Writing in 1928, a former Ministry of Health official maintained that the word "slum" was not officially recognised by the Ministry and that it was an extremely difficult word to describe with any accuracy.* He went on to quote the views of a Mr George H. Duckworth contained in a paper read to the RIBA in 1926. We are not told who Mr Duckworth is or was, but his views make illuminating, if not fascinating, reading: ". . . a slum is a street, court or alley which reflects the social condition of a poor, thriftless, irregularly employed and rough class of inhabitant." It seems that it did not occur to Mr Duckworth that "irregularly employed" people might tend to be poor and might even find it difficult to be thrifty. He goes on:

> Bread and litter in the streets; windows dirty, broken and patched with brown or white paper; curtains dirty and frayed, and blinds half drawn and often hanging at an angle. The street doors are usually open, showing bare

*B. S. Townroe, *The Slum Problem*, London, Longmans, Green & Co. 1928.

158

passages and stairways lacking banisters, while the door jambs are generally brown with dirt, and rubbed shiny by the coats of the leisured class, whose habit is to lean up against them. The cats are seldom lean, for in a working district lean cats are more often a sign of vice than of poverty.

Although he avoids the subject of lean cats, Mr Townroe himself has much to say in this offensively patronising style: Discipline and order are essential in the waging of our domestic war. Medical Officers of Health have reported that new housing estates, erected at the cost of millions from the public purse, are already "filthy and insanitary hovels", and that there is unfortunately a type of tenant who always makes a slum, wherever and however he is housed. He can only be prevented from wrecking a new house by discipline. The same man who as a private soldier in his unit was compelled to keep himself clean and to pay respect to the laws of sanitation in the trenches, has since gone back to his former undesirable ways.

Mr Townroe's plea for "Homes for Heroes" to be subjected to C.O.'s inspection fortunately fell on deaf ears.

Dr Hanschell's claim, that the slum denizen is a sub-species of Homo sapiens, has already been noted in Chapter 7 but his further views, also contained in Mr Townroe's book, were unfortunately widely held at the time: "There exists evidence for the probability that some, at least, of this sub-species' young are like the parent, hopeless and helpless by reason of stamped-in mental defect ... it is now plain that their children are not ordinary children; that their parental and physical environment from birth makes it obligatory ... that they be removed from parent and environment." Mr Townroe quotes these views with apparent approval; Mr Townroe was also at one time a senior official at the Ministry of Health, Chairman of the Housing Committee of Hampstead Borough Council, and had acted as consultant to the Building Research Board. He was, in short, the kind of man on whom the efforts of the State to promote better housing conditions chiefly depended. If his views were at all typical, it is a great wonder that municipal housing achieved anything at all.

We can accept that some candidates for local authority housing, whether through slum-clearance or otherwise, will have low standards, but so will some families living in privately-rented or even (dare one say it?) owner-occupied homes. The fact remains that there is overwhelming evidence that the great majority of council tenants, and those seeking to become council tenants, are ordinary decent people, well able to manage their own affairs and quite capable of looking after their accommodation in a proper manner. One could add that living in cramped, insanitary and crumbling dwellings is not necessarily conducive to habits of cleanliness and high standards of housekeeping.

Up to 1954 the standard of fitness or unfitness of a dwelling depended on the wording and interpretation of local bye-laws and the extent to which "by reason of disrepair or sanitary defects" houses fell short of them, but the 1954 Housing Repairs and Rent Act laid down criteria which are still largely in use today. The 1954 definition was repeated in Section 4 (1) of the Housing Act, 1957. It reads:

In determining for any of the purposes of this Act whether a house is unfit for human habitation, regard shall be had to its condition in respect of the following matters, that is to say —

(a)   repair;
(b)   stability;
(c)   freedom from damp;
(d)   natural lighting;
(e)   ventilation;
(f)   water supply;
(g)   drainage and sanitary conveniences;
(h)   facilities for storage, preparation and cooking of food and for the disposal of waste water;

and the house shall be deemed to be unfit for human habitation if and only if it is so far defective in one or more of the said matters that it is not reasonably suitable for occupation in that condition.

To which the Housing Act, 1969, has added a condition regarding bad internal arrangement and deleted the reference to storage in item (h). What is a slum is still clearly a matter of judgement and probably this is inevitable, but in 1965 the

Government of the day clearly felt that some more objective criteria might be laid down. The Central Housing Advisory Committee (this is the Minister's own Committee, appointed by him) set up a Sub-Committee in February 1965 with these terms of reference: "to consider the practicability of specifying objective criteria for the purposes of slum clearance, rectification of disrepair and other housing powers relating to minimum tolerable standards of housing accommodation; and to make recommendations."

The Sub-Committee, with Mrs Evelyn Denington in the Chair, was remarkable for its high-powered membership, and equally high hopes were being entertained that its deliberations might lead to some improved definition of what constitutes a slum. The Sub-Committee's Report, published in 1966 with the title *Our Older Homes: A Call for Action* was on the whole disappointing. They had come to the conclusion that as there were 824,000 dwellings classified as slums they could not recommend raising the standard: ". . . we consider it would be unrealistic to raise the fitness standard substantially at the present time." As it turned out the stated number of slum dwellings turned out to be a gross under-estimate, but in any case to decline to consider what a proper level of housing fitness might be, regardless of how few or how many unfit dwellings might thereby emerge, is not being objective. The Report in fact devoted much of its space to how the housing stock might be prevented from falling into obsolescence, which may well have been a worth-while exercise; to the author's way of thinking they failed to address themselves with sufficient application to the first part of their terms of reference.

In common with many other writers and commentators the author, in evidence to the Denington Committee, suggested that a minimum standard of housing fitness might very well be the twelve-point standard of fitness which was required of a dwelling before it was eligible for a discretionary improvement grant. For this the dwelling must:

(1) be in good state of repair and substantially free from damp;
(2) have each room properly lighted and ventilated;

(3) have an adequate supply of wholesome water laid on inside the dwelling;

(4) be provided with efficient and adequate means of supplying hot water for domestic purposes;

(5) have an internal water closet if practicable; otherwise a readily accessible outdoor water closet;

(6) have a fixed bath or shower in a bathroom;

(7) be provided with a sink or sinks with suitable arrangements for the disposal of waste water;

(8) have a proper drainage system;

(9) be provided in each room with adequate points for gas or electric lighting (where reasonably available);

(10) be provided with adequate facilities for heating;

(11) have satisfactory facilities for storing, preparing and cooking food;

(12) have proper provision for the storage of fuel (where required).

The Milner Holland Committee felt that even this "is lower than we would like to see . . . and it is far below that suggested by the Parker Morris Committee. . ." This does of course highlight one of the eternal dilemmas of slum clearance. Parker Morris standards are in the British context quite high. Local authorities were not obliged to observe them until 1969 and private builders are not required to build to this standard to this day (1973), twelve years after the Parker Morris Report was published. Whatever standard is set as the lower limit of fitness is clearly going to be well below Parker Morris or anything remotely comparable. But the occupants of unfit property are likely, once the local authority takes action, to be rehoused in a dwelling which is not just above the fitness level but in all probability a long way above it. This in turn brings in questions of finance and rent-paying capability, it also raises issues of fairness between one section of the community and another. Those below the "fitness" level will be rehoused at a high standard and will overtake by a wide margin those whose homes only just qualify as fit, who will not be rehoused at all and for whom the community will refuse to accept any responsibility whatsoever. This is a situation which will be cured only when public authorities accept a more comprehensive role in housing matters and will have at their disposal a whole range of housing of varying ages, standards and rents and who will be capable of rehousing applicants of all kinds within a comparatively short time.

After two years' delay, the Government in April 1968 published a White Paper (*Old Houses into New Homes:* Cmnd 3602) accepting most of the Denington Committee's recommendations, thus preparing the way for the Housing Act, 1969, and the massive switch in emphasis from redevelopment to rehabilitation as a principal means of improving housing conditions.

The argument about whether obsolete houses are best dealt with by improvement or by redevelopment is taken further in a later chapter; there seem to be considerable grounds for thinking that an improvement policy is a palliative, an expedient which can be effective only in the short-term and that by failing to demolish obsolete or unfit housing this generation of administrators is piling up trouble for the next.

Slum clearance is part of the "sanitary idea", the feeling that insanitary conditions ought not to be tolerated and that it is the State's duty to prevent them. The earlier legislation, indeed almost all legislation up to the First World War, was based on this concept. It escaped the notice of the early reformers that slum clearance without new building merely made conditions worse in those dwellings that were left. It is surprising how difficult it was to eliminate this particular blind spot. To quote Townroe again: "But . . . human factors played havoc with the well-meaning schemes of our legislators. Those who lived in poor houses scuttled like rats into the nearest available lodgings when their own houses were pulled down." What, may one reasonably ask, did he expect them to do? SHELTER, not one would suppose a reactionary body, came out heavily against slum clearance in a 1972 Report (*Reprieve for Slums*): "That's a hamfisted way of doing things. For the families that have suffered most gravely from slum life it is tragic . . . For them there is often no solution in rehousing. Most do not find themselves on a spanking new estate, or at least not for long, but in another condemned or soon-to-be condemned area of housing." The reasons given for this unhappy state of affairs are: (*a*) that occupants move before the council has a chance to offer them rehousing, (*b*) many families are unauthorised tenants, and therefore do not qualify for rehousing, and (*c*) rents of the dwellings provided by the council are too high. The answers to these objections appear to be: (*a*) one doubts whether this is generally true, (*b*) councils ought to be under a positive obligation to rehouse anyone displaced by slum clearance, and (*c*) no one should ever be excluded from council housing just because he cannot afford the rent.

It was Greenwood's Act of 1930 that laid the foundation of the modern concept of slum clearance accompanied by an obligation on the part of the local authority to see that the persons displaced were properly rehoused. It did so by arranging the subsidy to be related to the number of persons rehoused, which seems a simple, direct and effective way of doing things. The slum clearance programme did not get under way until the Act of 1933 when it was announced that it was hoped to clear the slums in five years. Local authorities were required to submit programmes for this purpose; they gravely underestimated the problem facing them. London found only 33 thousand unfit homes out of a total of 750 thousand; Manchester 15 thousand out of 180 thousand and Newcastle only 2 thousand out of 60 thousand. In England and Wales the total came to not more than a quarter of a million. (Bowley, op. cit.) In 1935 came a five-year programme for eradicating overcrowding; this was intended to follow the five-year slum clearance drive. By 1938 it was at last recognised that slums and overcrowding were but two faces of the same evil and the two subsidies were merged.

Overcrowding was first defined and made a potential offence in 1935; the definition of overcrowding was, however, disappointing. There were two separate tests, one of which was whether in any dwelling the sexes were capable of sleeping in separate rooms (if over ten years of age and not including husband and wife). As Marian Bowley very properly points out, on this basis only one-room houses would be overcrowded (and kitchens could be counted as rooms if they could be used as living rooms). The other test was contained on a scale relating the numbers of persons to the number of rooms (infants under a year excluded, children between one and ten counted as a half). On this scale a one-room house could be occupied by two people and a five-room house· could have ten. On this basis too, the little terraced house in which the author was born and brought up could have been occupied by ten people instead of the four who in fact lived in it; he recalls that it seemed quite cramped enough with four, never mind ten. Less than 4 per cent of all housing in the country at that time could be held as being overcrowded on this criterion; of these more than half were occupied by exceptionally large families and nearly half were very small houses. An exceptionally large family was one with more than five units (infants under 1 year ignored, children 1 to 10 years counting as half a unit). The Registrar-General in the Report of the Overcrowding Survey calculated that if living rooms had not been counted as available for sleeping purposes, the number of overcrowded families would have been 853 thousand instead of the 341 thousand reported. (Bowley, op. cit.) The number of slum dwellings to be cleared was revised in 1937 to 378 thousand and two years later to 472 thousand. In practice less than a quarter of a million of slums were cleared by 1939, to which may be added about 24 thousand houses built specifically for relief of overcrowding. So that by the time war broke out in 1939 nearly half the admitted slums (which we know was a gross underestimate) were still standing and being lived in. The Ministry of Health reported in 1939 that "further reviews by the local authorities have revealed more houses which can only be dealt with satisfactorily by demolition". This reluctance of local authorities to estimate realistically is seen again in 1955 and in 1965; presumably they report only that number of unfit dwellings they feel they can deal with, or perhaps it is an inevitable result of lack of objectivity in defining and reporting a slum.

No slums were in fact cleared after 1938 in view of the probable onset of war, and slum clearance was held in abeyance until public pressure forced a resumption in 1954. The Housing Repairs and Rent Act of that year required local authorities to submit proposals for dealing with their slums. As in the thirties they again underestimated the size of the problem. They reported that no more than 855,000 dwellings were unfit and this no doubt led to the increasingly optimistic reports from official sources from time to time as to the diminishing slum problem. Dr Charles Hill put the figure at 600,000 in 1962, the next year Sir Keith Joseph was prophesying the end of the slums in 1973, and even the Government Housing Survey thought in 1964 that there were no more than 515 thousand unfit dwellings, to which however had to be added a further 218 thousand with an estimated life of less than five years; this meant that 733,000 "accommodation units" would have to be replaced within the five years 1964-69. The Ministry called upon local authorities, in Circular 11/65, to report the number of unfit dwellings in their districts during the first quarter of 1965. The findings were summarised in the Denington Committee's Report, and showed, ominously, nearly 824 thousand unfit after more than ten years of slum clearance. But the Minister, not convinced that local estimates were accurate, called for an independent survey, carried out for the Ministry early in 1967 by public health inspectors seconded for the purpose from their authorities and working to a common brief.

The results were astounding. The number of unfit dwellings, far from being well under a million, came to very nearly two million (1.836 million). Of these nearly 1.1 million were likely to have to be dealt with in clearance areas and the other 737 thousand dealt with individually. Not only that, but the unfit houses were more spread out than had previously been thought. The returns made in 1965 suggested that half the unfit dwellings were concentrated in twenty-four large towns and cities. But the 1967 survey revealed that over two-thirds of unfit housing was located in rural areas and urban areas outside the conurbations. The White Paper containing the 1967 House Condition Survey (*Old Houses into New Homes,* Cmnd. 3602) recognised that numbers had been underestimated in the past and proposed an increased rate of slum clearance (para. 43). But housing policy by this time (April 1968) had already changed direction following the 1967 devaluation and the switch away from replacement towards rehabilitation had already begun. And the rate of slum clearance which had been running at about 63 thousand a year (1960-67) increased to about 69,000 a year but fell back in 1972 to just over 66 thousand, which for the purpose of the exercise is more or less where we came in.

The Government which came to power in 1970 undertook a new House Condition Survey in 1971 based on the same sample that had been used in the 1967 survey. Once again the results were remarkable. The number of unfit dwellings had apparently fallen from over 1.8 million to 1.244 million which meant that the total number of unfit dwellings had been reduced by 600,000 or nearly one-third. This surprising reduction was accounted for in this way: 400,000 dwellings unfit in 1967 had been demolished by 1971, 50 thousand dwellings had been converted to non-housing uses and 550,000 dwellings, unfit in 1967, had been made fit by 1971. Against this, 400 thousand dwellings became slums during the period.

There seems to be very good ground for questioning these figures. For a start the number of slums demolished does not agree with the published figures. The first survey was undertaken in February 1967 and therefore one should exclude the first two months of that year. But to be generous we will allow the figures for the whole of 1967, 1968, 1969, 1970 and the first half of 1971. These add up to 317.4 thousand which puts the 1971 survey figure adrift by nearly 83 thousand. There may be factors which explain this discrepancy but they are not obvious from the report. Second, the estimate of over half a million slums made fit in the four-year period is both startling and difficult to accept. Accepting that some owners particularly in London may have rescued their dwellings without grant aid, on the whole it seems likely that improvement on such a scale must have been made with the aid of grants. On the present definition of a slum one feels that standard grants are unlikely to make an unfit dwelling fit, so one must look to the figures for discretionary grants. From the beginning of 1967 to halfway through 1971 about 286 thousand discretionary grants were approved (we do not know how many were actually implemented), and of these about 120 thousand were for local authorities, leaving not more than just over 162 thousand for private owners. But we know that about four out of five grants for private sector housing go to owner-occupiers. Even if 100,000 grants had been applied to unfit housing (and the conditions attached to grants make this unlikely), it is still difficult to believe that 450 thousand dwellings have voluntarily been made fit by their owners without any government aid. Mr Reg Freeson, a Junior Minister in the Labour Government speaking in the House on 27 November 1972, suggested that there had "been some basic inaccuracy". This is also the author's view. One does not accuse those responsible, local and central government officers who cannot answer back of dishonesty, but if the 1971 figures are accurate then the 1967 ones cannot have been. And they were both based on the same sample of dwellings and for the most part inspected by the same inspectors. If eradicating bad housing had been that easy, one can very properly ask why it hadn't been done years before. One cannot avoid observing that the dramatic improvement suggested by the 1971 survey results must have come as a very welcome windfall to the Government whose housing performance was, by 1972, coming increasingly under fire. The first results moreover were announced in May 1972 by the then Minister, Mr Amery, who promised that the whole of the report would be available "in the autumn". In fact it was July 1973 before the report was published. One would like to have some explanation for the delay.

Ministers were not slow to announce the imminent end of slum housing. Mr Amery forecast that there would be no slums by 1980, in which he showed a lamentable failure to learn from the errors of a long line of his predecessors who had been making similar predictions for more than half a century. And Mr Paul Channon, speaking in the same debate as Mr Freeson (mentioned above), announced that Manchester hoped to clear its slums by 1975 and Birmingham and Liverpool by 1980. But Manchester itself admitted to 54,700 unfit dwellings in 1965, Birmingham to 41,733 and Liverpool to 92,166. And one knows that local authorities generally very much tend to underestimate the scale of their unfit housing. Ministers in their simplicity may regret that others may not share their optimistic expectations, but they ought not to be surprised.

They should also remember that slum clearance is an on-going process and that dwellings inevitably wear out in the longer or shorter run. The 1971 survey itself drew attention to 400 thousand dwellings, not unfit in 1967 which had become unfit by 1971. And this despite a comparatively high level of improvement activity. At this rate more than 800 thousand additional unfit dwellings will emerge between 1971 and 1980. Have these been taken into account? One doubts it. The sad truth is that, despite anything politicians may tell us, slums will never be eliminated completely and that current emphasis on short-term improvements will make the long-term obsolescence problem very much more difficult to deal with. And what is more, the 1971 estimate of 1.2 million slums seems low only by comparison with the 1967 survey; compared with any other estimate arrived at over the whole history of state involvement in housing, it is still lamentably high.

OVERCROWDING

Overcrowding, although still widespread, is undoubtedly diminishing. The average number of persons per dwelling, according to census figures in England and Wales, increased from 1911 to 1921 but fell away thereafter:

1911	—	4.69
1921	—	4.79
1931	—	4.18
1941	No census	— —
1951	—	3.46
1961	—	3.11
1966	—	3.05

Note: These figures relate to "private households".

The 1971 census when available will probably indicate a continuation of this decline. The increase from 1911 to 1921 was the result of the cessation of building during the First World War. The period from 1931 to 1951 might well have shown a corresponding increase had not the period from 1931 to 1941 taken in the very high rate of house-building of the 'thirties. The standard for overcrowding laid down by statute is contained in the Housing Act, 1957, which in effect re-enacted the provisions of the 1935 Act. The number of people a house may contain before it is overcrowded is:

No. of habitable rooms		*Permitted no. of persons*
1	—	2
2	—	3
3	—	5
4	—	7½
5 or more	—	2 per room

As in 1935, children under the age of one are ignored and those between one and ten count as half. The Housing Survey of 1964 found that less that 1 per cent of all households in England and Wales were statutorily overcrowded (76,000 households). In view of the very low standard, this is hardly surprising. One shudders to think of the condition under which the statutorily overcrowded families were living. The 1964 survey also tabled two alternative estimates of occupation density: (*a*) the number of persons per habitable room, and (*b*) the "bedroom standard" devised by the Social Survey in 1960 (but this was intended to be an index of under-occupancy rather than overcrowding). About 315 thousand families were living at a density of 1½ persons per room (2.1 per cent) and over a million (6.9 per cent) at a density of more than 1 person per room, which is about the maximum density most families would find acceptable. But by the Social Survey's bedroom standard approximately 1.391 million families (9.4 per cent) were below the standard, i.e. did not have enough bedrooms to meet their needs.

If nothing else this demonstrates how inadequate is the statutory definition of overcrowding. Because the standard is so ridiculously low, public health inspectors have taken to using the term "badly overcrowded", which sidesteps the statutory limit. It also tends to support the view held by SHELTER among others that there are 3 million families living in slums, near slums or grossly overcrowded conditions, and that despite the improvements over the years, overcrowding is still a major housing evil. And yet the legislation of the 'thirties, re-enacted in the 'fifties, is still largely ignored, one reason being that if action is taken against overcrowding the persons displaced will become homeless and will require further action by the local authority. One further point arises from estimates of occupation density. According to the 1964 survey less than 1 per cent of owner-occupiers were living at a density of more than 1½ persons per room, whereas 3 per cent of local authority tenants were in this position, 4 per cent of tenants in uncontrolled rented accommodation and no less than 19 per cent of tenants in furnished accommodation. This shows that (a) council tenants use their accommodation more intensively than owner-occupiers (this was confirmed by findings of the Milner Holland Committee), and (b) those who are overcrowded tend to be the poorest. This latter point is confirmed by evidence produced by the 1964 survey that social classes III (manual) and IV and V were more likely to be overcrowded than other groups.

For our purposes we may take slums and overcrowding together, since both are aspects of, indeed results of, a major shortage of decent dwellings. Whether there are 1.8 million slums or 1.2 million or some other figure, there are obviously far too many of them and their continued existence ought not to be tolerated by any society with pretensions to civilised and socially sensitive attitudes. Whether there are 76 thousand or 1.4 millions of people living in overcrowded conditions, there are obviously too many of them, and whatever the figure, the continued acceptance of such conditions is an affront to human dignity and a blot on a civilised society. SHELTER defined such people as homeless and they were not far wrong. The failure to remedy these twin evils (each of which overlaps the other to a considerable extent), despite legislation which goes back more than a hundred years, is one of the most abject failures of British housing policy. The remedy lies in a massive programme of new building, new houses to relieve overcrowding and to replace the slums, such a programme to be carried on ruthlessly and with determination for many years, not, as has

171

been the typical experience, a short period of comparatively intense activity, followed by long periods of inactivity. This and only this can change the failure of the slums into success.

12 The homeless

People who are homeless have nowhere to live. This does not mean they necessarily sleep out in the park at nights, although unfortunately some of them do. Nor does it mean those who, having lost the roof over their heads, are living in the temporary accommodation which local authorities (welfare authorities, i.e. counties and county boroughs) are, until 1974, required by law to provide. When the new structure comes into effect the new welfare authorities (counties and metropolitan counties) will have the power, but not the duty, to provide such accommodation, which may appear as further proof of the Government's intention to divest itself and local authorities of responsibility for those in dire housing need. These people are of course homeless and will probably find a roof if only that of the reception centres which are another name for the old poor law workhouses. But in the main most of those without a home will find some shelter somewhere, somehow, maybe with relatives or friends or perhaps, all else having failed, they have applied to the Welfare Department for temporary accommodation and (this by no means follows) they have been granted it. It is in fact only these latter families in temporary accommodation who are officially described as homeless, although clearly they represent the tip of a very large iceberg. And since in most cases such temporary accommodation as the Welfare Department may possess has always more applicants than space available, the numbers of people thus accommodated tells us not how many homeless people there are, even within this narrow definition, but broadly how much space there is in temporary accommodation. Which tells us very little about homelessness at all.

The number of people in temporary accommodation is rising. In 1966, when public uneasiness about homelessness was beginning to show, the figure was 13,031. Only five years later it had more than doubled to 26,879. On our own argument this may not mean that the number of homeless persons has doubled overall, it could mean, though this is unlikely, that local authorities have made twice as much temporary accommodation available and that they are now meeting a greater proportion of the total need. One can discount this.

We have already argued that those in temporary accommodation are only a fraction of those who ought to be described as homeless. SHELTER, an organisation formed in 1966 with the specific aim of helping the homeless, published a report in 1971 with the title "Face the Facts", and this suggested that the number of those truly homeless could be anywhere between the 18,689 officially in temporary accommodation at that time and the three million or so people who "live in slums, near slums, or in grossly overcrowded conditions". There were those who felt at the time, and the author was among them, that by exaggerating the problem in this way, SHELTER were doing no good service either to their own campaign or to the homeless people themselves. Subsequent experience does not seem to provide evidence that would refute this point of view. People who are living in slums or in overcrowded or otherwise unsatisfactory dwellings do at least have a roof over their heads; they may live in conditions which no civilised society ought to tolerate, but their problems are less immediate and less acute than those facing families who have lost their roof. On the other hand the definition relating only to families in local authority temporary accommodation is clearly inadequate and one suspects that the truth may lie somewhere between the two. Bryan Glastonbury's team which surveyed homelessness in South Wales and the South-west of England (subsequently reported in Bryan Glastonbury's *Homeless near a Thousand Homes,* London, George Allen & Unwin 1971) attempted to steer a middle course; their definition included all those without a roof over their heads, whether or not they qualified for help by the local authority or by some other organisation, and in addition also included those who had a roof, but "in circumstances that were clearly seen as temporary — a derelict railway carriage, or a caravan only available until the holiday season began, for example..." This is still a fairly tight definition but it must be remembered that Glastonbury was reporting on a provincial situation many miles from London and without the housing stress that is a usual feature of the capital's housing problems.

More than that one cannot say. There will be many definitions of homelessness and these will vary not only according to who is doing the defining but also other factors such as the geographical location of the area under discussion and the presence or absence of what is commonly called "housing stress" (shortage accompanied by overcrowding, multi-occupation, unfit housing and so on). In short we cannot say how many truly homeless people there may be at any given time; we cannot say because we do not know, the information is not there. This is one of the reasons why public concern flared up so suddenly and unexpectedly after the showing of *Cathy Come Home;* it is also a reason why public interest subsequently ebbed away. With slums you more or less know where you are, the definition is there, the figures are available and it is possible to maintain an informed public opinion on the subject; with homelessness this is not so. There may be public unease about the situation of the homeless, but there is no informed public opinion (SHELTER notwithstanding) because there is no accepted definition and there are no reliable figures.

Not that there is anything new in being homeless. Although the figures were never kept it seems likely that a large proportion of those who lived in grossly unsatisfactory housing during the last century were in fact without homes of their own but had been "taken in" by others only slightly better placed, partly out of compassion and partly to help to pay the rents of their own dwellings. The very large numbers of common lodging houses, particularly in London, would tend to support this view, but whether these were occupied by individuals "of no fixed abode" or whether they were men separated for a shorter or longer term from their families is hard to say. London and to a lesser extent other large cities have in short always had their homeless to deal with, but up to the First World War and to only a slightly lesser extent between the wars homelessness was considered a problem of destitution for which the workhouse was the appropriate and probably the only remedy. Even the large municipal building programme since 1919, only part of which has been undertaken specifically for those living in bad conditions, has brought relatively little benefit to the very poorest who are the section of the community most likely to become homeless.

After the Second World War the old Poor Law was abolished and with it came the intention to provide, by humanitarian and socially sensitive means, accommodation for those who would otherwise be literally without a roof over their heads. Throughout the voluminous literature on homelessness will be found reference to Part III of the National Assistance Act of 1948, Section 21(1)(*b*) of which placed on those local authorities who were welfare authorities the duty of providing and administering temporary accommodation. "It shall be the duty of every local authority to provide temporary accommodation for persons in urgent need thereof, being need arising in circumstances which could not reasonably have been foreseen, or in any other circumstances as the authority may in any particular case determine." Now when Aneurin Bevan as Minister of Health steered the Act through Parliament, what he probably had in mind was not homelessness in the present sense at all but rather the provision of accommodation for temporary use (maybe a few hours, certainly not more than a day or two) by people who had lost their homes because of such emergency as fire or flood, these being the sort of circumstances that cannot "reasonably have been foreseen"; homelessness by eviction, for example, can usually be foreseen although the hapless tenant may not be in a position to do anything about it. However nothing in the 1948 Act prohibits temporary accommodation being provided for evicted cases or indeed any other cases, since it is within the power (though it may not be the duty) of the authority to do anything they want to do, being "other circumstances" which "the authority may in any particular

176

case determine". Bevan, or his officials at the Ministry must
have seen what was coming. In Para. 15 of Ministry of Health
Circular 87/48 (June 1948) they amplified the duty of an
authority under 21(1)(*b*) as including fire, flood *or eviction*.
Eviction is one of the major causes of homelessness and the
Minister's inclusion of this circumstance as a duty on which
the authority must act probably represents one of those
second thoughts that all wise men, not to mention wise
administrators, entertain from time to time.

Eighteen years later, a Joint Circular from the Ministry of
Health, Home Office and Ministry of Housing laid further
emphasis on this point, even going so far as to say that any
distinction between foreseeable and unforeseeable homelessness was "artificial". That of course was in 1966 when public
concern about the homeless situation was at its height. It
conflicts somewhat with the wording of the Act (if the
distinction between "foreseeable" and "unforeseeable" was
all that artificial, Parliament would not have made it in the
first place), but as authorities in any event were required to
carry out their duties under the direction and guidance of the
Minister, we can safely say that almost from the start local
welfare authorities have been under a duty to provide
accommodation for people who have been evicted from their
former homes and probably for a great many other reasons
besides.

It is a duty that authorities have, for the most part,
consistently and persistently avoided. From the beginning,
authorities have never, almost without exception, applied the
Act to "persons" in the sense of individuals. There has been
an understanding, which may or may not be justified, that
the Section applied only to families with children. Clearly
families with children are in much greater immediate need
than those without and indeed the 1966 Joint Circular
thought that couples without children "will normally be
expected to find accommodation for themselves", though it
did go on to say that the admission of such persons should not
be excluded especially if they are elderly. The only instance
of the National Assistance Board (now the Supplementary
Benefits Commission) exercising the limited default powers
they possess in the matter occurred more than twenty years

177

ago when the County Council of the East Riding of Yorkshire were ordered by the Board to provide accommodation for a childless couple in their fifties. The major default powers vested in the Minister to deal with authorities who have failed to discharge their Part III liabilities have never, so far as the author is aware, been used at all. And this places those wrongfully refused temporary accommodation (and they must number thousands) in an impossible position, if they are not in one already. For it means that they are debarred from seeking redress in the Courts but can seek their remedy in a complaint to the Minister. Now it may well be that to contemplate people in a homeless situation taking Court action is on a par with the mediaeval exercise of estimating the number of angels that could dance on the point of a pin, but to think that they could be able to persuade the Minister to declare an authority in default on the basis of one individual case appears to have no parallel in the realm of philosophical probability. The failure of the central government to declare in default those local authorities (they are a majority) who have failed to provide for the homeless must be rated as one of the long list of housing failures (not yet complete) which it has been the purpose of this book to discover.

Who are the people who are likely to come knocking on the welfare authority's door? We have some information on this subject, in particular the two reports on homelessness published in 1971 (Glastonbury, op. cit., and Greve *et al., Homelessness in London*, Edinburgh, Scottish Academic Press). Such information must be treated with caution as it will be based for the most part on the circumstances of those who have been admitted to temporary accommodation, although Greve undertook some survey work on the *applications* for accommodation. First they are more likely than not to be young. Glastonbury found that at the time of entering temporary accommodation 17.5 per cent of mothers were under 21 and a further 45.4 per cent were under 31. Greve found a corresponding figure of 59 per cent under the age of 30 (this was in 1969; ten years earlier the proportion was 48 per cent). These mothers will have young children. Glastonbury found that one-fifth of the children were "in

178

nappies", i.e. were under 2, and a further 30 per cent were between 2 and 5 so that half the children were under school age. As financial difficulties are a factor in most cases of homelessness this is significant as it means (*a*) the mother cannot work to supplement the family income, and (*b*) those families in privately rented (particularly furnished) accommodation are vulnerable to those landlords who regard children as a nuisance and will if possible get rid of a family with numerous children and sometimes even those with only one or even none. It is beyond comprehension how a society which regards itself as civilised can permit young families at a crucial and vulnerable point of their lives to be denied the benefits and security of a home, especially at the very time when for their own sakes and that of the children they need it most.

Second, such families may probably be in arrears of rent. Glastonbury found this to be a main cause in nearly 43 per cent of cases whereas the Greve study put the figure lower at about 10 per cent. This illustrates one of the major differences between homelessness in London and in a provincial area. In London homelessness is mainly a housing problem, i.e. an aspect of the shortage of dwellings, and although the households concerned will probably be low-paid they are less likely to be in difficulty over money. On the other hand private landlords will in London tend to take action for reasons other than rent arrears. This action will range from court action for possession to outright harassment, and in mid-1969 such action accounted for no less than 37 per cent of cases of homelessness. And Greve went on to point out that for at least 7 per cent homelessness was probably caused by unsuccessful use of the very legal procedures such as recourse to the Rent Tribunal which had been designed for the tenant's own protection. A third major cause of homelessness appears to be domestic friction/marital breakdown which Glastonbury identified as a reason in 26 per cent of his cases, though Greve found a lower proportion in London (17 per cent). This is explicable, since if domestic affairs come to such a pitch that one partner feels constrained to leave, it will in practice usually be the husband who will then leave. If his income is inadequate he may fail, either because he will not or cannot, to make provision for his wife and family to continue to live in the family home. With this rather obvious fact in mind, one finds it difficult to understand the attitudes of those welfare authorities who, when families become homeless for non-marital reasons, deny the husband accommodation along with his family in temporary accommodation. Nothing could be more calculated to break down the unity of family life and conjugal and parental responsibility. It is reported that most authorities do not now follow this infamous practice, but one would like to be assured that it has ceased altogether; of this one is far from certain.

There is finally the attitude of those who deal with homeless cases as well as those of the public at large. These tend to be critical and censorious. The whole system of providing relief for the needy grew up with the Poor Law and apart from a period at the end of the eighteenth century when poverty was clearly seen as an aspect of inadequate income instead of personal inadequacy, it has been clearly based on deterrence This was particularly the case after 1834 when the New Poor Law was based by law on the principle of "less eligibility" so that conditions in a workhouse would be worse to endure than any conceivable set of circumstances outside it. These attitudes developed and hardened over a period of more than a hundred years, most of which occurred during the Victorian era which was itself a period of harsh moral judgements. The vivid accounts written by Jack London in the early 1900s are a damning indictment of the harsh and inhuman attitudes of those responsible for administering the workhouse system.* Although a Royal Commission of 1905-9 came out against "less eligibility" and proposed instead a "principle of restoration", no new legislation followed and in any case homelessness was still a condition requiring the attachment of a social stigma. Professor Bernard Bosanquet, writing in the *Sociological Review* for April 1909, put it this way: "a failure of social self-maintenance . . . a defect in citizen character, or at least a grave danger to its integrity" (quoted in Glastonbury, op. cit.). One can say that the principle of "less eligibility"

*Jack London, *People of the Abyss*, London, Panther 1963.

continued to exist right up to the Second World War and although the 1948 National Assistance Act put it that the "existing Poor Law shall cease to have effect", the attitudes which were generated and refined over a century of the worst kind of social repression could not be jettisoned overnight. They were still manifest in the attitudes of many local authorities after 1948 and in the policies towards homeless people who claimed their assistance and those to whom they gave their grudging help. Glastonbury describes it as manifest in the "form of restricted contact between husband and wife, employment as wardens of authoritarian ex-service N.C.O.s, the widespread acceptance that isolated and sub-standard accommodation was quite in order for such families, and the ultimate threat of removing children into care". He further found that when it came to people actually homeless, "none of the local authorities in the survey area accepted full responsibility for them. The various restrictions imposed on the use of temporary accommodation have resulted in the majority of the homeless not qualifying to receive help".

Moral judgements still persist, too, between the "deserving" and the "undeserving", great pressure being put on the latter to get themselves out of the mess they have got themselves into. This could for example include much chivvying of wives in temporary hostels to do pointless work, to go out during the day with their children regardless of the weather, to conform with petty regulations and to remind them constantly that the time limit, after which they would be ejected, was fast approaching. Nor were such attitudes limited to the Welfare Departments. Housing Managers, concerned as we have seen with the orderly and efficient management of their estates, were and are reluctant to take responsibility for families which do not conform to the accepted canons of behaviour. And please note that this attitude accepts that "homelessness" presupposes personal inadequacy or moral delinquency. Glastonbury again:

> . . . the criteria by which housing managers selected the families for whom they were prepared to make emergency provision involved a strict assessment of tenancy standards. . . . The onus was placed on the family, or more commonly a welfare or child-care officer, to convince the

housing manager not only that there was urgent need for a house but that the family "deserved" a house. Such things as a poor tenancy record or suspicion of immorality would certainly be major impediments to immediate rehousing. And finally: "At best the work being done by local authorities at the end of the 1960s offered real opportunities of improvement for a limited number of families, and temporary relief for many more. *But there remained many homeless people, needing help, asking for help, and being turned away"*. (My italics — Author) Nowhere in the whole field of local authority activity and endeavour, certainly nowhere in this book, will you find words more damning of the abysmal failure of British local authorities to carry out the humanitarian duties that the law has cast upon them.

For this failure there is no excuse. Leaving aside the SHELTER contention that all in inadequate housing are homeless, we know that the number of the literally homeless is not infinite. We know that the number of "official" homeless families in temporary accommodation on the night of 31 December 1971 was 5,630. To rehouse these families even at the current low rates of local authority house-building would take no more than a fortnight's housing output, taking the country as a whole. It is not suggested of course that the homeless could be rehoused in a fortnight but the comparison is made so as to emphasise the point that homelessness, defined in this restricted way, is a comparatively small problem, not to be compared in size or even complexity with slum clearance or overcrowding. Its continued acceptance in a prosperous community can only be regarded as ghastly administrative failure of central and local government alike.

Before we leave the question of homelessness altogether, we ought to consider the attitudes and reactions of the public at large. There is a tendency to adopt much the same attitudes as Glastonbury reported as endemic in South Wales and the south-west. This equates the homeless with "riff-raff", "workshy", "deadlegs" who do not deserve help, and in extreme cases with delinquency, crime, psychosis and worse. But public compassion can also be aroused as we have seen in the case of "Cathy". Jeremy Sandford, journalist and writer, had reported in *The Observer* (September 1961) about conditions in Newington Lodge, an L.C.C. hostel for the homeless. Sandford had in particular condemned the atrocious physical conditions under which the families housed there had to live. His account caused some stir, but partly because *The Observer* is not a mass-circulation newspaper and partly because bad housing conditions seem in some way to be accepted, if not acceptable, provided they occur in London, its effect was little more than minimal. It was not until Sandford's TV play *Cathy Come Home* was shown in 1966 that the storm broke. Housing Minister Anthony Greenwood ordered his officials to see a private showing, TV commentators and opinion-moulders kept the subject on the boil for days and representatives of local authorities were duly arraigned as the villains of the piece. Such reaction was understandable. Housing had now been a matter of state concern for more than a century and had been a positive duty, with Exchequer subvention, for over half a century. If despite all this effort, worse still all this money, conditions such as Cathy's were still possible let alone widespread, then something was very wrong indeed. Moreover these revelations (and they were treated as such although the play was really a piece of documentary-style fiction) came close on the heels of the public scandal which had brought to light the abuses and misdeeds of Perec Rachman. It is a sobering thought to entertain, that had it not been for the salacious public rapacity for the carryings-on of those in high, and not-so-high places, the great wave of public concern for the homeless might never have erupted in 1966. Such is life. As it was, Cathy would have turned out to be nothing more than a nine-day wonder (as far as public interest is concerned that was the case) had it not been that a New Zealand-born Public Relations man by the name of Des Wilson was planning a national campaign to combat homelessness. With an exquisite sense of timing which to this day he insists was coincidental, his campaign, shortly to be labelled SHELTER, was launched within a few days of Cathy appearing on the TV screen. Coincidence or not, SHELTER achieved success almost overnight and went on to become a million-pound-a-year organisation. This chapter is not the place to assess the merits and defects of the SHELTER campaign or the worth of its work. It is remarkable enough that it could have happened at all when its reforming predecessors, establishment-minded to the last, and as near defunct as makes no difference, slumber on from year to year stirring only to exchange their annual self-congratulations and then to sleep return.

SHELTER in short was different. For a start its team was remarkably young, the average age being not much more than twenty-four. Although it had powerful establishment figures at its head, these kept wisely in the background while its youthful director and his helpers went on from strength to strength. Wilson left in 1970 to take over the Consumer Council, a move which the newly elected government in as petty a piece of political spite as we are ever likely to see, countered by abolishing the Council. SHELTER's Housing Officer, John Willis, took over. Willis was an older man with a sober dark-suit image which probably added to his stature and certainly was good for SHELTER. Of all the SHELTER team it was above all Willis who really knew what he was about when it came to housing and it was a great loss to the organisation when he decided to leave at the end of 1972. Judging from the reports of bickering and dissent emerging from SHELTER since, it is clear that Willis's departure dealt it a blow from which it will take some time to recover.

As for Cathy, she is hardly remembered. If Sandford's play were to be shown today there would be widespread switching to the other channel. For it is a fact that the British conscience can only take so much, after which it switches off. The Oxfam photographs are a case in point. When the Greve and Glastonbury reports were published in 1971 they caused hardly a ripple. And yet they contained the hard evidence, the chapter and verse, of all that Sandford could only assert five years earlier. To repeat Marian Bowley's words, it is a dismal story.

Nothing in this chapter should be taken as detracting from the splendid efforts, often in circumstances of great difficulty, of those authorities or more often those officers who have strained every nerve, and put in every available ounce of effort, to help homeless people. No words, certainly no words of mine, can adequately describe the thankless, gruelling, punishing task to which they have applied and continue, against the odds, to apply themselves. My strictures do not apply to them. But they are a minority and although their candle shines out like a good deed in a naughty world, the candle is small and the world is very large. Homelessness represents, no, not represents, *is* the ultimate housing disaster and the measure of British housing failure is the fact that homelessness is the one factor of housing stress which was and is within the power of central and local government to remedy within a comparatively short period of time. It is the most abject failure of them all.

13 Rehabilitation and grant systems

In any given year not more than about 2 per cent will be added to the housing stock. Therefore 98 per cent of the housing supply already exists and most of it will have been in existence for a long time. Houses do of course wear out but they take much longer to do so than say motor cars or clothes or those items which we laughingly describe as household "durables" which all too often turn out to last not much longer than a couple of years. But a house seems to go on for ever. A hundred years is quite usual and there are examples still to be found which are three or four hundred years old and are a source of great joy, not to say expense, to their owners.

Because the supply of houses cannot be rapidly expanded and because they take so long to produce, it must obviously be an act of prudence to make the best use of what we have, to keep them in good repair (which is easier said than done) and from time to time improve them by adding amenities which rising affluence and expectations will increasingly lead their occupants to expect. Improvement work therefore will include putting in baths, washbasins, hot water systems, W.C.s, and so on. It may also include replacing such things as doors and windows with more effective ones or with ones of a more modern design. Allied with this work will be items such as attending to defective plaster, floorboards and joinery and dealing with pests and rot and rising damp, possibly by putting in a dampcourse. Externally, work may include attending to defective pointing, drains and gulleys and may run to quite expensive items such as stripping, felting and retiling roofs. Much of this kind of work is not very different from repair; one could argue that if the house-owner had done all those things that he ought to have done, his dwelling would not be in the sort of condition which calls on public assistance to rectify.

Allied with this kind of work is the matter of conversion where a larger, possibly dilapidated, house is properly converted into a number of smaller, more convenient dwellings with the necessary alterations to layout and installation of additional equipment that this change of user requires. For the purpose of this chapter conversion work is lumped together with improvements of other kinds and indeed in the legislation dealing with improvements, conversions are distinguished mainly by the level of grant they can attract.

Considerable advantages are claimed for giving older houses this sort of treatment instead of knocking them down and building new ones. In housing jargon rehabilitation is held to have advantages over redevelopment and the superiority of one approach over that of the other has been a matter of debate for many years, is not yet resolved, and seems likely to continue.

Some of the advantages claimed for rehabilitation may well be true. Improvement work can sometimes be carried out more quickly and at a lower cost. The Deeplish Study undertaken by the Ministry of Housing and Local Government in 1966 claimed that even the most expensive of the three improvement schemes proposed for this twilight area of Rochdale would cost not more than 45 per cent of the capital cost of redevelopment. Smaller building firms can be put to this sort of work, firms of the kind that specialise in alteration and repair rather than new building. Such firms employ something like 40 per cent of the nation's building labour. Most improvement work is carried out indoors and is less liable to be interrupted by bad weather. If an area is "rehabilitated" rather than "redeveloped", the existing community is left largely undisturbed; community break-up is one of the more serious charges levelled against slum clearance and rebuilding. Moreover as the prices of new houses continue to rise steeply, they are becoming more and more beyond the reach of younger first-time purchasers and it may be that young couples, priced out of the market for new and modern housing, could still afford an older dwelling which they might then proceed to improve with the aid of a government grant. And a further "advantage" which may be considered to be political rather than practical is that such dwellings will remain in the private housing sector, whereas municipal redevelopment will mean more council houses which some consider undesirable. Such arguments have been supported in recent years by academic, theoretical propositions strongly favouring rehabilitation policies. One thinks for example of Dr Needleman whose book *The Economics of Housing* (London, Staples Press 1965) contained a number of calculations of how much it is worth spending on houses with different life spans and different rates of interest.

Needleman's argument is based on the assumption that modernisation will be worth while if its cost, plus the present cost of rebuilding in 'x' years' time, plus the present value of the difference in running costs (i.e. between an improved dwelling and a new one), is less than the cost of rebuilding. According to his calculations if, for example, the rate of interest is 7 per cent and the improved dwelling has an expected life of twenty years, it will be worth spending up to 70 per cent of the cost of rebuilding on improvement. If the rate of interest is 8 per cent and the expected life is thirty years, the proportion rises to 86 per cent. Such figures seem to the author to have an air of unreality about them, particularly as they seem to ignore the effect of inflation. For it is surely true that inflation will greatly affect the "cost of rebuilding in 'x' years' time" as well as the "present value of the difference in running costs". If the current rate of inflation is not less than the current rate of interest, why delay rebuilding at all? And in any case the difference in running costs is very difficult to assess and has almost certainly been underestimated.

But his figures attracted a great deal of interest and much argument has been based on them. The rehabilitation *v.* redevelopment debate continues and is not likely to be resolved in the near future. In any case, no matter how sophisticated the economic arguments on either side, one weakness remains: one is not comparing like with like. An improved house will in most aspects be inferior to a new dwelling and will usually have a shorter potential life. In most cases, too, the new house will be better laid out internally and will stand in a better environment and have better facilities for, say, access and car-parking. If one is going to attempt to cost these factors in money terms one will run up against the subjective difficulties frequently encountered in conventional cost-benefit analysis, bringing with them the usual uncertainty about the conclusions drawn.

Whether in fact improvement work is undertaken as a genuine alternative to redevelopment or whether its purpose is to make older housing more comfortable and attractive to live in until it has to be knocked down, Parliament has decided that the owners of such property may receive state help when they carry out improvements. Even Addison's Act of 1919 contained provisions whereby local authorities could *lend* money to private owners for improvement or conversion work. The first Act actually to give money away was The Housing (Rural Workers) Act of 1926 under which local authorities in rural areas had the power to make grants for improvement work costing not less than £50. The amount of grant could be up to two-thirds of the cost of the work and the maximum grant was £100. Half the grant came from the Exchequer and half from the local authority and this was extended by amending Acts right up to 1945.

The first improvement grants as we know them today were introduced by Bevan in 1949. The Housing Act that year gave the local authority power to make a 50 per cent grant available for work costing not less than £100, or more than £600 (increased to £800 in 1952). Three-quarters of the grant came from the Exchequer and one-quarter from the local authority. The dwelling so provided had to have an estimated life of not less than thirty years. The local authority fixed the rent for any new dwelling provided in this way and for any improved dwelling that had not been occupied during the preceding five years. Where it had been let in the preceding five years the landlord could increase the rent by 6 per cent of his cost of the works and this limitation lasted for twenty years. (This of course meant that the dwelling had to be retained for private renting for that time.)

Owner-occupiers accepting the grants also had to accept some limitation if they subsequently sold the property. And when the property was improved it had to come up to a sixteen-point standard.

The Housing Repairs and Rent Act, 1954, retained these grants but removed the upper limit on the cost of the work, the maximum grant remaining at £400. The thirty-year life expected of an improved property could be reduced to fifteen years, a landlord could raise the annual rent by 8 per cent of his share of the cost and the sixteen-point standard was replaced by a reduced, twelve-point standard.

Up to 1959 improvement grants were made at the discretion of the local authority and many authorities were reluctant to make them. Some felt that such grants were a subsidy to the private landlord which they were reluctant to support, others that resources devoted to improvement impeded the building of much-needed new dwellings. The House Purchase and Housing Act of that year introduced a new kind of grant to be given "as of right" to applicants wishing to install five basic amenities. These were bath (or shower), wash handbasin, hot water supply, a W.C. in, or contiguous with, the dwelling and a ventilated food store. The dwelling when improved had to have all the amenities, had to have an expected life of at least fifteen years, and the maximum grant for all five amenities was £155. The same limitations applied as with discretionary grants. The grants authorised by the 1949/1954 Acts were continued, but the landlord's period of limitation was reduced from twenty years to ten. The Housing Act, 1961, raised the rent increases following improvement from an annual 8 per cent to 12½ per cent of the landlord's share of the cost.

So far, the grants had been made available for individual dwellings, but the Housing Act of 1964 introduced the concept of improving whole areas. If a local authority felt that in any area at least half the dwellings could be brought up to the five-point standard, with a fifteen-year expectation of life, they could designate it an improvement area and could with certain limitations compel improvements within it. Landlords could appeal against the authority's proposals and tenants could veto them for five years. Local authorities could also compel the improvement of tenement blocks and houses outside improvement areas if the tenant asked for it. The maximum standard grant of £155 could be increased to £350 if the work required a septic tank, a piped water supply or a bathroom built on. The period during which conditions attached to a grant would apply was reduced from ten years to three. And the maximum conversion grant was increased from £400 to £500 per unit in houses of three or more storeys.

Shortly after the passing of the 1964 Act there was a change of Government. The new Government had come to power with a commitment to increase the rate of house-building to 500,000 houses a year and its first housing White Paper confirmed this pledge. The magic 500,000, hitherto rejected as impractical, was to be reached by 1970 and to be maintained thereafter. Many of the writers and commentators on housing, the author included, had for years come to the conclusion that in the long run the answer to the housing problem was houses and that only by a massive and sustained programme of house-building could the evils that had been endured for so long by so many of our fellow men be at last eradicated; to them the Government's apparently firm commitment to such a large programme could only come as the best of good news. The house-building figures rose sharply. Up to and including 1963 they had been running at about 300,000 a year for Great Britain; there was a sharp upturn in 1964 and this increase was maintained up to 1968, the total number of houses completed annually rising during this period from 373,676 to 413,715. This was the largest number of houses ever built in a calendar year in Great Britain. (The largest number ever built in a period of twelve months was 419,338 built during the year ending on 31 August 1968.)

This fine achievement was short-lived. Following a long period of economic uncertainty the pound was devalued in November 1967 and almost immediately afterwards measures were announced to reduce government spending. After some prevarication by the government it became obvious that the half a million a year target was being abandoned.

Housing: the great British failure

Anthony Greenwood, the Minister of Housing, made this clear at a Press conference on 18 January 1968:

Housing has had to make its contribution to economic recovery along with the other social services. Local authority programmes for 1968 and 1969 are being reduced below the levels originally planned, and that means that performance in the public sector, although increasing, will be less than originally intended ... The Government do not therefore now expect 500,000 houses in 1970 to be completed. There are too many uncertainties for it to be possible for anyone to say exactly how many houses will be built in 1970, but I am confident that the number will be large — well beyond 400,000. Because of the large increase in programmes which have already been approved, and which are now moving into the stage of building, completions in the public sector will continue up to 1970 at an even higher level than in 1967.

But Mr Greenwood (he is now Lord Greenwood of Rossendale) had got it wrong on almost every count. Even as he was speaking, public sector completions, far from increasing, were entering a long period of decline from which they have not yet recovered. Public sector completions in the record year of 1967 came to 203,918 (Great Britain) which was by no means a record. Macmillan had done considerably better than that when he completed 234,973 council dwellings in 1954. By the end of 1968 the figure had fallen to 191,722. This decline in fact had little to do with devaluation — it was far too soon — or indeed much to do with government policies at all; the fall in public sector completions during this period was due to the fact that an unusually large number of urban authorities had changed political control and had decided to reduce their housing activities.

Nor was it likely that more than 400,000 houses, despite Mr Greenwood's confidence, would be completed in 1970 (the out-turn was in fact 366,793). The disturbing thing about this miscalculation is not so much the error itself, though that was bad enough, but rather that the evidence of the coming decline was already in the Ministry's hands at the time the Minister was speaking. It seems more than likely

192

that the decision had already been taken within the Ministry, with or without the knowledge of the Minister (probably without) that the expansion in the rate of house-building was costing too much, particularly in view of the rising cost of subsidies under the 1967 Act which were linked to interest rates which in turn were rising fast. There is supporting anecdotal evidence for this contention, for example it was taking much longer to get Ministry approval to a clearance order at that time. Moreover there was evidence that the revision of the housing cost yardstick, which limits the cost at which a house may be built, was being purposely delayed so that the higher housing tenders brought about by inflation could not get through the yardstick net. This was not the first time that administrative action (or inaction) had been deliberately used to cut back the house-building programme and it was surely not the last.

The switch from redevelopment and new building to rehabilitation, at which Mr Greenwood had already hinted, was not long delayed. The White Paper *Old Houses into New Homes* (Cmnd 3602, April 1968) made it very clear

. . . as the result of the very large increase in house-building in the last few years, it is possible to plan for a shift in the emphasis in the housing effort . . . the balance of need between new house-building and improvement is now changing. . . The Government intend that within a total of public investment in housing at about the level it has now reached, a greater share should go to the improvement of older houses.

The intentions of the White Paper were clothed with reality by the Housing Act, 1969. The powers of compulsory improvement introduced by the 1964 Act were taken away. They had proved cumbersome, had been little used, and not many were sorry to see them go. In their place the 1969 Act introduced a new conception, the general improvement area. In such an area authorities should "help and persuade owners to improve their houses". They could also be able to buy land and buildings and carry out work for improving the environment. To aid this latter work, the Government introduced a new grant of 50 per cent on approved expenditure, the grant-aided expenditure to be limited to £200 per house.

No powers of compulsory improvement were included and although there was always the reserve threat of compulsory purchase, it was clearly intended that improvement work should be carried out more or less with the approval of the occupants and owners. "The harsh and unconscionable" use of compulsory powers would not be supported by Ministers. (Mr Anthony Greenwood moving the Second Reading.) Other provisions of the act were:

1. Local authorities could act as agents for owners in improvement matters.
2. Loans could be made to help the owners pay for their share of improvement work. On such loans authorities could charge interest only, leaving the recovery of the principle until later on.
3. Local authorities could compel owners to repair their houses, and certain repairs and replacements were to be eligible for grant.
4. The normal discretionary grant was raised to £1,000 (from £400).
5. The standard grant amenities were varied, the ventilated food cupboard was no longer required but a sink was included; the total grant was raised to £200 (from £155). Moreover the basic amenities need not all be installed at the same time, the houses in which they are installed need not have a life of even fifteen years and the grant could be paid even if the work had begun before the grant was approved.
6. Housing associations could, under the Housing Subsidies Act, 1967, get assistance from the Exchequer towards buying houses for improvement or conversion; this assistance was now extended to local authorities as well and was increased to £2,500 per dwelling obtained (from £2,000).

Other provisions related to progress towards fair rents, multiple occupation, and compensation payments in respect of owner-occupied and well-maintained houses acquired for slum clearance.

We can now see the trend in the attitude of Government towards improvements. With each successive Act the Government has felt constrained to relax conditions previously thought necessary. Whether in the cost of the work, the conditions relating to the rent of the improved dwelling, conditions imposed regarding the future tenure of the dwelling, the required life of the dwelling: on every count the conditions have been modified, made less onerous, presumably to make them more attractive to the owners of older dwellings. For there is no doubt that up to 1969 the system of improvement grants had been no more than a moderate success. During the previous ten years the number of grants approved, standard and discretionary, had remained steady at between just under 110,000 and just over 130,000. (Average for this period = 117,779.) The principal beneficiaries had without any doubt been owner-occupiers who during this period obtained between 50 and 60,000 grants a year. The owners of privately rented dwellings were not so keen to undertake the improvement of their dwellings: their take-up was about half of that for owner-occupiers at between 24,000 and nearly 29,000 a year during this period.

There is a remarkable consistency about these figures which appears to have been almost totally unaffected by changes in legislation occurring after 1959 and before 1969. Private tenancy, the tenure group most in need of the refurbishing that the grant system could provide, appeared to do relatively badly, four out of five grants, in round figures, going to local authorities or owner-occupiers. The proportion moreover remained at about this level after the 1969 Act had started to bite in other directions. After 1969 the level of grants approved rose sharply: 156,557 in 1970, 197,481 in 1971 and a record 319,169 in 1972. (This latter figure may have been inflated because the Housing Act, 1971, had made a 75 per cent grant level available for the development and intermediate areas, where the need for a large take-up was particularly acute.) But the proportion going to privately rented dwellings remained obstinately "sticky" at 20 per cent. It is precisely because of the predominance of local authorities and owner-occupiers as candidates for grants that the figure claimed in the 1971 House Condition Survey of 550,000 dwellings made fit between 1967 and 1971 is so difficult to accept.

This is not to say that the 1969 Act has been a total

failure. Within the limits set by its claimed objectives it has been reasonably successful. What may be questioned is whether, by switching substantial resources from new building to improvement, the Act and the philosophy which lay behind it were really beneficial to the long-term prospects of good housing in this country. There are many who thought not. Colin Buchanan and Partners in a report prepared for the Nationwide Building Society felt that the 1969 Act would result in isolated houses being patched up while their general environment remained squalid. A policy of rehabilitation may "have the merit of economic sense at a time of high interest rates", but they went on to argue that "there is a danger that by shoring the fabric of elderly housing, we will deny ourselves the possibility of a much more positive and enduring renewal of the housing environment". This is precisely the author's criticism of Needleman's propositions (i.e. that inflation at the rates experienced in this country since the war to a large extent negative his calculations of the economic benefits accruing to a policy of rehabilitation. In any case an improved house is not the same thing as a new house and any cost-benefit analysis must take this imponderable into account, not to mention the probable estimated future life of both new and improved housing.) The author, in oral evidence, made much the same point to the House of Commons Select Committee on Estimates, Sub-Committee B: "An improvement policy will lengthen the life, one assumes, of many houses though it may not lengthen the life of some of them; you simply make them more bearable to live in while they exist and eventually they have to be replaced."*

So much argument has been heard about the benefits of an improvement policy, particularly since the Cambridge Conference (a conference called by the Ministry in 1967 of many of those who might have something to contribute to a discussion on the merits of a change of emphasis to rehabilitation — builders, planners, sociologists, academics, tenants, landlords and councillors, for example), that the case for concentrating on building new (and demolishing old) dwellings has gone largely by default. This is not altogether

*F. J. Berry, Oral Evidence, Question 4906, 7 July 1969.

surprising since it seems more than likely that the Ministry, led from the rear by the Treasury, had already decided to slow down on new building and were likely to ensure that official pronouncements wherever possible supported the new line. We have already mentioned some of the benefits, real or imagined, that a rehabilitation policy might bring with it, so that it is worth examining one or two of the arguments leaning the other way.

1. *That with improvement the work can be carried out more quickly.* This depends on what you mean by improvement. If one is talking of installing four or five "standard" amenities, then this is undoubtedly true. But if one is referring to the large-scale rehabilitation of a run-down area there is evidence to the contrary. To quote Simon Pepper:

> With the examples of Leeds and Newcastle before us [Professor Pepper had examined the operation of improvement policy in these cities in detail] we must constantly remind ourselves that improvement is not faster than other forms of development. Indeed it has been argued that large-scale improvement could most profitably be tackled by spreading council efforts more widely, and by operating at a low-key on a long schedule. A long period of time would elapse before any political pay-off could be delivered.*

2. *That redevelopment breaks up and scatters existing communities.* There is a good deal of force in this argument but again it depends on what you mean. "Existing communities" may in some cases exist only in the planner's mind: "There is no reason to assume, as Jon Davies pointedly observed that 'an area drawn on a map by some junior doodler in a planning department (should) suddenly become a substantive community'." (Pepper, op. cit.) And even where an existing community can be shown to exist it does not follow that it is something fixed and enduring; communities are changing all the time and one can often go back to what was apparently a well-established and stable community after say ten years and find that one hardly knows the place.

Housing Improvement: goals and strategy, London, published by Lund Humphries for the Architectural Association 1971.

197

3. *That rehabilitation is cheaper.* Well of course it is. Were it not so there would be no case for it at all. It does not follow that it is economic. Dr David Kirby of the Manchester Business School in a recent article quoted a case where a local authority has spent more than £1,000 each on modernising houses built in 1922. In the present make-up of the housing stock 1922 is comparatively recent; more than a third of our houses are older than that. This would not be the case in, say, Western Germany, where an "old" dwelling due for modernisation may very well mean one built in 1948 or thereabouts. (The German housing stock is newer than ours since they had to contend with the slum clearance policies of U.S.A.F. and Bomber Command.)

But if policies put forward by Needleman and others were to be followed we should now be thinking of spending upwards of £5,000 to 6,000 on the improvement of individual dwellings and to spend that sort of money on old property without examining very carefully indeed the relative costs and benefits smacks of economic imprudence of a very high degree, particularly if substantial government grants are involved. And without significant government subventions it seems unlikely that any rehabilitation policy can be maintained.

4. *The advancing age of the existing housing stock.* Improvement does nothing to contain this. It is possible to deal with all the ills that older housing is heir to — inadequate original construction, bad internal layout, the ravages of damp, decay, infestation, corrosion, not to mention age, on all the elements and equipment which go to make up a house — but, when all is said and done, when you improve a 100-year old house what you have at the end of the day is a house that is one hundred years old.

Whatever the merits of a concentration on rehabilitation may be, there is no doubt in the author's mind that the current emphasis has come about for almost certainly the wrong reasons. We have already mentioned how the Labour Government in 1968 abandoned the attempt to build half a million new dwellings a year. Ostensibly this was part of the backwash of the 1967 devaluation and although there is evidence that the Treasury actually believed that it was necessary to deny ourselves proper housing so that the pound might be stabilised (the subsequent devaluations since 1971 disproved this thesis), the real reason for the cut-back was the refusal of newly-elected councils to go on building council houses. The Government therefore needed some explanation for the houses that were not being built and the true reasons smacked too much of party-political point-making. But improvements, particularly if they were low-cost "standard amenity" installations, could be made to show results comparatively quickly. The Conservative Party, at that time in opposition, was being faced with demands from within its own ranks to reduce the amount of aid given to all kinds of "lame ducks" and was more than ever setting its face against further municipal housing. It should have come as no surprise therefore that the Housing Act of 1969 was passed through Parliament with such embarrassingly fulsome support from both sides. There is some evidence that the Government was concerned about the reasons for Opposition support for the measure, but given the situation there was not very much they could do about it.

The Minister responsible, moreover, seems to some extent to have been the victim of his own propaganda. When, in February 1969, Mr Greenwood moved the Second Reading of the Housing Bill, he introduced his remarks by reciting the achievements since the war: ". . . we have built nearly 6,000,000 new houses, cleared over 850,000 unfit ones in England and Wales, and over 1,250,000 old ones have been brought up to date. Great progress has been made." All very true, but in saying it Mr Greenwood was saying much the same sort of thing that Henry Brooke had said in 1959, or Dr Hill in 1962 or Sir Keith Joseph in 1963 or, for that matter, one of his own Ministers (Mr Kenneth Robinson) was to say subsequently. The essence of this kind of argument is that we have done as much as can be expected and should therefore take things easy. Yet in Mr Greenwood's case one can only express surprise; for in the very same White Paper that announced the Government's intentions to concentrate on improvements, were included also the results of the 1967 House Condition Survey which revealed that the condition of the housing stock was very much worse than had previously been thought and that the number of known and admitted slums was higher than at any previous time in the nation's history. (The author is not trying to say that there were *more* slums in 1967 than at any previous time though that may have been true; the argument is that there were 1.8 million slums and at no time in our history had this number or anything like been admitted officially.) Thus included in one and the same document were an admission of a need greatly to increase demolition and rebuilding *and* an announcement of the Government's intentions to do precisely the opposite.

It is not difficult to see where this policy might take us in the longer term. Colin Buchanan and Partners estimate that at least half of the family housing in use in the year 2000 is already built. To the author's mind it is likely that the proportion will be higher than that. Let us make a simplified projection. There are at the present time rather more than 17.1 million dwellings in England and Wales. Let us assume that the decline in housing completions levels out at round about 300,000 a year. (This is about the same figure as was usual over the period 1952-64.) As for slums we will assume, for the purposes of the argument, that the clearance rate will rise to about 90,000 a year (including dwellings demolished for other purposes). This means that by the year 2000 about 8.1 million dwellings will have been added to the housing stock and about 2.43 million demolished, leaving about 22.77 million nett at that date. Of these, 14.67 million (64 per cent) are already in existence, so we could say, unless these projections are wildly adrift, that two out of every three dwellings in use in the year 2000 are already built. A.D. 2000 is only twenty-seven years away, but if one thinks back twenty-seven years (to 1946) one can now say that of all the dwellings in use in 1973, half were already in existence then. And if one thinks on beyond A.D. 2000 to the year 2027 the proportion of dwellings already in existence at the turn of the century will almost certainly be greater than two out of three. It is an escalating process. We used to share with France the doubtful privilege of possessing the oldest stock of housing in Europe; the French are now moving ahead leaving us to occupy this unenviable position unchallenged. And this leaves out of account the further decline in

200

environmental standards which the general improvement area arrangements seem unlikely to arrest. Nor does it take into account rising expectations about the standard of the dwellings themselves; surely one must assume that by 2000 much of our present housing stock would be counted as grossly inadequate.

Nor does concentration on improvement bring trouble only in the future, it has brought quite enough problems in the here-and-now. Not the least of these is the misuse of improvement grants. There had been misgivings from the beginning about the possibility of such grants being used in a way not intended (or even envisaged) by those responsible for introducing them. Nor did such a possibility seem to weigh very much in the minds of those responsible for the 1969 Act. Some slight disquiet began to be felt round about 1970 at first in relation to cottages converted for holiday use and later to other kinds of rehabilitation work. In 1970 the author was asked as part of his professional duties to enquire how widespread was the practice of converting holiday cottages with the aid of grants. At that time the practice appeared not to be widespread and even where it occurred the local authorities expressed no great concern. They felt that the important thing was to get the dwellings improved regardless of possible future use. In a slightly different context Pepper writing in 1971 (Pepper, op. cit.) dismissed the importance of possible misuse: ". . . there seems little justification for the concern frequently expressed at the possibility of people making money out of house improvements". And again: "The general principle of money being made out of improvements does not greatly worry me". It was certainly worrying some people and by 1972 it was worrying a great many people, though not, it seems, Her Majesty's Ministers. On 5 November 1972, *The Observer* carried an article by Jeremy Bugler indicating that in London there was widespread exploitation by property developers, although such a charge had been denied by the Minister for Housing and Construction only a week previously. Ten days later, the Secretary of State for the Environment, Mr Rippon, was maintaining that "tenants of larger landlords [should] have an opportunity for grants, as well as owner-occupiers or tenants of small landlords". Put this way it sounds eminently reasonable, the snag was (and is) that although tenants may benefit from an improved dwelling (if they do not get kicked out before they have a chance to enjoy it), they do not get the benefit of the grants. (For some years there had been pressure to make grants available to tenants in certain circumstances, a pressure which the governments of the day quite properly resisted.) But while Mr Amery and Mr Rippon had been busy denying the possibility of widespread misuse (in fact Mr Amery had said on television on 18 September 1972 that he could not "get any evidence at the moment that anybody has been made homeless as a result of improvement"), SHELTER had commissioned Philip Pearson and Alex Henney to report. The outcome of their investigations (published by SHELTER under the title *Home Improvement – People or Profit?*) was that because of "improvement" large numbers of so-called "protected" tenants in rented accommodation had been thrown out of their homes by fair means or foul, that "gentrification" (invasion of traditionally working-class areas by middle and upper income groups) was increasing, that rents were rising far beyond the reach of existing tenants (furnished tenancies in the Lanhills/ Marylands General Improvement Area [Westminster] had increased from an average of £5.70 before to £22.39 after improvement), and that large profits were being made. The SHELTER report was sent in due time to the Ministers, but at the time of writing no great impression seems to have been made. What surprises the author is not that such abuses occur, they seem in the circumstances to be inevitable; what puzzles him is that it should not occur to the Ministers, or to SHELTER for that matter, that organisations established for the purpose of making profit will pursue any course of action which will tend to maximise that profit. So long as the opportunity is there, and so long as the most rigorous checks and controls are not imposed, for so long will such "abuses" occur, and for anyone to think otherwise seems simple-minded beyond belief.

The other kind of widespread abuse, i.e. the use of grants to convert cottages into holiday homes, seems similarly deplorable. In a free society it is not possible, nor indeed

202

desirable, to prevent people from owning more than one home. What is objectionable is the use of public funds to help such people, who are by definition the more affluent members of society, not only to acquire but to improve them as well, particularly when, as with seaside cottages, they will be used for only a few weeks a year.

It may be that all this sounds like wholesale condemnation of the improvement grant system. This is not entirely so. Clearly the expenditure of so much public money must have had some beneficial effect on housing conditions. The 1971 House Condition Survey has already been mentioned and doubts expressed about its accuracy, but it does contain the only information available about the effect of the improvement policy between 1967 and 1971, even though the figures may turn out to be optimistic. According to the Survey, 3.951 million dwellings lacked one or more basic amenities in 1967; by 1971 this had reduced to 2.866 million, a reduction of 27.5 per cent. More than three-quarters of the dwellings still lacking one or more of these amenities were built before the First World War. Of the 2.866 million dwellings lacking amenities approximately 0.994 million were classified as unfit; this still leaves 1.872 million "fit" dwellings without one or more of the *basic* amenities. But there is plenty of evidence to show that owner-occupiers were getting most of the benefit from improvement. More than half (53 per cent) of the dwellings lacking at least one basic amenity in 1967 but having all five in 1971 were owner occupied; so were 55 per cent of those in which an internal W.C. had been added, 57 per cent where a bath in a bathroom had been added, and 52 per cent where hot and cold water at three points had been added. The corresponding percentages for "other tenures" (almost entirely private tenanted dwellings) were 21 per cent (lacking one or more in 1967 but having all in 1971), 24 per cent (W.C.), 33 per cent (bathroom), 24 per cent (hot and cold water). This seems to confirm the contention that, after allowing for the incidence of discretionary grants, about four out of five grants did not benefit private tenants (the tenure group most in need of the benefits that improvement can bring). 10.9 per cent of owner-occupied dwellings lacked one or more amenities in 1971 but the corresponding proportion of dwellings held on "other tenures" was 40.2 per cent.

Both the House Condition Surveys of 1967 and 1971 had been carried out by public health inspectors seconded by the Ministry from their authorities. Their professional association, the Association of Public Health Inspectors, published in 1973 a valuable piece of research into the operation of improvement policies. They found that people renting houses from private landlords were not getting their fair share of the improvement grant scheme. They also reported that 15 per cent of the replies had shown that landlords were forcing tenants out in order to improve and sell their properties, mostly in London and other big cities. (One of the drawbacks of the A.P.H.I. report is that it is based on the *number* of responding authorities and not their size. The results therefore give insufficient weight to the problems of large authorities and too much to small.)

Other figures included showed that 79 per cent of authorities expected that all dwellings in their areas would achieve the standard grant standard by 1982 but that only 53 per cent would reach the twelve-point standard by that date. 87 per cent felt that all unfit houses would have gone within ten years (approximately 1982). The question was also asked, "What percentage of private houses in your area could qualify for grant?" One reply said "none", which takes some believing; 37 per cent said between one and ten per cent; 95 per cent said up to fifty per cent; the remaining 5 per cent thought that more than half of such houses could qualify. Of these, fourteen replies indicated that more than 70 per cent of private dwellings could qualify for grant. The report does not indicate the number of dwellings involved, but it is clear that a very large number of them still require improvement even to the very low standards at present accepted. The Association make other points which, coming from officers so close to the problem of bad housing, ought to be heeded: "There is a continuing need for more houses to let and it is clear that they must be provided mainly by the local authorities. The record is, however, disappointing." Or, referring to the need to compel landlords to improve their property: "The Housing Act 1969, however, . . . removed virtually in their entirety, the compulsory powers for securing house improvements. This was regretted by the Association."

Attitudes to improvement grant policy vary widely from high commendation to downright condemnation and we have seen enough to tell us that the debate surrounding "improvement *v.* rebuilding" is complicated and not susceptible to economic analysis alone. It may well turn out in the end to be mainly a value-judgment. We can conclude with some telling remarks made by Professor John Greve in the *Report on Homelessness in London:*

The 1969 Housing Act places the responsibility — not for the first time — on the local authorities to take the lead in promoting a campaign for improving houses. But in the areas where houses and environments are most in need of improvements, local authorities are already incapable of discharging their multifarious and expanding housing and planning responsibilities. How is it foreseen by central government that they can become more vigorous and effective at the same time as taking on new burdens and holding down rate levies?

The grant-aided improvement of large numbers of the older houses can be no more than a relatively short term palliative — making do for the time being only because the general housing situation is so bad that many thousands of obsolete, ill-equipped houses in poor environments cannot be dealt with by demolition and renewal as was intended.

Much of the improvement work only raises sub-standard houses up to a minimum acceptable level, it does not turn them into well-equipped desirable residences in attractive neighbourhoods. It is a delusion to pretend otherwise. Deterioration is a continuous process. It is not halted for ever when a house is improved, though it may be held up for a while or slowed down.

The great majority of the houses which have been improved in the past decade, or which are improved in the next ten years, will have to be replaced some time between 1980 and 1995.

Here is the nub of the argument. The commitment to a rehabilitation policy is a vast exercise in putting off the evil day and not putting it off for very long. One can indeed wonder just what problems for the next generation our present-day administrators are building up. In the meantime improvement work, which is highly labour-intensive, is getting in the way of new building; Government moreover seems all too willing to accept that rehabilitation is a valid substitute for replacement. There is evidence for this in the way that the improvement grant figures are included in the D. of E. monthly housing progress reports as if they represented some sort of addition to the housing stock. They are nothing of the kind, in fact some schemes of rehabilitation result in a reduction in the stock of dwellings.

Meantime the production of new dwellings continues to flag and we cannot feel any sort of satisfaction until this trend has been substantially reversed and the production of new homes returned to its rightful place in national policy. The immediate aim should be the replacement of the pre-1919 stock within the next twenty years. We cannot afford to leave it any longer.

14 Standards for the future

This chapter is about standards; standards which houses now being built should achieve. This is quite a different matter from the standards discussed in Chapter 11 where we were thinking of minimum tolerable standards or in other words standards below which no dwelling should be allowed to fall. Standards in the context now being considered refer to such things as space, equipment, layout, heating, lighting, car parking provision; we are not really concerned with other aspects affecting the method of construction and the stability of the structure as these are covered by other controls, by what used to be known as the bye-laws but which are now incorporated in a national code of building regulations.

We have seen how, even in the nineteenth century, some dwellings provided for working-class families were constructed to what was then a very high standard, some even including bathrooms, an unheard-of provision in those days. These were very much the exception, and at this distance in time it is difficult to understand why, when so many Victorians were preaching that cleanliness was next to godliness. We can say that very few working-class dwellings, right up to 1919, were equipped with this elementary necessity; nor was it uncommon for it to be necessary for example to pass through one bedroom in order to reach another, or to find that the W.C. was not only not inside the building but might very well be situated well away from it. Hundreds of thousands of small dwellings with these shortcomings were still being built right up to the First World War.

The housing reform movement which became active at the turn of the century did not confine itself to pressure for municipal building. Many famous architects and philanthropists were associated with its activities and it is not surprising that their aims included provision of homes of a high standard. It was this pressure that led to the setting up of the Tudor Walters Committee during the First World War, whose recommendations were to revolutionise concepts of working-class housing. Nearly all the inter-war municipal dwellings were built to standards recommended by Tudor Walters and there is no doubt they had their effect in raising the quality of privately-built housing although there was no requirement that such housing should meet the Committee's standards.

That was more than fifty-five years ago and there is no point in going into any detail except to note two points of particular significance. The first was the requirement already noted that council houses should be equipped with baths (though not necessarily in a bathroom — that was to come later) and the second was a stipulation that such houses should be built at a density of not more than twelve to the acre. This may be regarded in some respects as a "spin-off" from the low density campaign which was being waged by Ebenezer Howard and the Garden Cities and Town Planning Association. These were remarkable innovations and much condemned at the time; baths were considered completely unnecessary for working-class people who, unused to such strange contraptions, would probably keep coal in them (some no doubt did, especially where the local authority had omitted to build a coal shed), and the low-density requirements were attacked for all sorts of reasons of which cost, dispersal and consequent high cost of travel to work were only some. Such attitudes were widely held and no doubt were part of a general feeling that such amenities were the prerogative of the better-off and definitely too good for ex-slum dwellers and other seekers after council-housing, erstwhile heroes though they may have been.

Prejudice dies hard, but in the end these particular prejudices did die and by the time the Second World War had come to an end the standards being required by the Ministry of Health were not only higher than Tudor Walters, they were also higher than had been common between the wars for middle-class private housing. The three-bedroom council

208

house built between the wars had a floor area of about 860 sq.ft.; those built in 1946 had a floor area (including outbuildings where provided) of 1,026 sq.ft. Despite economic difficulties the size of the three-bedroom house grew each year until in 1949 it had reached 1,055 sq.ft., dropping slightly in 1950 and 1951 to about 1,032 sq.ft. Although the early 'fifties were a time of comparative prosperity, the new Government with Macmillan as Minister cut the size of a three-bedroom house in 1952 to 947 sq.ft. and later years saw successive reductions until by 1960 it was down to 897 sq.ft., still higher than in 1938 but not much.

The Dudley Committee of 1944 which laid down the standards for post-war housing could only have thought in pre-war terms since the innovations and improvements in household equipment still lay ahead in the 'fifties and 'sixties. By 1960 it became clear that the whole question of standards for public and private sector alike would have to be rethought. A sub-committee of the Central Housing Advisory Committee under the chairmanship of Sir Parker Morris published its report in 1961 under the title of *Homes for Today and Tomorrow*. It was enthusiastically received and proclaimed, as were so many previous reports, as the herald of a new age. The new age seems to be a long while coming; the major recommendations of the Parker Morris Committee were made obligatory for New Town Housing in 1967, for local authorities in 1969 (nearly eight years after the report was published), but they are still not mandatory for private enterprise housing and it is fair to say that a good deal of housing built for owner-occupation falls short of them. And yet the Committee were convinced that "the problem of designing good homes is the same whoever provides them. . ." and that their recommendations applied "to private enterprise and public authority housing alike". Although some speculative developments advertise their dwellings as being up to Parker Morris standards, presumably because they find it an additional selling point, most do not. It is at least arguable that the majority of the buying public have never heard of Parker Morris and wouldn't recognise Parker Morris standards if they saw them.

Adherence to these higher standards is justified in new

town and local authority housing because "we are building for the future" and therefore what is built now ought to be at least acceptable in thirty or forty years or longer time. With greater emphasis in recent years on private rather than public ownership it is difficult to say why some attempt has not been made to introduce, and ultimately enforce, these standards in the private sector. To settle one point straight away, we ought to be clear that neither existing planning law nor the building regulations can be used for this purpose; it will be necessary to introduce some new kind of legislation and this would probably be more difficult than it sounds because it involves an entirely new principle. We have never tried to lay down by law what people will eat or wear or the quality of the goods they will buy, so long as these products do not fall below some predetermined minimum; so up to now it has been with housing.

As for the standards themselves, they range over the whole business of home design, but they concentrate particularly on the undoubted fact that most of our houses are too small and are inadequately heated. In fact one goes with the other for one can say with certainty that in the case of most dwellings built until very recently, at least half the house cannot be properly used for more than half the year. This presumably is why British bedrooms are equated in the European mind with medium-sized refrigerators, both in size and temperature. No wonder our bedrooms are only just big enough to accommodate a bed and the minimum of accompanying furniture; no one in his right mind would want to use them for any other purpose than sleeping during a British winter, not to mention most British springs and autumns as well. So when the weather proves sufficiently clement for the room to be used for some other purpose, a child playing or doing homework for example, there is not sufficient room. Parker Morris and his Committee could truly say that a home built without satisfactory heating is built to the standards of a bygone age.

The Committee clearly recognised that new modes of life developed in the last two or three decades had revolutionised our expectations in the matter of good housing. People, in all income groups, had more possessions and engaged in a much

210

wider range of activities. To cope with the mid-twentieth-century patterns of living a home needs more space and, to be usable all the year round, it must be adequately heated. Previous recommendations had concentrated on laying down minimum room sizes which sooner or later came to be regarded as maximum room sizes, particularly in the public sector. They felt that rooms could be put to more than one use, provided they were large enough: a bedroom, for example, need not be only a bedroom and where children are concerned should be more in the nature of a bed-sitting room. Bathrooms are usually too small and make it difficult to dry oneself and even more important to wash and dry young children. Kitchens should be large enough to accommodate the extra equipment which advancing affluence has brought within the reach of many, if not most, households; they should also be big enough to eat in since in most homes at least one meal a day is taken there, even if there is a separate dining-room. Houses built on two or three storeys should have two W.C.s of which one ought to be on the ground floor (or entrance floor if this is off the ground). While this may not always be possible, a second W.C. should be provided for families of five or more in two/three-storey dwellings, which of course includes nearly all three-bedroom houses; the second W.C. can be located in a bathroom.

Young families are going to need a pram, perhaps for quite long periods in their lives, and space should be provided for it inside the dwelling; it should be big enough to take a folding push chair as well and there should be enough room to manoeuvre. When such space is provided the pram can be used as a day-time cot without cluttering up some other part of the house.

Other categories of household are not forgotten, e.g. childless couples, persons living alone, single-parent families, elderly people, and so on. In the case of the latter, Parker Morris makes the point that the elderly need as much space as other people plus the additional safety devices which ought to be installed as a matter of course. But all houses, for whatever category, should be adaptable to cope with the changes that occur over the twenty or thirty years in which a family develops. Some dwellings have been designed so that the internal walls can be moved easily so as to re-arrange the room pattern when the need arises. Even the much criticised "open-plan" type of dwelling can offer advantages in this direction. But whatever happens to the layout, now or in the future, the Committee recognised the need for privacy and suggested that homes for four or more people should have set aside in the living area one room where peace and privacy can be found.

The Committee also made a most useful suggestion that all house plans should have the furniture marked on; at least this makes the architect think about what is going into the rooms he designs. The suggestion was taken up by the Ministry of Housing who have insisted on it being done since 1967.

Heating has already been mentioned as a major factor in raising home standards. Up to the 'sixties most dwellings were heated in the main living-room only, partly on the ground of expense and partly because the necessary equipment was not available at a reasonable cost. The Committee recommend that, as a minimum, the kitchen and circulation spaces should be maintained at a temperature of 55°F and the living areas at 65°F when the outside temperature is 30°F. With such an installation the bedroom temperature can be "topped-up" at little additional cost and if the bedrooms are used for other purposes, as in the larger dwellings, they should be capable of being heated to 65°F as well. As a concomitant the Committee saw the need for better thermal insulation. They did not think that double-glazing was an extravagance though they thought that perhaps more attention should be paid to properly sealing the outside doors.

The Committee felt that storage space in most existing homes is woefully inadequate, even for essentials, quite apart from the natural human tendency to hoard. At least 50 sq.ft. of storage space, well placed, ought to be provided in houses for four or more people. This is quite apart from the space needed for the dustbin and for fuel. Flats and maisonettes should have 15 sq.ft. inside the dwelling with a separate store of 20 sq.ft. elsewhere. Cupboards should be provided for clothes and linen though, for some reason, the Committee did not regard a wardrobe cupboard in the main bedroom as essential. This apparently was because the bedroom ought to

212

be big enough to accommodate a full bedroom "suite" which included a wardrobe; this appears to be one aspect where events have already overtaken Parker Morris. Solid fuel needs a store of up to 20 sq.ft. in a place convenient both to the householder and the coalman who ought to have direct access without coming into the house.

The Committee recognised the flexibility and the greater number of outlets possible with electric power circuit ring mains and they recommend that at least fifteen sockets should be provided in a five-person house and really it ought to have twenty.

The Report went on to recommend various improvements in standards for flats, two of which concerned sound insulation, to which more attention should be given, and refuse disposal. In the case of the latter the Committee thought that some technical breakthrough was required, since none of the traditional means of refuse disposal in flats, even the expensive hydro-mechanical arrangements, was entirely satisfactory. The new standards for heating have already been described; the recommended floor space standards are shown in Table 2.

Other aspects of the report dealt with the housing environment and the "externals" of housing development, landscaping, car parking, play spaces for children, gardens and layout generally. Housing can become obsolete in layout just as much as in its internal design and it was felt that much housing then being built (1961) was obsolete before it left the drawing-board. The report concluded by maintaining that "Good homes are worth paying for, even at the sacrifice of some other things . . ."

Twelve years have passed since the Parker Morris Committee put out its report. It took seven years for part of its proposals to be made compulsory for all public sector housing and even to this day some parts of the report remain as pie in some future sky. It has never been made mandatory for private building and it is extremely unlikely that it will ever be so. The reason is not far to seek: good housing costs money, a fact only half recognised by the Committee itself. The 'sixties, a decade in which great strides in housing design and standards could have been made, was a period of great inflation in the price of land and in the cost of money, quite apart from increases in building costs. Mr Mellish, then

TABLE 2 — *Recommended floor standards in square feet*

| | Number of persons per dwelling | | | | | |
	1	2	3	4	5	6
Houses						
1-storey	320	480	610	720	810	900
2-storey (semi-detached or end terrace)				770	880	990
2-storey (intermediate terrace)				800	910	
3-storey (excluding garage if built in)					1010	1050
Flats	320	480	610	750*	850	930
Maisonettes				770	880	990

*720 if balcony access

Parliamentary Secretary, complained in 1969 that house-building costs were increasing in real terms at the rate of 5 per cent a year. In the 'seventies the rate has been a good deal higher than that; couple this with the high cost of borrowing (at the time of writing the going building society lending rate is 9½ per cent and is being held down to that level only by temporary government intervention; there is talk of the rate rising to 10 or 11 or even 14 per cent) and the escalation in land prices, and we can see that superior standards of design and construction are being priced out of the market. In such a situation it seems unlikely that even present standards can be held for very long either in public or private development. It is all very well to argue that "we are building for the future" so that anything built now ought to be acceptable in forty or fifty years' time; has it occurred to anybody that we do not know what will or will not be acceptable that far ahead? And ought we to build for it even if we did know? A duty to posterity is all very well, but we also have a more pressing duty to the present, if you like to those millions who, because of misguided and sometimes downright vicious policies, are being denied access to adequate housing here and now.

From time to time it has been suggested that, at any rate until we have sufficient houses of acceptable quality, we should be concentrating on providing small dwellings with the minimum of frills and occupying the minimum of space. The County Architect of Buckinghamshire, Mr Fred Pooley, has from time to time put forward similar suggestions and has frequently been taken to task for his pains. To the author there seems to be great virtue in building this kind of dwelling. What shelter is all about is to have a roof over one's head and to be able to keep wind and weather out. To the young couple anxious to set up home, to the homeless mother at the end of her tether, to those crammed into insanitary hovels, such homes, basic though they might be, would nevertheless be a godsend.

A programme for building "mini homes" need not necessarily be confined to the public sector, though if the further escalation of house prices is to be contained there seems to be a good case for doing so. Moreover, government subsidy could be especially channelled to public sector building of this kind. And public authorities could bring to bear their undoubted expertise in finance, in design, in management, in land assembly and in construction, all of which would be of immense value in any large-scale long-run programme of this kind.

It could be held that small homes of reduced standard would be regarded as second-class homes for second-class people. I think that it would be difficult to refute such a charge; on the other hand it should be remembered that from time immemorial it has been accepted that half a loaf is better than no bread. And in housing terms these homes would amount to a good deal more than half a loaf, in the sense that they would be infinitely preferable to the likely alternatives of slums, sharing, multi-occupation and of course homelessness itself. It is greatly to be regretted that the management of the national economy and the housing policies, national and local, pursued for the greater part of the last half-century, have made it necessary even to entertain such a suggestion. However, we do neither ourselves nor those in urgent need of housing any good service by refusing to face the facts. The facts are that we are falling farther and farther behind our European neighbours in economic performance of all kinds, not least in house-building and construction generally. This is no place to seek out why the British are fast becoming the "peasants of Europe". We can and should face the fact that one of the consequences will be reduced housing standards at a time when most of Europe are raising theirs. There is in fact some evidence that already standards are falling. Compare most houses being built in 1973 with those built ten years earlier and you can see how the shoddy is replacing the quality article, how inferior products are replacing the superior, how the cheap and nasty has become the norm both in structure and in finishes, how in fact everything has gone down except the price. This is but one way that economic necessity has of teaching us lessons we are otherwise reluctant to learn. Would it not be far better to acknowledge that we can no longer afford to raise our sights in housing matters, at least not without a change in political attitudes and economic policies which, within the foreseeable future, seem unlikely to occur.

And if we can leave British standards for a moment, we can have a look at the rising European housing standards which not so long ago were inferior to ours on almost every count but which have already overtaken Parker Morris, which itself has not yet been generally adopted in this country. The

216

European equivalent to Parker Morris Standards are "The Cologne Recommendations". These were first drawn up in 1957 at a Joint Meeting of the Committee for Family Housing of the International Union of Family Organisations, and the Standing Committee Rent and Family Income of the International Federation for Housing and Planning (see page 266). Thirteen countries took part in this work together with representatives of the International Labour Organisation, the European Coal and Steel Community and the International Union of Architects. The Recommendations were by and large confined to laying down minimum space standards for families of different sizes.

The Cologne Recommendations have proved, without question, to have been a major influence on European housing policy as one by one countries have related their building requirements and financing arrangements to the space requirements laid down. However, the participating countries recognised that rising affluence and increasing expectations will render existing standards obsolete and the Recommendations were revised in 1971. As with Parker Morris, the Cologne Recommendations are concerned mainly with space related to the number of occupants. However the number of occupants is also related to the number of bedrooms by means of a capacity index. This comprises two digits, the first giving the number of bedrooms and the second the number of people who will occupy those bedrooms, e.g. 3/5 means a dwelling with three bedrooms designed for five people. Table 3 shows the previous Cologne Recommendations, the revised areas, and a comparison, as near as can be managed, with Parker Morris.

As an illustration of the equipment now thought to be essential in European housing we can mention that the main bedroom is expected to accommodate two beds, room for a cot, a small table and two armchairs, storage space (or a separate dressing room) a private washroom with shower, heating arrangements and connections for T.V. and radio. A kitchen is expected to have a double sink, dish-washing machine, refrigerator, freezer and a ventilation system. It is assumed that there will be need for separate provision for washing machine, spin drier, ironing board and other

217

apparatus for washing, drying, ironing and mending clothes. Clearly Parker Morris has been left far behind. But the European countries, almost without exception, have the expanding economic base from which rising housing standards, among other things, can spring. Such a situation seems increasingly unlikely to occur in Britain, but even if it changed there is such a large leeway to be made up that it would still make sense to build to a lower standard until all urgent needs had been met.

Here there seems to be a multiplicity of failures. First a failure to keep pace with the improved standards first introduced after the war but abandoned in the early 'fifties. Second there is the failure to adopt Parker Morris and make it a recognised standard in the early 'sixties. Third there is the failure, not strictly a housing failure, to provide the economic climate in which existing housing standards could be maintained, never mind raised. Fourth there is the failure to recognise that either an inadequate number of good dwellings or an adequate number of inadequate dwellings (but not an adequate number of good dwellings) is about all we can afford and that sooner or later existing standards will have to be reduced or, at best, not raised from their existing level. In all this we can find little comfort, but then those seeking comfort should not be reading this book.

TABLE 3 – The Cologne Recommendations

Capacity of dwelling (area expressed in square metres)

	0/1	1/2	2/3	2/4	3/4	3/5	3/6	4/6	4/7	4/8	5/8
1957 Cologne Recommendations			51.5	56.5	60.5	69.2	76.2	80.2	86.7	93.7 101.7*	97.7 105.7*
Parker Morris† (approximate equivalent)	33.0	48.5	61.0	71.5	71.5	80.0	88.5	88.5	114.5		
1970 Cologne Recommendations	35.5	51.0	64.5	69.5	74.5	92.0	102.0	107.0	115.0	121.0	126.0

* includes an additional room.

† includes certain areas which are excluded from Cologne Recommendations, e.g., corridors, stairs, partitions, etc. The difference between Parker Morris and the revised Cologne Recommendations is therefore even more marked than the figures would suggest.

15 Conclusion

Throughout the whole history of state intervention in housing we have seen the conflict of two opposing philosophies underlying the part the State should play. On the one hand we have observed the proclaimed desire to help all those who, for whatever reason, are unable to help themselves and on the other the depreciation of assistance to all kinds of lame ducks and a firm reliance on the principles of self-help and sturdy independence. This conflict has never been far removed from the general debate on housing policy and it is just as alive today as it was fifty or a hundred years ago. Indeed it is a conflict which makes itself manifest in a wide range of matters of social concern and lies perhaps at the root of the many disagreements which, sometimes with great violence, erupt in council chambers throughout the land and in Parliament itself.

It is right that this should be so. For this debate is political and it is a proper thing to bring housing into the arena of political argument. From the time the author was first involved in the field of housing he has heard countless pleas to "keep politics out of housing". This is rather like asking to keep surgery out of medicine. It is not possible and even if it were, it would not be desirable. For what such pleas usually intend is to keep out of housing the kind of politics to which the author happens to subscribe. It is an unappealing British characteristic to regard the other fellow's politics as dogmatic prejudice whereas one's own are no more than rather obvious common sense. But this is no reason to eschew politics; what politics is all about is the place of the State in the great society and the way the nation's affairs are run; without politics such debate is sterile and unavailing.

From the time of the Greeks it has been usual for political thinking to polarise into two schools of thought, those who wish by and large to keep the world as it is and those who wish to change it. This division has occurred at all times in the civic development of man and in all countries; it is not special to Britain nor to the twentieth century. To bring the matter to housing terms, those who are seeking change in society will be more likely to advocate state involvement in housing provision than those who do not; this is borne out by the attitudes of extremists on both sides. Only politicians on the extreme right will advocate that the State should have no truck with any kind of housing involvement, only those on the extreme left will maintain that housing should be provided by the State alone. It is customary at this stage for observers to say with much hypocrisy that either may be right. This the author cannot do, for he is as much the prisoner of his political convictions as the next man, and having arrived at the point where he is convinced that certain truths are self-evident, he sees no reason to throw them overboard on the first occasion they may be of some use to him. It should not at this late stage come as a surprise to any reader that the author is in favour of the State getting itself involved in the nation's housing and in a good many other things besides. It is also obvious that many will take an opposite view and indeed if it were not so there would be no need for argument and no need for this, or any other similar, book.

All the same such conflicts can bring unfortunate results in their train. From the time the first philanthropists thought about working-class housing and the housing reformers initiated their campaigns, there has been opposition, vociferous and bitter, to every step towards state housing provision. This was particularly evident in the 'twenties when it was widely asserted and commonly held that it was not worth while giving working-class people decent housing as they would not know how to use it. Keeping coals in the bath was only one aspect of this unsavoury picture of working-class life. Such views are not commonly expressed today, though the attitude behind them still persists; it may appear, as Donnison puts it, as a belief that people prefer

221

T.V. sets to decent housing. As an aside one may reflect that society has made it possible for quite poor people to equip themselves with television; at the same time it has denied them the possibility of proper housing. (It is surprising how the old arguments persist; when the author was a youngster it was the radiogram that was evidenced as the epitome of working-class irresponsibility.) When it became obvious that opposition to state housing was proving ineffective, its opponents changed tack and switched to insisting that state housing (to all intents and purposes this means council housing) should be reserved only for the very poor. This is a policy that has been widely followed and has been implicit, and occasionally explicit, in much housing legislation.

There are extreme dangers in such a policy. It has led to the sort of segregation of particular kinds of people in one-class housing estates, purposely cut off from the rest of the community, the kind of ghettoes that James Tucker railed against so vehemently in his book (*Honourable Estates,* see page 105). It has meant unfairness in the sense that families of a particular income level or social category have been helped to improve their housing situation substantially while others, only slightly more affluent, have been denied any help at all. There are the kind of social implications that seem to surround any kind of state help, the stigma that the Government has purposely attached to, say, supplementary benefit; these are bound to make themselves manifest in any kind of social housing confined to one section of the community. And if the policy is pursued logically it entails a notice to quit being served on any householder so ill-advised as to improve his income or position in the world. In practice, fortunately, this happens less often than one might imagine, but there remains the fact that council tenants who no longer qualify on income grounds may be subject to all kinds of pressure to leave and may in the case of some authorities actually be at risk of eviction. And of course there is the danger that policies which are defensible on moral or practical grounds will not be vigorously and equitably pursued. Compassion for one's less-fortunate fellow men is thinly and unevenly spread and in any case tends to evaporate when it starts to cost money.

It is in fact difficult to distinguish any philosophy whatever behind the great mass of housing legislation since 1919. At different times state effort has been concentrated on housing for general needs, working-class housing, slum clearance, overcrowding, multi-occupation, accommodation for the elderly, and improvement of existing property. Added to this, housing policy has always been considered as expendable, a suitable case for Treasury treatment as soon as the economy gets into difficulty, or to be jettisoned because of changes in the political climate. Housing programmes have many times been axed as part of the regulation of the economy, though in fact housing makes a very bad regulator. In broad terms it takes two years for the brakes to be put on and another two for them to be taken off again, long after the precipitating crisis has been forgotten. Not only housing, but the construction industry generally, not to mention the building materials supply industry, have been clobbered unceasingly in this way since the last war and even to some extent between the wars; there is small need to enquire why their performance has not been better than it has. As a result housing policies have tended to be makeshift, hasty and ill-conceived. The great lack, indeed one can claim the great failure, of British housing is the failure to work out a clear, logical approach and then to pursue it with single-minded vigour. In short to determine who needs help, what help do they need, and how are they to be enabled to get it.

When the first draft of this book was being prepared, the Housing Finance Act had just been passed and this was hailed as a turning point in housing policy that would at last lead to the millennium. Now, even after only a few short months it is becoming obvious that the strictures heaped on it by its opponents were on the whole justified and that its prime purpose was to raise rent income and reduce Exchequer liability. Its effect on future house-building, if any, will be mainly on the split between public and private housing rather than on the total numbers built. Some adjustment of rent levels was in fact necessary and long overdue in both public and private sectors, certainly the previous levels could hardly be justified. But it did not need this kind of steam hammer to crack this particular nut. Nor is there any virtue in a high rent

Housing: the great British failure

level in itself, apart from the help it can give to others. In the public sector higher rents from older houses can mean that the rents of new, expensive dwellings can be lower than would otherwise be the case. And in the private sector there is no doubt that a low rent level meant that there was great injustice to many landlords, though no one should be simple-minded enough to believe that any income from increased rents would necessarily be spent on repairs and improvements to privately rented houses.

Since 1919 successive governments, though anxious to reap the political rewards of a comprehensive and generous housing policy, have throughout the period regarded the situation at any given time as somehow abnormal, that the circumstances were exceptional so that no really drastic action was called for. When normality returned the old economic laws would see to it that private enterprise could and would supply nearly all needs, with state housing becoming little more than a minor balancing factor. In those circumstances there can be little wonder at the lack of enthusiastic forward planning or even a realistic assessment of current and future needs, at either local or central government level. If local authorities' involvement in housing was to be only temporary there was no obvious need for either. We have already seen how central policy flitted from one palliative to another and we cannot exclude central government from at least part of the blame for the Great British Housing Failure.

But they are not alone to blame. From the time local authorities were first charged with the duty of securing acceptable housing, it was obvious that here was a duty that most would seek to avoid. Let us be clear that there have been honourable exceptions, authorities who have done everything humanly possible to secure the very best housing situation for their citizens; but they are not typical. The majority have never built enough houses for their requirements and though many of them blamed central government for their shortcomings it has been made very clear by the wide variation in performance by different authorities that available housing powers are sufficient provided they are properly and enthusiastically used. Marian Bowley, writing in

224

1944, was quite definite about it: "There is no doubt that the organisation of the provision of houses through the local authorities has not been satisfactory." (Bowley, op. cit., Chapter XIII.) And although the total output in the post-Second World War years has been a good deal higher than in the inter-war period, the same charge can still be made. Dr Bowley goes on:

> It is clear that if the authorities are to remain housing authorities they must be provided with a cut-and-dried policy about which there can be no misunderstanding; moreover, their attempts to carry out these programmes must be supervised and controlled. There must be some authority who can and will oblige local authorities to perform duties laid on them by Parliament or supersede them altogether.

These are strong words and most apposite, although they were written almost thirty years ago.

It has already been noted that local authorities became housing authorities almost by accident, mainly because "they were there", or as Marian Bowley puts it: "local authorities have tended to accumulate powers and duties for which they have no particular qualifications, except their existence." We have already suggested that local authorities are unsuitable agents for housing policy, but Doctor Bowley had already seen that this was so thirty years ago. Let her have the final word on this matter:

> . . . they have endeavoured to achieve the minimum instead of the maximum, and there has been no outside authority to force them to do otherwise. . . It is possible that the whole difficulty is just an illustration of the inferiority of state organisations in matters of initiative and imagination. . . On the other hand there are one or two considerations which suggest that the local authorities are a peculiarly unsuitable form of state organisation for housing purposes. In the first place there is no defined standard in housing matters to which they must conform. In education, for instance, there is at least a definition in that free elementary education must be provided for all. . . In the second place, there are in each district large groups of ratepayers whose interests are definitely contrary to

those of a progressive housing policy. It is clearly not in the interest of the owners of slum houses that they should be cleared away; it is not in the interests of landlords in general that there should be rigid limits placed on the number of persons who can live in a particular house; finally, it is not in the interest of property owners as a whole that the supply of houses should be increased! This is a formidable list of opposing interests rivalled perhaps only in the case of town planning... All these groups of interest have a maximum opportunity for obstruction of the building plans of the local councils which have the duty of making and carrying them out. It is noticeable that it is only when the housing shortage has been so acute that the demand for houses has become a political factor of first-class importance that local authorities have shown real energy and enthusiasm... *The solution must be in an improved state organisation.** [My italics — Author]

The author has quoted from Dr Bowley at some length, partly because her work was the most brilliant and comprehensive appraisal of inter-war housing policy ever undertaken and partly because her words, sadly, have a strangely familiar ring and could apply, with very little modification, to the situation in 1973. That this could and should be so is a measure of the extreme failure of British housing policy and of its chosen instruments, the local authorities. Only Bevan, of all post-war Housing Ministers, made it clear that local authorities were going to do as they were told. Succeeding Ministers have been only too ready to emphasise, at least for so long as it suited them, the freedom of local authorities and their independence from central control.

There is no doubt about it, if the nation is to be adequately housed, the job must be taken away from the local authorities. It must be given to some other kind of organisation which is at least one stage divorced from local politics and preferably removed from them altogether. Some national body, similar in organisation to the Scottish Special Housing Association, seems to be called for to which all existing council housing could be transferred. This would give the very maximum advantage that rent- and loan-pooling can

*Bowley, op. cit., pp. 259-60.

226

bring, it would enable Exchequer aid to be directed to the areas and for the purposes where it is most needed, it would put an end to the local patronage still exercised in the grant of a council tenancy, it could employ technical, professional and managerial staff of high calibre and could plan and use its power and prestige to enter into large-scale contracts on advantageous terms. It would admittedly be a large and bureaucratic body, shortcomings which are formidable but which pale into insignificance against the sheer lack of drive and efficiency which are characteristic of the local authority. It would not be removed from the political process altogether and, as has already been argued, there is no good reason why it should be. It would, however, be free from the petty, trifling and occasionally semi-corrupt local political arena.

Nor does the reorganisation of local government offer a more hopeful future. It has been frequently stated that the new framework would ensure among other things that much of the old "dead wood" among officers and members would be discarded; as it turns out it is clear that much of the "dead wood" is being carried forward into the new authorities, and there seems no good reason to suppose that the new authorities will turn out to be any more effective than the old.

The problems of land prices and interest rates have already been mentioned, and need not detain us long here. The price of land which has risen so astronomically in the last few years has been a symptom not a cause of high house prices. Nonetheless if some sense is to be brought to a large-scale building policy it is essential that the price of land be controlled and certainly reduced from its present level. In this context the Land Commission, whose abolition owed much to political dogma and little to common sense, was not given a chance to prove its worth particularly in the field of land assembly; it could have brought great benefit to housing. Similar powers of compulsory purchase and land assembly could conveniently be given to a new National Housing Authority. Interest rates have already been noted as a crucial factor in housing finance, public or private. (It is a measure of the rate of inflation as well as the rise in interest rates that Appendix 2 which deals with the subject at some length has had to be rewritten three times while this book was being prepared.)

The author has already made his view quite clear, that the solution to the housing problem is houses, in short that only a large-scale building programme sustained over many years will suffice. It is not a view universally held. Let us consider a passage from a paper presented by Professor Cullingworth to a Conference in 1971 (J. B. Cullingworth, *Who Needs Housing,* Housing Centre Annual Conference, 1 July 1971):

> When I was Chairman of the Scottish Committee on Unfit Housing, it was repeatedly put to us that all problems would be solved if only we could produce more houses. The same idea has been expressed in relation to numerous housing problems for generations: but it simply is not true. Indeed it is perniciously misleading. Building more houses enables housing problems to be met: it does not ensure that they will be.

It is difficult to follow Professor Cullingworth's reasoning. If it is "perniciously misleading" to suppose that the solution is more houses, are we to suppose that the position will be improved by building fewer? To the author one thing is certain beyond argument, the problems cannot be solved unless the houses are built. The business of ensuring that the new dwellings go to those in need is a comparatively simple matter; it would be simpler still if there were an adequate supply of houses of all kinds, and their management were in the hands of a national authority. With one-and-a-quarter million slums at least and with a larger but indeterminate number of dwellings barely fit to live in, it does not seem likely that we shall be in any danger of over-provision for many years, even at any enhanced rate of building likely to be forthcoming.

And while we are on the subject of the rate of building we must constantly remind ourselves that our performance in this respect is almost the worst in Europe. This is so whether we calculate the number of houses built annually per thousand head of population or whether we consider the proportion of the Gross National Product devoted to housebuilding. At no time do we seem to have spent more than 3.7 per cent of our G.N.P. on building houses, whereas since 1955 West Germany has allocated between 5.2 and 5.7 per cent, Italy 5.2 to 7.2 per cent, Sweden 5.0 to 6.0 per cent and even the Republic of Ireland has overtaken us (1970) by devoting 3.8 per cent of her G.N.P. to our 2.9 per cent. Partly this is due to the unwillingness to spend, either as private citizens or as public authorities, enough money on putting roofs over our heads; partly it is due to the fact that Britain's construction industry is far too small. A recent report by the Federation of Master Builders makes this abundantly clear: 5.7 per cent of the labour force here is employed in construction as against 7.7 per cent in Ireland, 8.0 per cent in West Germany, 9.1 per cent in Sweden and 10.7 per cent in Holland. (W. S. Hilton, *An Expansion Programme for Construction,* 1973.) Half of all the construction output in this country is commissioned by public authorities and is responsive to their demands. It cannot be claimed that in this matter the construction industry has let the country down, on the contrary by failing to plan sufficiently far ahead and on an adequate scale the public authorities have ensured that the construction industry has been kept below the level at which it could satisfy the major demands made on it. The solution is obviously in government hands. If the economy of the country is to expand at the rate now regarded as essential it is necessary that the construction industry expands at an even faster rate. The situation probably does not call for a massive direct labour organisation either with or without a parallel private sector; though there are many excellent examples of what direct labour can do. Aims of Industry notwithstanding, the problems of management alone in such a large organisation would be too daunting.

It has been frequently asserted that bad housing is but a manifestation of poverty and that when poverty has been eliminated all will be well. At the very least this is arguable, but in any case we have no proof. Poverty is still very much with us with one household in nine below the poverty line. These are the "submerged tenth" of the twentieth century and no Government, Labour or Conservative, has paid much attention to them. This is almost inevitable. While people are poor or unorganised or homeless they are unlikely to cut much ice politically; it is no accident that British housing policy has benefited most the skilled worker (who is used to saying, and getting, what he wants) and the middle-class who exercise political influence totally out of proportion to their numbers or value to society. The elimination of poverty is a stated social objective by both parties though performance by either leaves much to be desired. It is singularly unfortunate that even Britain, the country of the "Welfare State", has been left behind by almost every other country in Europe. What chance does housing stand?

Housing in Britain has been a failure, and the evidence of that failure has been catalogued, however inadequately, in this book. There are some lessons to be learned. At the beginning it was made clear that one of the major causes of housing problems was a sharply rising population and it does not need much imagination to see what benefits a stabilised population level would bring long-term; it is equally evident that to enforce this remedy may well be beyond the reach of Government. Second, housing should be taken away from local authorities and put in the hands of some public national organisation. Certainly it should not be left to private enterprise, which is plainly not interested in the kind of problems most in need of solution. Third, the people of this country should be educated in the need to spend enough money on housing themselves. This does not mean setting some absurd proportion such as 25 per cent of gross income on housing, equally it is certain that many local authority rents and most controlled private rents were until recently too low to make any kind of sense. The author at conference after conference has heard representatives of some authorities declare that they had undertaken never to raise the rents of their houses again. This is an utter absurdity; only by raising the rents of older properties in a sensible way could the money be found to keep down the rents of new, expensive dwellings to a level that the prospective tenants could afford. (Even this possibility has now been swept away by the 1972 Housing Finance Act.) If householders are ready to spend more on food and clothing, never mind more expensive, less essential spending, and if they are to insist on higher wages, there is no justification for them to retain the rent levels of ten or twenty years ago if a rise would help the tenants of more recently built dwellings.

This is by no means all. At almost every point housing policy is capable of some, occasionally much, improvement. There is an obvious need, for example, to plug the gap which releases public aid to the tune of £300 million a year to owner-occupiers, quite apart from permitting them to make capital gains. But perhaps enough has been said here to persuade the reader that this sphere of social activity has turned out to be, despite all the money and all the effort, one of the greatest British failures of them all.

Appendix 1 Families on low incomes

The then Secretary of State for the Environment, announcing the Government's policy on Housing Finance to the House of Commons on 3 November 1970, made the following statement: "In spite of the fact that the 1968 Family Expenditure Survey disclosed that a far higher proportion of households in the private unfurnished sector had incomes below £1,000 per annum than in the public sector, no form of rent rebate has been available to private tenants." This statement, although undoubtedly true, needed further examination particularly as it had been adduced to support a fundamental change in British housing policy.

The first difficulty arose from the Secretary of State's reference to incomes of £1,000 per annum. The Family Expenditure Survey did not measure incomes annually, only weekly. As £1,000 per annum was £19 3s. 7d. per week, the nearest classification available in the Survey was £20 per week and the figures in this appendix have been calculated on that basis.

That Mr Walker's statement was true was supported by the 1968 Survey, the relevant statistics from which are summarised in Table 4.

Just over 45 per cent of households in private rented accommodation had weekly incomes of less than £20, whereas the corresponding percentage of households in local authority accommodation was 32 per cent. This should have caused no surprise since unfurnished dwellings to rent in the middle range have largely disappeared over the last fifty years and have been replaced either by local authority rented or by owner-occupied property.

In order to assess the validity of Mr Walker's argument one

TABLE 4 — *Proportion of each tenure in*
each income bracket

Household weekly income (£)	Local authority rented		Private rented	
	%	Cumulative %	%	Cumulative %
Under 6	1.56	1.56	8.44	8.44
6-8	7.16	8.72	7.73	16.17
8-10	4.18	12.90	4.50	20.67
10-15	9.22	22.12	10.80	31.47
15-20	9.91	32.03	13.72	45.19
20-25	15.74	47.77	14.59	59.78
25-30	14.82	62.59	11.99	71.77
30-35	12.21	74.80	8.91	80.68
35-40	8.17	82.97	5.84	86.52
45-50	9.09	92.06	6.86	93.38
50-60	4.54	96.60	3.79	97.17
60	3.40	100.00	2.84	100.00

would have liked to know the average size of family in each
of the various income ranges and in each type of tenure.
Unfortunately the Survey did not provide information from
which these comparisons could be made. In any case it would
have been more helpful to know what proportion of those
families earning under £20 per week was in local authority
and what proportion in privately rented accommodation
respectively. On this basis one found that households with
incomes less than £20 per week were distributed over the
tenures as shown in Table 5.

TABLE 5 — *Households with incomes less*
than £20 per week

	No. in survey	%
Local authority rented	698	31.23
Private rented	573	25.64
Other tenures	964	43.13
Total	2,235	100.00

This showed a very different picture with the proportion in local authority dwellings being appreciably above those in privately rented dwellings. On the other hand the proportion in "other tenures" was lower than the national average and this was not surprising since this classification included owner-occupiers.

It would also have been helpful to know whether households earning less than £20 per week differed significantly from the rest of the population (apart from the fact that they were on low incomes). There were in fact significant differences:

(*a*) This sector contained an unusually high proportion of elderly and retired persons or other persons drawing social security. Reference to Table 6 emphasises the point.

TABLE 6 — *Weekly household income*

	Under £6	£6-8	£8-10	£10-15	£15-20	All house-holds
Average income (shillings)	102.17	137.39	180.81	246.24	352.91	599.62
Social security retirement and widows' pensions	79.39	107.70	111.35	90.61	43.01	35.94
Other Social Security benefits	8.44	7.60	15.18	26.83	19.64	16.58
Total Social Security	87.83	115.30	126.53	117.44	62.65	52.52
Social Security as percentage of average income	% 85.96	% 83.92	% 69.98	% 47.69	% 17.75	% 8.76

(*b*) 38 per cent of the people in this sector were over 65 years of age compared with 10.8 per cent of all households.

(*c*) This sector contained a larger proportion of households in which no member was working. In fact there were no working persons in 55 per cent of such households. To put it another way, 27.5 per cent of people in this sector were working compared with 47.5 per cent of people in all households.

(*d*) This sector also contained a larger proportion of small

234

households. In fact 43 per cent of all households with incomes of less than £20 per week were one-person households and a further 39 per cent were two-person households.

Taking all the above factors into account, the majority of households in receipt of very low incomes could be expected to receive supplementary benefit in support of rent. It could further be argued that this category was receiving state aid towards rent and that Mr Walker's statement that "no form of rent rebate has been available to private tenants", although true, was misleading. Pursuing the point that households with the very lowest incomes may be assumed to be in receipt of supplementary benefit in support of rent, it immediately became less important whether these households occupied privately rented or local authority housing in the sense that those in both tenures were in receipt of public aid.

By eliminating the lowest income category, i.e. those earning less than £6 per week, the tenure pattern was approximately as shown in Table 7.

TABLE 7 — *Tenure pattern*

*Households with incomes of £6 per week
and less than £20 per week*

| | Weekly incomes | | | | Total no. in survey | % |
	£6-8	£8-10	£10-15	£15-20		
Local authority rented	156	91	201	216	664	32.45
Private rented	98	57	137	174	466	22.78
Other tenures	120	125	333	338	916	44.77
Total	374	273	671	728	2,046	100.00

It will be seen that in all four of the income categories quoted in Table 7 the proportion occupying local authority rented accommodation exceeded the proportion in privately rented dwellings and taken together the percentages were approximately 32.5 per cent and 22.75 per cent respectively.

The next point concerns the proportion of income spent on rent. Table 8 shows the average weekly household income in the various categories, the average amounts spent on rent

TABLE 8 – *Weekly household income*

	Less than £6	£6-8	£8-10	£10-15	£15-20	£20-25	£25-30	£35-40	£40-45	£45-50	£50-60	£60+
Mean weekly household income (shillings)	102.17	137.39	180.81	246.24	352.91	451.86	550.64	648.50	746.23	887.05	1085.77	1651.84
Average rent (shillings):												
In local authority dwellings	31.79 (31.11%)	36.55 (26.60%)	39.11 (21.63%)	46.28 (18.79%)	45.41 (12.87%)	51.16 (11.32%)	52.36 (9.51%)	52.94 (8.16%)	55.68 (7.46%)	57.42 (6.47%)	55.51 (5.51%)	62.21 (3.77%)
In privately rented dwellings	20.26 (19.83%)	27.03 (19.67%)	30.28 (16.75%)	34.80 (14.13%)	38.04 (10.78%)	45.27 (10.02%)	44.74 (8.13%)	53.62 (8.27%)	49.91 (6.69%)	60.42 (6.81%)	68.58 (6.32%)	135.75 (8.22%)

Note: Figures in brackets show rent as a percentage of mean household income.

in local authority dwellings and the average amounts spent on rent in privately rented dwellings. It also shows the amounts spent on rent as a proportion of the average household income. The table shows that the proportion spent by households in local authority dwellings was higher than those in privately rented dwellings for all income brackets up to £30 per week and that even above this income level the difference was not significant until the "£60 and over" level and this no doubt reflected the luxury end of the privately rented market. So it could be seen that in the lower income categories households in privately rented dwellings were paying a smaller proportion of their income than local authority tenants despite the subsidies given to the latter. Moreover households in local authority dwellings were larger than those in privately rented accommodation and so have a lower *per capita* income.

We may conclude that low-income families in privately rented dwellings were not worse treated than those in other tenures. This is not to say that many of them may not have needed help. There may well have been valid reasons for granting rent allowances to private tenants but the information disclosed in the Family Expenditure Survey was not one of them.

Appendix 2 Interest rates

Nearly all local authority capital expenditure is financed by borrowed money. If this were not so, an authority's capital expenditure would be limited to what its revenue in that year could stand and a great deal of capital work would not be undertaken at all. There is the further point that much of the work undertaken today will be enjoyed not only by the present but also by future generations and that in consequence it is not unreasonable for posterity to meet some of the cost. In an inflationary situation, particularly when interest rates are rising fast, we can say that posterity is on to a good thing; certainly many authorities must be thankful that their predecessors had the foresight to carry out the many projects which are still an asset to the community but which would be prohibitive at present-day cost levels.

To borrow money costs money and usually loans are available only because someone has a surplus he is ready and willing to lend at a profit. The payment exacted for the hire of the money is the rate of interest and is usually expressed by the number of units (pounds) charged each year for each hundred units (pounds) borrowed. When we speak, therefore, of the rate of interest we are referring to the annual rate of interest *per centum.*

The major concern of recent years is not with the *fact* of interest payments (these are to all intents and purposes inevitable) but rather with their *level,* which is felt to be unduly high, and the purpose of this appendix is to examine the effect of different rates of interest on loans taken out for varying lengths of time.

238

PUBLIC SECTOR

Money to build council houses, in common with other local government expenditure is borrowed either on the open market, from the Public Works Loan Commissioners or from internal sources such as balances in the authority's super-annuation fund. It has to be repaid within sixty years. In practice the borrowed money goes into the council's loan "pool" and the cost of the housing developments are met from the "pool". In this way the benefit of lower interest rates on money borrowed in previous years is used partly to offset today's higher rates.

Open market borrowing may be by the issue of bonds, stock, or by way of mortgage loans. Money borrowed from the Public Works Loan Commissioners commands varying rates of interest depending on the period of the loan, whether

TABLE 9 — *Interest rates*

Last day of	Bank rate %	Deposits with local authorities		Building society rates %
		7 day %	3 months %	
1960	5.0	5.1	5.2	6.0
1961	6.0	6.8	6.7	6.5
1962	4.5	4.8	4.8	6.5
1963	4.0	4.3	4.6	6.0
1964	7.0	8.0	7.7	6.0
1965	6.0	6.3	6.4	6.75
1966	7.0	7.4	7.3	7.125
1967	8.0	8.4	7.8	7.125
1968	7.0	7.3	7.8	7.625
1969	8.0	8.9	9.0	8.5
1970	7.0	6.8	7.3	8.5
1971	5.0	4.4	4.6	8.0
1972	9.0*	8.0	8.2	8.5

* Minimum lending rate

the loan is repaid periodically or at maturity, and finally whether the loan comes out of the authorities' quota or not. The quota is a proportion of the authority's capital expenditure for the year, the amount of which is laid down from time to time by the Treasury.

Interest rates have varied considerably over the years as Table 9 shows.

It has generally been the practice when interest rates are low to borrow for as long a period as possible and to borrow short when they are high. Table 10 illustrates the point.

TABLE 10 — *Loan Costs on £1,000*

Annual Repayments (to nearest £)

Rate of interest	Period of repayment (years)							
%	10	20	30	40	50	60	100	ind*
	£	£	£	£	£	£	£	£
3	117	67	51	43	39	36	32	30
4	123	74	58	51	47	44	41	40
5	130	80	65	58	55	53	50	50
6	136	87	73	66	63	62	60	60
7	142	94	81	75	72	71	70	70
8	149	102	89	84	82	81	80	80
9	156	110	97	93	91	91	90	90
10	163	117	106	102	101	100	100	100
11	170	126	115	112	111	110	110	110

* indefinite, i.e. interest only

Lenders of course take a different view. As Table 10 also shows, the higher the rate of interest, the less advantage there is in borrowing long. Of course no Treasurer in his right mind would borrow for sixty years at current rates, he will borrow for as short a period as possible in the hope that when he comes to reborrow the money interest will have fallen. But if, as seems likely, we are entering an era of high interest rates, one might well consider the desirability of amortising development debts over a shorter period than sixty years.

Even at 9 per cent, to reduce the period of repayment of £1,000 from sixty to forty years would increase the annual repayments by only £2.45. And the total repaid would be reduced by more than £1,700.

But it is the rate of interest itself which has the major effect, as Table 11 shows.

TABLE 11 — *Loan of £1,000 repaid over sixty years*

Rate of interest	Annual repayments £	Total repayments £	Interest as % of total repayments
5	52.83	3,169.69	68.45
6	61.88	3,712.54	73.06
7	71.23	4,273.75	76.60
8	80.80	4,847.88	79.37
9	90.51	5,430.85	81.59
10	100.33	6,019.77	83.39
11	110.21	6,612.61	84.88
12	120.13	7,208.03	86.13

As will be seen, even at what now seems the fantastically low rate of 5 per cent, over a period of sixty years interest accounts for £68.45 out of every £100 repaid and this rises to £83.39 at 10 per cent.

So far the tables in this appendix have assumed equal annual instalments of principal and interest ("the annuity method"). There are two other methods of repayment. One is payment at maturity in which no principal is repaid until the end of the loan. This demands a sinking fund to amortise the loan, and assuming that money in the sinking fund can earn the same rate of interest as is being charged on the loan, the costs will be roughly the same as in the case of annuity repayments. The third method is that of equal annual repayments of principal plus interest on the balance outstanding. Table 12 provides an example.

TABLE 12 — *Loan of £1,000 at 10 per cent repaid over 10 years*

Year	Repayment of principal £	Interest £	Total payment £
1	100	100	200
2	100	90	190
3	100	80	180
4	100	70	170
5	100	60	160
6	100	50	150
7	100	40	140
8	100	30	130
9	100	20	120
10	100	10	110
Total	£1,000	£550	£1,550

By this method the annual payments decrease during the period of the loan. In the example quoted the total repayments amount to £1,550. Had the annuity method been adopted, the annual repayments would have amounted to £162.75 and the total amount paid would have increased by £77.50.

From what we have already seen the benefits of low interest rates are obvious and it seems all the more regrettable that the subsidy provided by the Housing Act, 1967 (which provided an effective rate of 4 per cent) has been jettisoned.

PRIVATE SECTOR

In speaking of the private sector we are of course talking about owner-occupation. No one is going to invest money in housing to rent (except in the luxury class) at current rates and possibly not in any circumstances. Similarly, co-ownership schemes financed by the Housing Corporation are not going to flourish in an era of high interest rates coupled with high rates for building society mortgages. In any case the principal advantage of this kind of finance, i.e. repayments over a long period of time, possibly forty years, is, as we have already seen, largely lost when interest rates are high.

Assuming that building societies are willing to lend on the basis that annual repayments shall not exceed some percentage of annual income, say 25 per cent, then one obvious effect of an increase in interest rates is to decrease the amount of the loan obtainable. In preparing Table 13 it has been assumed that annual repayments will be £500, being 25 per cent of an annual income of £2,000, at different rates of interest and with periods of repayments of twenty, twenty-five and thirty years.

TABLE 13 — *Maximum mortgage loan available assuming annual repayments of £500 (i.e. 25 per cent of £2,000)*

Rate of interest	Period of repayments		
	20 years	25 years	30 years
%	£	£	£
5	6321	7047	7686
6	5735	6392	6882
7	5297	5827	6205
8	4909	5337	5629
9	4564	4911	5137
10	4257	4539	4713
11	3982	4211	4347

One can see that over a period of twenty-five years a decrease in the rate of interest from 11 per cent to 5 per cent will increase the amount of loan theoretically available by 67 per cent. Moreover a 5 per cent, increasing the period of the loan from twenty to thirty years increases the amount of possible loan by 23.4 per cent; at a rate of 11 per cent the corresponding increase is only 9.2 per cent. One should also bear in mind that, inflation notwithstanding, the assumed income is comparatively high; in 1971 not more than 20 per cent of heads of households were earning as much as this.

When a building society increases its rate of interest, it endeavours to make things easy for existing borrowers by extending the period of repayment. High interest rates limit the extent to which this can be done. To take an example from the table above, if a borrower obtained a loan of £7,047 (which he could have repaid over twenty-five years at 5 per cent) at 10 per cent and assuming the same annual repayments, he could never repay. He would in fact have to pay £704 a year just to keep himself from going further and further into debt. If he were to repay over twenty-five years at this higher rate of interest he would need to increase his annual repayments to £776.37 a year which is nearly 39 per cent of his assumed income level of £2,000.

All this is damaging enough in itself, but it is of course happening in a period of inflation in which house prices are rising at a much greater rate than most other prices. So that we shall not be accused of culling examples from the present "abnormal" situation (but what is normal?), let us take an example from the period 1964 to 1969. Let us take the average prices for new houses in those years and also let us assume a twenty-year repayment period. The annual repayments and the minimum income required are shown in Table 14.

TABLE 14

Year	Interest rate	Price	Loan (90%)	Annual repayments	Minimum income required
	%	£	£	£	£
1964	6	3,433	3,090	269.4	1,078
1969	8½	4,782	4,304	454.8	1,819

It will be seen that the average price of new houses increased by almost 40 per cent but the annual repayments and therefore the minimum income required have increased by almost 70 per cent. It is likely that in 1964 28 per cent of all incomes were at or above the level required (£1,078), but in 1969 only 13 per cent of incomes amounted to £1,819 per annum or above.

To come nearer to the present day (1973), we know that the average price of existing houses in Great Britain at the end of 1972 was about £9,300. Assuming 10 per cent deposit this means a loan of £8,370 which over twenty-five years at 10 per cent requires an annual repayment of £922.12 or £17.68 a week. Even with tax relief the nett repayment in the first year will be £671.02 or £12.87 a week; it will of course increase thereafter. If gross repayments are not to

TABLE 15 — *Effect of tax relief*

Per £1,000 borrowed — Repayments over twenty-five years

Interest rate	Annual repayments	Total repayments	Interest gross	Tax relief	Interest nett	Effective rate of interest
%	£	£	£	£	£	%
7	85.81	2145.25	1145.25	343.58	801.67	5.17
7½	89.71	2242.75	1242.75	372.82	869.93	5.53
8	93.68	2342.00	1342.00	402.60	939.40	5.91
8½	97.71	2442.75	1442.75	432.83	1009.92	6.29
9	101.81	2545.25	1545.25	463.58	1081.67	6.66
9½	105.96	2649.00	1649.00	494.70	1154.30	7.05
10	110.17	2754.25	1754.25	526.28	1227.97	7.43
10½	114.43	2860.75	1860.75	558.23	1302.52	7.80
11	118.74	2968.50	1968.50	590.55	1377.95	8.18
14	145.50	3637.50	2637.50	791.25	1846.25	10.43

Assuming borrower is paying standard rate of tax (30%)

exceed 25 per cent of income, then no one earning less than £3,688 p.a. (£70.73 a week) can afford to buy on these terms. It seems unlikely that more than 3 per cent of all heads of households have incomes of this order. At the time of writing mortgage rates have not yet risen to 10 per cent though they would have done had not the Government stepped in with a temporary subsidy. But there is talk among building society chiefs even now of the possibility of mortgage rates going up to 14 per cent; if they do, the Conservative concept of a property owning democracy will have become an historically interesting anachronism.

Before we leave the subject we ought to have a look at the effect of tax relief. We have already seen that the benefits of

Housing: the great·British failure

tax relief on mortgage interest payments can be considerable and that it exceeds the subsidies given to the public sector. Table 15 shows the effect of a tax relief situation where the borrower is paying tax at the standard rate of 30 per cent on all the income which he devotes to repaying his mortgage. Remember that the figures refer to a loan of £1,000 repaid over twenty-five years.

The effective rate of interest quoted in Table 15 is that rate which would lead to the same overall repayments as the interest rate quoted, less tax relief. It differs somewhat from the figure usually quoted in this regard but it is felt to be more accurate. The table shows the effect of tax relief in mitigating the impact of rising mortgage rates.

Appendix 3 Housing cost yardstick

Although the appropriate government department had always required that tenders obtained by local authorities for housing work should be submitted for approval, they did not until 1967 impose limits which such tenders must not exceed. Indeed, apart from the 1919 Act which placed on the Treasury any burden over and above the product of a penny rate, the liability of the Exchequer had not been affected by the cost of the scheme since the subventions had taken the form of a lump sum per dwelling granted for a stated number of years. The 1961 Act, for instance, had laid it down that the basic subsidy should amount to either £8 or £24 (according to circumstances) per annum per dwelling for a period of sixty years. To put it mildly, this was neither a scientific nor satisfactory method of allocating government aid; it took no account of subsequent rises or falls in building costs or rates of interest, nor of the decreasing need for subsidy arising from the operation of a system of rent "pooling" in an inflationary situation.

Realising the onerous burden that high interest rates impose on housing finance, local authorities and others had for many years pressed for loans to be made available at low and stable rates of interest for housing finance. This after all was, and is, a usual method of housing subsidy in Europe and one which, it was felt, could be adopted here. Successive Governments had resisted the idea until the 1967 Act virtually brought about that state of affairs by providing a subsidy which made up the difference between current rates of interest (strictly speaking a "representative rate of interest" for the previous year) and a rate of 4 per cent.

This was no longer a lump sum subsidy since it would vary

with the total cost of the project and therefore with the amount of money borrowed to finance it. It was, in fact, a percentage grant, though the amount of the percentage would vary according to the year in which the loan was raised. Once fixed, the same annual subvention was intended to be paid throughout the loan period, i.e. sixty years.

No subsidising department will countenance such an "open-ended" subsidy without retaining some strict control over costs, particularly if, as was the case with the 1967 Act, the new subsidy is substantially higher than the old. In introducing the new subsidy arrangements, therefore, the Ministry took power to impose upper cost limits. This control took the form of a "housing cost yardstick".

The yardstick was contained in a table which laid down the upper limit to the amount to be spent per person housed (i.e. per designed bed-space provided) according to the level of density and the average number of persons per dwelling in the scheme under examination. The yardstick totals were divided into three parts: substructure, superstructure and external works. To allow for different levels of costs in different areas, the country was divided into regions in each of which the yardstick figures could be increased by some stated percentage (in the original yardstick table this percentage was fixed at 0 per cent in the North, Yorkshire and the East Midlands, rising to 12½ per cent in part of the Greater London area). Alteration of these regional variations formed a convenient method of revising the yardstick levels.

The successful tender attracted subsidy up to but not beyond the yardstick figure for the scheme. Loan sanction was forthcoming up to the yardstick figure plus a further sum, if required, amounting to not more than 10 per cent of the yardstick figure. This became known as the "ten per cent tolerance" and was intended to be used for innovation and experiment in design. It did not rank for subsidy and no loan sanction was forthcoming for expenditure in excess of the tolerance figure. In fact, the tolerance factor came to be used very widely to absorb rising costs instead of its original purpose.

The circular (36/67) which first announced the yardstick details promised that the Ministry would review the cost levels annually and might revise them from time to time to take account of changes in cost levels, design practice and other relevant circumstances. This promise was not kept and although changes were in fact made from time to time they were always tardy and inadequate. From the beginning the Ministry were empowered to agree to *ad hoc* yardstick levels to meet special circumstances, but when inflation really took hold in 1972 the then Secretary of State introduced a "market forces" allowance which in effect made every tender a possible candidate for an *ad hoc* yardstick.

From the beginning the yardstick was unpopular with most authorities. It was of course not intended to be merely a cost limit; it was also meant to encourage cost-consciousness during the design period. But it is clear that the benefits of cost-planning were not universally appreciated. This is understandable. Because of departmental delays in revising the yardstick levels, authorities found it increasingly difficult to keep their costs within its bounds. In a survey undertaken by the author towards the end of 1968, about half the responding authorities reported difficulty in keeping to the yardstick; by the spring of 1971 this proportion had risen to 82 per cent; by that time 60 per cent of authorities were using the 10 per cent tolerance to absorb rising costs instead of its proper purpose. Other criticisms maintained that constant pruning of specifications so as to keep costs down to yardstick levels resulted in inferior dwellings built of poor materials and that this would mean high maintenance costs later on. And although the yardstick table had been deliberately constructed so as to make high-rise building unattractive from a cost point of view, by 1971 more than half of the local authorities were complaining that the yardstick was inhibiting low-rise and low density development as well.

At the time of writing (September 1973) the yardstick position is out of hand with many influential people and organisations calling for its abolition. Obviously in an era of runaway inflation any form of cost-planning may be difficult almost to the point of impossibility. None-the-less the author feels that the yardstick was correct in principle and an essential discipline, provided the superintending department is prepared to revise cost levels frequently and rapidly to accord with current requirements. There is no doubt that failure to do so laid the former M.H.L.G. and the D. of E. open to the charge of reducing council house building activity by administrative inaction, a charge which it seems contains more than just a grain of truth. But although changes in subsidy arrangements may have reduced the need for a yardstick from the Treasury point of view, the general benefits of working within the discipline of cost-planning are such that it would seem desirable for it to be retained.

Appendix 4 Option mortgages

Option mortgages are so called because the borrower can, when he takes out a mortgage, opt to forego tax relief on his interest payments and be granted instead a lower, subsidised rate of interest. The scheme was introduced by the Housing Subsidies Act of 1967 with the idea of giving to the lower paid borrower, who might not be paying much tax, or none at all, roughly the same advantages as those enjoyed by the higher-paid borrower who can claim tax relief on the interest paid on his mortgage debt and who thereby obtains considerable help from the State with his housing costs.

When the scheme was first introduced in 1968 all existing borrowers were given the opportunity to change to an option mortgage though in the event less than 5 per cent did so. The number of new borrowers opting for the scheme varied from about 10 per cent in 1968 to just over 6 per cent in 1970. Since then there has been some revival of interest in option mortgages though the proportion of borrowers actually opting is still not high, especially when one remembers that the scheme has advantages even for the borrower paying full tax.

Since January 1970 the amount of option subsidy has been based on a sliding scale which varies according to the rate of interest as shown in Table 16.

The option subsidy reduces the going rate of interest by the percentage stated so that at present the building society rate is 9½ per cent but the option rate is 6¾ per cent. The difference is paid by the Government direct to the lender. The figures above relate to ordinary mortgages repaid on an annuity basis; the option subsidy for endowment mortgage is ¼ per cent less. If the ordinary mortgage rate falls below 6

Housing: the great British failure

TABLE 16

Rate of interest %	Option subsidy %
6 - 7	2
Over 7 - $7\frac{7}{8}$	$2\frac{1}{4}$
Over $7\frac{7}{8}$ - $8\frac{3}{4}$	$2\frac{1}{2}$
Over $8\frac{3}{4}$ - $9\frac{5}{8}$	$2\frac{3}{4}$
Over $9\frac{5}{8}$	3

per cent the rate charged on an option mortgage does not fall below 4 per cent (4¼ per cent for endowment mortgages).

When the scheme was first introduced it was thought that it would be of benefit only to those not paying tax at the standard rate and this was the advice which the Ministry of Housing hoped that building societies would give to their customers. In fact this advice could have been misleading as there have from time to time been circumstances when the option scheme has been of some benefit to some borrowers paying full tax (though not surtax) and occasionally to all of them, depending on the circumstances. Three factors in particular affect the benefit borrowers can obtain from the scheme:

(a) The rate of income tax. Obviously the lower the rate, the less will be the amount of tax paid and therefore the less will be the benefit of tax relief.

(b) The actual level of the mortgage rate. Consider Table 17.

TABLE 17

Mortgage rate %	Effective rate after tax relief %	Option mortgage rate %
6½	4.85	4.50
7	4.90	5.00
7½	5.25	5.25
8	5.60	5.50
8½	5.95	6.00
9	6.30	6.25
9½	6.65	6.75
10	7.00	7.00

From this table it will be seen that the option rate is advantageous to the standard rate taxpayer when the going building society rate is 6½ per cent, 8 per cent and 9 per cent, the normal tax relief arrangements may be more beneficial at 7 per cent, 8½ per cent and 9½ per cent, and there is no difference at 7½ per cent and 10 per cent. It should be noted that the effective rate quoted above differs somewhat from the equivalent figures quoted in the appendix on interest rates: the latter are valid only if the mortgage runs to its full term, whereas the figures above apply to interest as it is paid, irrespective of the term.

(c) The length of time the mortgage runs before it is redeemed. If the mortgage runs to its full term the total repaid will be less under an option mortgage than would be the case with a tax relief mortgage, and the longer the term the greater this advantage will be. Because more interest is paid in the early years of a mortgage, the greater will be the benefit of tax relief in those years and so the nett repayments will be less with tax relief than with an option mortgage. Against this, because of the way annuity repayments are calculated, under the option scheme the borrower will pay off more of his principal debt in the early years. Tables 18 and 19 illustrate these points quite clearly (they are calculated in accordance with the situation in 1972 when conditions were to some extent more "normal" than the very fluid situation obtaining at the time of writing (1973)).

These tables assume:

(*a*)   A building society rate of 8½ per cent.

(*b*)   The option mortgage rate is 6 per cent.

(*c*)   The borrower is paying tax at the standard rate of 38.75 per cent.

(*d*)   He is entitled to earned income relief of two-ninths. The tax arrangements were altered in April 1973 with a standard rate of 30 per cent but no earned income relief. This makes very little difference to the calculations. Table 19 shows the situation at the end of the eighth year; eight years is about the usual life of a mortgage regardless of the term of years for which it was taken out.

In broad terms, option mortgage borrowers pay between £5 and £7 more per annum in the first year for each £1,000

TABLE 18 – *Comparison between mortgage with tax relief and option mortgage subsidy loan of £1,000 taken out for the number of years shown*

No. of years	Option			Tax relief mortgage		
	20	25	30	20	25	30
Annual repayments (gross)	87.18	78.23	72.65	105.67	97.71	93.05
Total repayments (gross)	1743.69	1955.67	2179.47	2113.42	2442.79	2791.52
Total subsidy/ tax relief	369.73	487.12	612.05	335.57	434.84	539.94
Total repayments (nett)	1743.69	1955.67	2179.47	1777.85	2007.95	2251.58
Interest as % of nett repayments	42.65	48.87	54.12	43.75	50.20	55.59

TABLE 19 — The position at the end of the eighth year in respect of option and tax relief
mortgages of £1,000 taken out for a period of 20, 25 and 30 years

Loan period	Total repayments (nett)		Total subsidy received		Total capital repaid	
	Option	Tax relief	Option	Tax relief	Option	Tax relief
	£	£	£	£	£	£
20 years	697.44	658.05	147.92	187.31	269.00	223.87
25 years	625.84	587.57	155.84	194.11	180.41	137.64
30 years	581.20	571.50	163.20	198.09	125.20	87.18

borrowed and between £15 and £20 less in the last year, the actual amount depending on the rate of interest and the length of the mortgage. The changeover point at which the option borrower starts to pay less than a mortgagor receiving tax relief is about halfway through the mortgage term.

To sum up, it seems that the borrower cannot lose by going for an option mortgage (unless he pays surtax); there is a definite advantage at the usual period of eight years and some advantage at any stage. There is an additional point: under the mortgage scheme the borrower actually pays less "over the counter"; with tax relief the monetary advantage, although just as real, is less obvious since it is tied up with tax allowances and "take-home pay". Some borrowers prefer the option scheme for this reason alone. The Government have recently proposed changes in the tax system (*Proposals for a Tax-Credit System*: Cmnd 5116) which would lead to the abolition of the option scheme. This, however, is not likely before 1977 at the earliest.

Appendix 5
Housebuilding performance

It has been the habit of British political parties, until 1970 at any rate, to proclaim at times of general elections how many houses they intend to build during their tenure of office should the electorate decide to entrust them with the conduct of affairs. Such promises, in which the contestants occasionally appeared desperately anxious to outbid each other, were considered to be very important electorally and although performance almost always failed to live up to expectation (the Conservative record after the 1951 election is an exception) nevertheless some attempts to translate such undertakings into reality were usually made and were considered an essential prerequisite of continued political credibility. Cynics on the other hand were prone to dismiss these declarations of intent as mere "targetology", rather unfairly, one may think, since on the face of it there is nothing wrong in setting yourself a target even if you don't manage to hit it. The purpose of this appendix is to examine and compare performance with prediction in the post-war world.

We have already seen in Chapter 5 how the Conservative Party were encouraged, if that is not an understatement, to accept a target of 300,000 houses a year at the time of the 1951 Election. By 1953 this target had been exceeded and thereafter up to 1963 the annual production of houses in Great Britain continued at around the 300,000 mark. Table 20 and Figure 3 illustrate the point. They also show the sharp upturn in 1964 with the coming of the Labour Government.

The undertaking to achieve a rate of completions of 500,000 a year by 1970 is well documented and does not need much reiteration here. The magic figure of half a million

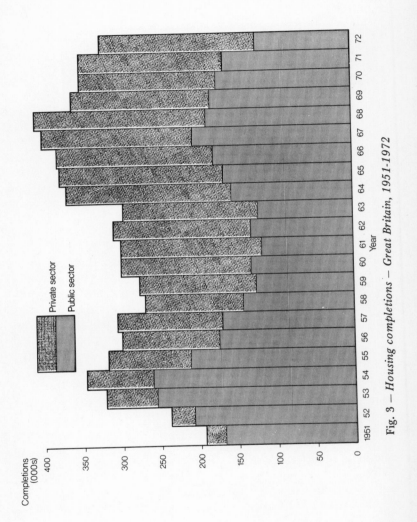

Fig. 3 — *Housing completions – Great Britain, 1951-1972*

TABLE 20 — *Housing completions Great Britain 1958-72*

Year	Public sector	Private sector	Total
1958	145,547	128,148	273,695
1959	125,966	150,708	276,674
1960	129,189	168,629	297,818
1961	118,549	177,513	296,062
1962	130,628	174,800	305,428
1963	124,008	174,864	298,872
1964	155,582	218,094	373,676
1965	168,498	213,799	382,297
1966	180,137	205,372	385,509
1967	203,918	200,438	404,356
1968	191,722	221,993	413,715
1969	185,090	181,703	366,793
1970	180,129	170,304	350,433
1971	158,908	191,612	350,520
1972	122,827	196,323	319,150

apparently first appeared in the now almost-forgotten National Plan prepared by the Department of Economic Affairs in 1965. It was at once accepted by the Government as a target; for example it appeared in the first paragraph of the White Paper, *The Housing Programme 1965 to 1970,* Cmnd. 2838) published in November 1965: "... The rate of building will be pushed up as fast as resources and improving techniques allow. In 1964, 383,000 houses were completed (United Kingdom). The first objective is to reach half a million houses a year by 1970. *Even that, however, will not be enough... The 1970s should see still bigger programmes"* (My italics: author).

It was generally accepted that the 500,000 target referred to Great Britain but on the other hand the White Paper specifically mentioned the United Kingdom though it did not go so far as relate the target figure to it. This is one of the perennial difficulties in dealing with housing statistics; the ministries concerned seem rather prone to switching from England and Wales to Great Britain to the United Kingdom and back again according to how they want the figures to look. If in fact the half million target did refer to the United Kingdom then the record year of 1968 saw just over 425,000 houses completed or about 85 per cent of the target figure.

And let there be no doubt that 1968 *was* a record year. Whether one is speaking of England and Wales or of Great Britain or of the United Kingdom, more dwellings were completed in 1968 than in any other year of our history. Whatever else one can say about Mr Greenwood's policies, and elsewhere in this book I have been extremely critical of them, nothing can take away from him the achievement of having presided over the greatest output of dwellings this country has ever seen. 1968 was not a record year for public sector building (that was 1954) or of private sector building (that was 1935, though 1968 was a post-Second World War record) but overall the figures from both sectors combined were sufficient to produce a record that does not look like being beaten for many a long year.

We have already seen in Chapter 13 how the 500,000 target was tacitly abandoned early in 1968 (the record year ironically enough) and how Mr Greenwood's predictions of high output in subsequent years proved disastrously wrong; it is still worth while comparing the output actually achieved not only with the stated targets but also with the known need. The White Paper already referred to stated that a programme of half a million houses a year is modest in the light of housing needs. It then went on to pinpoint a minimum need of 3.7 million houses accompanied by an annual figure of 180,000 to keep up with new household formation and to replace losses for roads and other forms of redevelopment. This is indeed modest. The author, when giving evidence to Sub-Committee B of the Estimates Committee in 1969, suggested that a programme of 500,000 was a *minimum* requirement and on statistics alone it would be quite easy to make a case for a much higher figure. The collapse of the upward trend after 1968 must not be regarded as merely unfortunate, it is a disaster.

Completions in 1972 came out at less than 320,000. This was the lowest figure since 1963 though it was still higher any of the years 1946-52 and 1955-1963. The number of public sector dwellings completed at 122,800 was less than any post-war year though it was higher than any pre-war year. 1973 completions look like being even lower.

The Ministry of Housing, or rather the Department of the Environment publish each month a housing report in which they give the number of dwellings started, under construction and completed by public authorities and private owners in England, Wales and Scotland during the previous month. The report usually gives some other information such as the number of Improvement Grants approved and the number of slum dwellings cleared. This clearly is very useful information for the student, the journalist, the politician and the man in the street who happens to be concerned about housing. Of course in any year completions (and starts) will be higher in some months and lower in others because of seasonal factors such as weather, holidays and so on; generally speaking these factors tend to keep the figures low in the first half of the year and to raise them in the second half. Moreover they tend to make comparisons with previous years unreliable.

The Department of the Environment, in common with other Government Departments, try to get over this defect in the raw figures by presenting them as "seasonally adjusted" in a table of monthly averages. This is a useful and legitimate statistical exercise and for some purposes it is essential but such figures should be used with caution. If the non-statistician knew what had happened to the figures during the process of "seasonal adjustment" he would be less happy about using them. An alternative method which tends to reduce the effect of seasonal influences is to add together twelve consecutive months. The figures can then be presented as a series of such totals which are sometimes known as Moving Annual Totals. This, in the matter under discussion, means that the figure stated against any month is the total of completions (or starts or whatever) in the twelve months immediately preceding the end of that month. All the months, busy and slack, are therefore taken into account and this will reduce, though may not eliminate, the effect of seasonal influences.

The further advantage of presenting figures in this way is that one is using true figures which have not been "messed about with". Moreover if a Moving Total drops it means that the position is deteriorating and a continuing fall indicates that current results are continuing to fail to equal the previous year's results. Conversely a rising Total indicates an improvement.

Moving Annual Totals in monthly stages for the six-year period 1967-72 are given in Table 21. A study of these figures will show the way things are going. They also pinpoint the arbitrary effect of choosing a calendar year as a basis. For example it will be seen that the highest figure in any period of 12 months was in fact for the year ending 31 August 1968; at 418,604 they are 1.18 per cent higher than those for the calendar year. Moreover the total for the calendar year (413,715) was a lower figure than the Annual Totals based on the preceding and succeeding months.

The Totals have been plotted graphically at Figure 4 which brings out even more clearly the sharp downward trend in new housebuilding.

TABLE 21 — *Housing Completions — Great Britain — Moving Annual Totals in monthly stages*

1967 - 1972

Month/year	Public sector	Private sector	Total
Jan., 1967	181,417	203,691	385,108
Feb.	185,008	203,986	388,994
March	186,644	201,993	388,637
April	189,057	199,185	388,242
May	191,248	197,305	388,553
June	193,291	196,757	390,048
July	194,579	195,504	390,083
Aug.	197,456	195,544	393,000
Sept.	198,846	195,006	393,852
Oct.	201,756	196,701	398,457
Nov.	201,788	198,140	399,928
Dec.	203,918	200,438	404,356
Jan., 1968	201,945	203,330	405,275
Feb.	200,868	205,574	406,442
March	202,438	210,742	413,180
April	199,624	213,281	412,905

Month/year	Public sector	Private sector	Total
May	200,954	217,497	418,451
June	198,844	217,754	416,598
July	198,232	220,372	418,604
Aug.	196,862	222,476	419,338
Sept.	194,573	222,254	416,827
Oct.	193,320	223,046	416,366
Nov.	193,734	222,336	416,070
Dec.	191,722	221,993	413,715
Jan., 1969	194,171	220,694	414,865
Feb.	191,712	217,603	409,315
March	187,631	211,955	399,586
April	188,249	209,883	398,132
May	185,257	204,863	390,120
June	184,756	204,279	389,035
July	185,194	200,250	385,444
Aug.	184,502	196,388	380,890
Sept.	185,362	194,390	379,752
Oct.	185,711	190,861	376,572
Nov.	184,202	186,599	370,801
Dec.	185,090	181,703	366,793
Jan., 1970	182,732	178,816	361,548
Feb.	184,754	177,708	362,462
March	187,027	176,261	363,288
April	186,656	174,409	361,065
May	187,201	172,890	360,091
June	187,642	170,574	358,216
July	188,378	171,125	359,503
Aug.	188,140	170,399	358,539
Sept.	187,352	169,245	356,597
Oct.	186,231	168,984	355,215
Nov.	185,126	169,890	355,016
Dec.	180,129	170,304	350,433
Jan., 1971	181,247	171,461	352,708
Feb.	179,359	171,328	350,687
March	178.911	173,699	352,610
April	178,454	173,811	352,265
May	175,698	174,937	350,635
June	172,623	177,633	350,256

Housing: the great British failure

Month/year	Public sector	Private sector	Total
July	169,232	179,075	348,307
Aug.	166,384	180,327	346,711
Sept.	164,805	182,560	347,365
Oct.	162,622	183,734	346,356
Nov.	159,961	185,332	345,293
Dec.	158,908	191,612	350,520
Jan., 1972	156,446	192,681	349,127
Feb.	155,230	195,512	350,742
March	153,465	196,635	350,100
April	151,747	197,742	349,489
May	149,033	199,419	348,452
June	147,950	200,910	348,860
July	144,354	199,873	344,227
Aug.	140,927	200,423	341,350
Sept.	136,146	200,142	336,288
Oct.	131,800	199,304	331,104
Nov.	129,557	199,952	329,502
Dec.	122,827	196,323	319,150

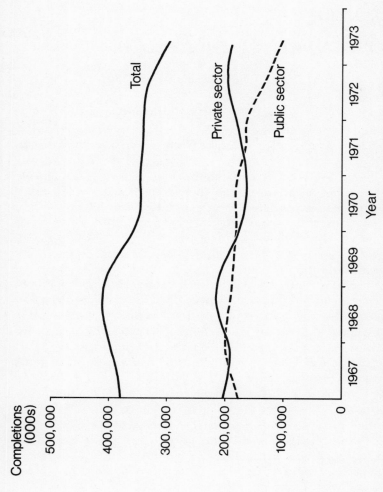

Fig. 4 — *Housing in Great Britain - Moving Annual Totals of dwellings completed, 1966-1972*

Appendix 6
Social housing in Europe

The manner of providing and financing "social housing" (i.e. assisted housing for those unable to afford what they need in the open market) varies widely from country to country. In most of Western Europe there is, for example, less emphasis on direct building by public authorities, or on private renting or on owner-occupation than there is in Britain; on the other hand there is a good deal more on non-profit-making housing associations and on housing cooperatives. Both these latter forms are widely subsidised, either directly or by personal subsidies given to the tenant to enable him to meet his housing costs.

As in this country, the housing associations are operated by one lot of people so as to provide housing for another lot, whereas the cooperatives are by one means or another leased or owned and operated by the tenants themselves. Because of the non-profit aspect, it is felt that communally operated housing makes its own contribution towards keeping rents down to a reasonable level.

It would be difficult enough to describe adequately any one of the following systems in an appendix such as this; as it is the outlines given must of necessity be brief and inadequate. Readers wishing to know more about housing in Europe could do worse than get hold of some of the many publications issued by the International Federation for Housing and Planning (address: 43, Wassenaarseweg, The Hague, Netherlands). Much of what follows is in fact taken from the Federation's Report *The Financing of Social Housing* which was prepared by their Standing Committee for Social Housing.

266

AUSTRIA

Austria's houses are old, the majority of its dwellings were built before 1918 and a quarter of them before 1880. In consequence it is felt that the state will continue to have a large part to play by encouraging the construction of new dwellings and the improvement of the best of the existing stock.

The Federal Housing and Homes Fund of 1921 and the Promotion of Housing Act of 1954 between them enabled loans to be available up to 90 per cent of the cost, repayable over 40 to 80 years at an interest rate of 1 per cent. Housing law was consolidated in 1968 and now social dwellings up to 130m^2 floor space (more in the case of families with more than four children) can qualify for assistance. About 60 per cent of the cost is provided by public loan and at least 10 per cent by the building owner, the rest coming from the ordinary money market. The down-payment can be partly or wholly met by means of a personal loan, without interest where necessary. Loans are for 50 years, interest is 1 per cent and amortisation comes to 2 per cent in the first twenty years and 3 per cent during the remainder. The purchase and the preparation of the site have to be met entirely from private capital. Occupancy of the dwellings so provided is restricted to families with low incomes and the rent is controlled. The rent is calculated from the repayments due on the public and private loans, plus certain allowances for maintenance, administration and operational costs. No profit is provided for in the rent calculations.

BELGIUM

Social Housing in Belgium means housing provided by the Société Nationale du Logement, the Société Nationale de la Petite Propriété Terrienne (in rural areas) and by approved societies operating under their aegis.

Government finance for housing comes partly from the Ministry of the Family and Housing and partly from the Ministry of Public Works. The Ministry of Finance also comes into the picture because of tax reliefs.

The two societies lend out money for building at a much lower rate of interest (e.g. 1½ per cent) than the rate at which they borrow; they also lend it out for longer periods (e.g. 66 years). The state makes up the difference.

The state also covers the cost of road construction or improvement where a development includes at least 25 "social" dwellings.

Other state help includes financing rent reductions granted to large families; covering losses on slum clearance whether undertaken by the municipalities or by the two national societies; guaranteeing loans for housing purposes made by the Central Savings Bank; and making payments to individuals of modest means to enable them to buy.

There are special provisions for miners. For example, for them the rate of interest can be as low as ½ per cent.

CZECHOSLOVAKIA

Most housing in Czechoslovakia is financed or subsidised by the Government. Housing cooperatives have become increasingly important during recent years (this is also true of Poland and possibly other Eastern European countries) and they now account for approximately 60 per cent of all housing construction. Cooperatives get a subsidy of 8,100 Kĉs (Czech Crowns) per dwelling unit plus 1,050 Kĉs per m² up to 85m². They can also get additional subsidy for special purposes, e.g. building for the disabled. The individual members of the cooperative must contribute shares of approximately 30 per cent of the state subsidy. The balance of the cost can be met by a loan raised by the cooperative from the National Bank, 30 years at 1 per cent, the first instalment being due two years from the time building starts.

Members of the cooperatives can build the dwellings themselves; if they do, their labour can be set against their share of the financing. Moreover, of members of the cooperative, their relatives or their friends do pay manual work on the site, they do not have to pay income tax on their earnings.

Individuals can in some instances build their own dwell-

268

ings, usually in rural areas or on the outskirts of towns. Workers can obtain a loan of up to 25,000 Kĉs from their employers (in some cases 35,000 Kĉs). These loans are interest-free and are cancelled if the borrower undertakes (*a*) to work for the same employer for at least ten years from the date of the loan, (*b*) to occupy the house himself and (*c*) not to sell it. The loan is also cancelled in the event of industrial disablement or death. Rents are calculated uniformly throughout the country.

DENMARK

State aid in Denmark takes the form of credit guarantees in respect of that portion of a loan which exceeds 60 per cent of the value of the mortgaged property. By this means it is possible to obtain loans of up to 94 per cent of the capital required. In addition there is a subsidy, the purpose of which is to keep rents low, this brings down the effective rate of interest to 6½ per cent for the first five years. The subsidy is then phased out over the next three years.

Housing is exempt from "Moms" (Danish V.A.T.) and social housing associations are exempt from income tax.

Owner-occupiers get tax reliefs and in addition all tenants are entitled (assuming they qualify) to a rent subsidy which varies according to (*a*) the rent paid, (*b*) the size of the family, (*c*) the family income and (*d*) the size of the dwelling relative to the size of the family.

FRANCE

In France there are special arrangements for building houses to be let at moderate rents. These are controlled collectively by the National Union of Federations of Organisations for Dwellings at Moderate Rents (Habitations à Loyer Modéré or H.L.M.). These organisations may be public authorities, limited liability companies, cooperative associations or building societies but they all have the common aim of providing on a non-profit basis, dwellings let at modest rents; they may also undertake slum-clearance.

There is a special loan office which collects subsidy allocations from the national budget and which also raises money on what may loosely be called the "public capital market"; it can thus make finance available at a lower rate of interest than it pays itself. This money is used by the H.L.M. organisations to build houses to rent or for sale. The dwellings thus provided must reach certain minimum standards and must not exceed stated maximum costs.

The state also provides subsidies to private persons or to corporate bodies wishing to build to a higher standard than H.L.M. These dwellings must not exceed 150m² in area nor must the cost exceed certain limits which are however, somewhat higher than the H.L.M. limits. For example a four-room dwelling may attract a subsidy of 440 Fr. a year for 20 years or 735 Fr. a year for 10 years. The dwellings may be rented or sold and if the price is beyond the means of an intending purchaser a special mortgage loan is granted as well.

In addition the community can make available rent allowances for those whose rent is too high in relation to their means.

And finally the law requires employers to make an investment in social housing equal to 1 per cent of their wage bill.

ITALY

Social housing in Italy is financed by levies on employers and employees plus further funds provided by the state. At least half the funds thus provided goes towards the construction of dwellings for lower-paid workers and 15 per cent is allocated for the provision of dwellings by cooperatives. In the latter case the members help by meeting the cost of the land.

A further 15 per cent of the funds is put towards a "rotary fund" for buying or building dwellings for individual workers. This assistance takes the form of direct loans or mortgage guarantees.

LUXEMBURG

Here aid is given only to owner-occupiers, seemingly on the rather extraordinary premise that increasing the supply of owner-occupied dwellings would in some way increase the supply (and therefore reduce the rent) of rented dwellings. "The expected beneficial effects of this policy," I am told, "have been very modest up to now."

Aid takes the form of a building premium amounting to 28,000 Belgian Francs plus 9,000 Frs for the first and the second child, 12,000 Frs for the third and so on. Families with three or more children can obtain a reduction of the rate of interest on part of their loan.

Rent regulation is theoretically still in force but seems to be ignored in practice.

NETHERLANDS

The Netherlands has been subsidising social housing since the turn of the century but a unified system was adopted in 1965 to bring the social and private sectors into line with each other. Subsidies are intended partly to raise housing standards and partly to meet higher land, building and interest costs. As owner-occupiers have to pay income tax on the subsidies they receive, the latter are about 50 per cent higher than those for rented dwellings. In the first year the subsidy covers about 45-50 per cent of the initial economic rent but the subsidy is gradually eliminated by means of rent increases of about 6 per cent per annum. Owner occupier subsidies are phased out over a period of not more than ten years with a yearly reduction of not less than H.Fl.250.

Social housing attracts public loans amounting to 100 per cent of the total cost. These dwellings are provided by the municipalities or by non-profit associations, the latter having preference. Up to 1968 a special rate of interest of 4 per cent was charged on these loans but now they are at market rates. In consequence the subsidy has had to be increased considerably and may now amount to as much as the rent the tenant pays initially. Amortisation is over a period of 75 years for land and 50 years for other costs.

SWEDEN

By tradition house construction in Sweden has been financed by multiple mortgages and between 1942 and 1968 government aid mainly took the form of third mortgages granted by the state. Other institutions, e.g. banks, insurance companies, the Post Office Bank, mortgage institutions and so on, covered about 70 per cent of the cost by means of first and second mortgages, the third mortgage being granted by the State Loan Authority. The latter loan brought the amount advanced up to between 85 per cent and 100 per cent according to who was doing the building. The rate of interest was held down, rents were controlled and in addition rent allowances were made available to certain people with low incomes.

This was all changed in 1968. The state subventions which covered part of the interest payments on loans were abolished as was also the low-interest state loan itself. So that a substantial increase in rents could be avoided, the former subventions were converted into loans in the form of mortgages on the property and the total amount loaned could reach 110 per cent of the cost. The new state loan has to be amortised by means of a fixed annuity spread over 30 years. The other loans need not be amortised until the state loan is repaid.

The new system is extremely complicated and the foregoing is an over-simplification but it does give some indication of how things are done in Sweden. The aim is to even out the capital cost of the dwellings regardless of the year in which they were built; to even out fluctuations in the rate of interest; and by means of rent increases to make it possible to provide housing at reasonable rents without subsidy.

Housing allowances are still granted to needy families. These basically amount to Sw.Kr. 720 a year for a family with one child under 16 to which is added a further Sw.Kr. 240 for each additional child. There is a further grant in some cases for additional rooms and the whole scheme is graded according to income. As an example, a family with two children under 16 with an income of Sw.Kr. 17,000 and living in two rooms plus kitchen would receive a rent allowance of Sw.Kr. 1,680 per annum. Municipalities can grant additional allowances if the commune's rent level justifies it.

WEST GERMANY

The German miracle certainly seems to extend to housing. Despite the devastation of the war (some would say because of it) West German investment in housing has been at an extremely high level, no less than 20,230 billion DM between 1949 and 1969. During this period 10½ millions were constructed of which 5½ million were subsidised social dwellings, 2½ million were subsidised by exemption from land tax and the remaining 2½ million unsubsidised. The rate of construction had reached 623,000 a year by 1964 which puts British performance, even in its best years, pretty much in the shade.

Despite this very high level of activity the Germans do not believe that supply is yet in sight of demand and their programme for the 'seventies is to build half a million dwellings each year of which about half will be subsidised.

The first housing law of 1950 exempted certain dwellings from land tax for a period of ten years. This category of housing was intended for people not qualifying for subsidised social housing but who were unable to afford full market prices. Rents were fixed at a level about 30-40 per cent above the rent level for social housing. During the 'fifties more dwellings were built under these arrangements than were built for the private market. Rent control was relaxed in 1967.

Social Housing has been subsidised in a number of ways which in many cases have been in the form of 100 per cent loans, interest-free but with a charge of 0.5 per cent for administration and with amortisation amounting to no more than 1 per cent. Or state aid can take the form of expenditure aids which are effectively deficit grants and which diminish every third or fourth year and are phased out in 8, 12 or 16 years in different Laender. Rents must not exceed current expenditure (capital costs and management costs). A further alternative has been in the form of annuity aids granted by the Laender intended to decrease the rate of interest on housing loans.

Provided he fulfils the conditions, every citizen of the Bundesrepublik and of West Berlin has a claim as of right to social housing aid.

Appendix 7 Postscript

The world does not stand still and I have deliberately left the writing of this Appendix until the last moment (May 1974). Since my manuscript was delivered to the Publishers last year much has happened. An economic crisis, though not entirely unheralded, has burst upon us with unexpected ferocity. The oil sheiks have determined that our standards of living shall fall. We have survived the traumatic experience of industrial strife, severe restrictions and shortages, and a three-day working week. We appear to have acquired an enormous trade deficit for which at the moment there seems to be no solution. And if that were not enough we have, quite unexpectedly seen the Government defeated at a General Election and a minority Labour Government elected to office but not to power. All this has its implications for housing. My preductions of falling housing standards seem all too likely to come true. Large numbers of houses have been standing uncompleted for many weeks or even months because of the difficulty of obtaining the materials to complete them, a situation we usually associate with Eastern Europe or the Banana Republics. This has led to a further fall in housebuilding output in both public and private sectors, the latter appearing particularly depressed.

On the other hand the Building Societies, faced with a net outflow of funds, have for the second time in recent months accepted Government help by way of investment funds, subject to their agreeing not to raise mortgage interest rates even further. Thus the coming of the 14% mortgage appears to have been temporarily delayed. It seems likely that there will be more money available in the coming months but as there will be even fewer new dwellings on the market the stage seems set for a further disastrous round of house price increases. Clearly some stabilisation of the way funds are made available for house purchase must be high on the list of priorities for this or some future government.

As for legislation, the Conservative Housing Bill was lost because of the General Election. Labour's Housing Bill seems extraordinarily similar though obviously there are differences in emphasis and detail.

Both Bills envisaged a considerable extension of the role of the Housing Corporation which would be empowered to acquire, develop and dispose of land. Its functions in relation to Housing Associations would also be extended. The latest Bill aims to extend the power of local authorities in regard to house improvements, both generally and in General Improvement Areas. Local authorities would also be able to declare Housing Action Areas in areas of severe housing stress and to take direct action to improve living conditions. It seems likely that the 1972 Housing Finance Act will be repealed, either wholly or in part. But little or nothing has been said about extending the role of local authorities in providing new housing to rent.

I find this new bi-partisan approach curious to say the least. But although it would be beneficial to have some of the heat taken out of the housing debate, I cannot say that I am very happy about the proposals as they stand. Certainly those relating to the Housing Corporation suggest that the Government is turning away from the local authorities as the major house providing agency and is moving towards the idea, supported in this book, of a National Housing Authority which could in time become the principal provider of public sector housing and even perhaps take over existing council housing. But I am very concerned indeed about the continued emphasis on improvements rather than replacement and new building. I need not pursue the point unduly, I have dwelt on it at length in other parts of this book. Nevertheless it is worth considering the extent to which improvements are already out of hand.

Over the two-year period 1970-72 the cost of improvement grants increased by about 440%. Discretionary grants approved during the first three quarters of 1973 came out at

£277 million and thus exceeded those for the whole of 1972, itself a record year. If maintained it would represent an annual grant level of around £370 million. Figures published recently show that during 1973 the number of grants approved increased by about 13% overall which means that the cost of improvement grants at the moment of writing could be running at something over £400 million a year.

Compare this with the figure of £300 million a year which was held to be a totally unacceptable level of subsidy to council house building (and which would not have been reached until 1975-76). All this money and not a single new dwelling to show for it.

Some further points occur to me after reading over the proofs of the preceding chapters. On page 224 I say:". . . we cannot exclude central government from at least part of the blame for the Great British Housing Failure.". This was probably an understatement, in fact Henry Aughton calls it "an understatement of awe-inspiring dimensions" and goes on to say: "I would have thought that the overwhelming blame for the housing failure is the repeated changes of mind of central government, motivated sometimes by party ideology, sometimes by lack of understanding or more probably lack of will. In these conditions you cannot have an efficient building industry of the required size."* I think he is entirely right, but this does not invalidate my general argument which, reduced to a single sentence, is that local authorities have had the powers but have too often failed to use them.

The second point concerns the New Towns to which I have been accused of being less than just. To quote Henry Aughton again: "Here at Hemel Hempstead the great Lord Reith himself was Chairman. . . There are mistakes. . . But by and large the achievement and the standard is very high. It is moreover a town where it is not easy to tell which houses are tenanted and which owner-occupied. They did not pack them in like they do nowadays, and thank God for it. As time went on, the Treasury in my belief assumed a greater and greater dominance, and unless you have a great man like Reith to stand up to these fellows the effect is deadly."*

*Henry Aughton in a letter to the Author: 16 April 1974.

276

I agree; perhaps I did not show up the New Towns in their best light. But the great days of the New Towns were the early days, since then we have had greater emphasis on "maintaining and enhancing the value of the land" and later still (under Greenwood of all people) the insistence of building only for owner-occupation so that a 50/50 balance with tenancy could be achieved. This was a piece of dogmatic stupidity of which a Labour Government in particular ought to have been ashamed. But my contention was and is that the New Towns were intended to relieve congestion and housing stress in the big cities, London most of all. The congestion and the stress are worse than ever. In strictly housing terms I insist that the New Towns are a failure.

A final point; on page 122 I say that "Fair rents are therefore a compromise and on the whole it seems an acceptable compromise at that". Although I think the text makes it sufficiently clear, for the record I will say that here I am referring to the private sector only. In the public sector so-called "fair rents" make no sort of sense at all. I support the principle of pooled historic costs at the basis for council house rents supported if need be by a rising cost and a high cost subsidy. This was the basis for rents laid down in the 1972 Scottish Housing Finance Act and I believe that only political bigotry prevented it from being adopted in England and Wales as well.

Index